Hot
Appetizers

EURODÉLICES

HOT APPETIZERS

DINE WITH EUROPE'S MASTER CHEFS

KÖNEMANN

Acknowledgements

We would like to thank the following persons, restaurants and companies for their valuable contributions to this book:

Ancienne Manufacture Royale, Aixe-sur-Vienne; Baccarat, Paris; Chomette Favor, Grigny; Christofle, Paris; Cristalleries de Saint-Louis, Paris; Grand Marnier, Paris; Groupe Cidelcem, Marne-la-Vallée; Haviland, Limoges; Jean-Louis Coquet, Paris; José Houel, Paris; Lalique, Paris; Les maisons de Cartier, Paris; Maîtres cuisiniers de France, Paris; Philippe Deshoulières, Paris; Porcelaines Bernardaud, Paris; Porcelaine Lafarge, Paris; Puiforcat Orfèvre, Paris; Robert Haviland et C. Parlon, Limoges; Société Caviar Petrossian, Paris; Villeroy & Boch, Garges-les-Gonesse; Wedgwood-Dexam International, Coye-la-Forêt.

A special thank you to: Lucien Barcon, Georges Laffon, Clément Lausecker, Michel Pasquet, Jean Pibourdin, Pierre Roche, Jacques Sylvestre und Pierre Fonteyne.

Skill ratings of the recipes:

☆☐☐   easy

☆☆   medium

☆☆☆   difficult

Photos: Studio Lucien Loeb, Maren Detering
Copyright © Fabien Bellhasen and Daniel Rouche
Original title: Eurodélices – Entrées Chaudes

Copyright © 1998 for the English-language edition:
Könemann Verlagsgesellschaft mbH,
Bonner Str. 126, 50968 Cologne

Translation from German: Regina Bailey
English-language editor of this volume: Jana Martin
Coordinator for the English-language edition: Tammi Reichel
Typesetting: Goodfellow & Egan, Cambridge
Series project manager: Bettina Kaufmann
Assistant: Stephan Küffner
Production manager: Detlev Schaper
Assistant: Nicola Leurs
Reproduction: Reproservice Werner Pees, Essen
Printing and binding: Neue Stalling, Oldenburg

Printed in Germany

ISBN 3-8290-1127-X

10 9 8 7 6 5 4 3

Contents

Foreword

The Eurodélices series brings a selection of European haute cuisine right into your kitchen. Almost 100 professional chefs, many of them recipients of multiple awards and distinctions, associated with renowned restaurants in 17 countries throughout Europe, joined forces to create this unique series. Here they divulge their best and their favorite recipes for unsurpassed hot and cold appetizers, fish and meat entrees, desserts, and pastry specialties.

The series as a whole, consisting of six volumes with over 1,900 pages, is not only an essential collection for gourmet cooks, but also a fascinating document of European culture that goes far beyond short-lived culinary trends. In a fascinating way, Eurodélices explores the common roots of the different "arts of cooking" that have developed in various geographic locations, as well as their abundant variety.

For eating is much more than the fulfillment of a basic bodily need; cooking is often elevated to the level of an art, especially in association with parties and celebrations of all kinds, in private life and in the public sphere. Young couples plan their futures over a special dinner at an elegant restaurant, partners gather at table to launch new business ventures, heads of state are wined and dined. Every conceivable celebration involves food, from weddings to funerals, from intimacies shared over coffee and cake to Sunday dinners to Passover and Thanksgiving feasts.

We often have our first contact with the cultures of other lands, whether nearby or across an ocean, through their food. Precisely because the various contributing chefs are rooted in their distinct traditions, some flavors and combinations will be new to North American readers, and occasionally ingredients are called for that may be unfamiliar or even difficult to locate. The texts accompanying each recipe help elucidate and, wherever possible, suggest substitutes for ingredients that are not readily available in North America. A glossary is also included to explain terms that may not be obvious, listing some ingredients.

Because precision is often crucial to the success of recipes of this caliber, a few words regarding measurements and conversions are in order. In Europe, it is customary to use metric units of liquid volume or weight, that is, milliliters or grams. Every household has a kitchen scale and solid ingredients are weighed, rather than measured by volume. Converting milliliters to fluid cups and grams to ounces is straightforward, if not always neat. More problematic are ingredients given in grams that North Americans measure by volume, in tablespoons and cups. Throughout the Eurodélices series, the original metric measurement follows the North American equivalent. The conversions are painstakingly accurate up to 100 ml and 100 g (which necessitates some awkward-looking amounts). Thereafter, they are more neatly, and thus less accurately, rounded off. As with all recipes, measurements are approximate for many ingredients, and a wide variety of factors ranging from temperature and humidity to accuracy of kitchen implements to the way food is sold will affect the amount actually used. If the reader wants to recreate the recipes as given, however, the use of a kitchen scale is strongly recommended.

The unique collection of around 750 recipes contained in Eurodélices aims to excite its readers' curiosity. Classic dishes, which have been enjoyed for generations and thus form the foundations of modern cookery, are liberally presented. But there are also new and surprising pleasures, familiar foods prepared in novel ways, as well as culinary delights composed of ingredients from far away places that we experience for the first time. Allow yourself to be inspired by the European master chefs to try and, perhaps, try again.

Preparation time: 1 hour
Cooking time: 5 minutes
Difficulty: ★

Serves four

20 small green asparagus spears
2 truffles

For the truffle mousse:
2 tbsp / 30 g truffle juice
3/4 cup / 200 ml cream
2 shees of gelatin

For the decoration (if desired):
2 oz / 50 g truffles, finely chopped
1 bunch chervil (for the leaves)

Our Spanish chef, Fernando Adría, introduces us here to his very personal version of Irish Coffee. The traditional Irish Coffee is a drink made of very strong coffee with whiskey and thick cream, served in a tall glass.

This recipe follows the same idea. Our chef uses the same type of glass to present his version, which combines truffle jelly, asparagus soup, and a cream converted into truffle foam. He thus transforms this traditional drink, which normally rounds off a meal, into a warm appetizer to start a meal.

The prestige of truffles needs little explanation. In this recipe, the black variety of this most noble edible fungus is given preference over its white counterpart. Our chef also advises against

mixing the two types or disregarding in any way the old gastronomic adage that "a black truffle is as good as two white ones." In Spain the black truffle is exclusively found in Armorrera near Castellón de la Plana, and, Adría points out, is in no way inferior to black truffles from Périgord in France.

Use wild asparagus that is very fresh and green for this recipe. It should be prepared at the last minute so its delicious flavor does not break down over time. The main challenge when preparing this dish lies in layering the three components without mixing them (as in its inspiration, Irish Coffee). The truffle jelly needs to be prepared somewhat ahead of time, so it can set in the individual glasses before the other layers are added.

1. Cook the asparagus in salted water for three minutes, and puree in a blender or food processor. Add two tablespoons of water to achieve a smooth, fine soup.

2. Dissolve the gelatin into the hot truffle juice, stir, and refrigerate for 30 minutes. Whip the cream and, setting aside a small portion, carefully add some truffle juice to the remaining portion.

Asparagus and Truffles

3. Pour the truffle mousse in tall glasses until it reaches a third of the glass's height, and refrigerate.

4. Heat the asparagus soup and season to taste. Pour carefully into the glasses containing a base of chilled truffle mousse. Just as carefully, top with a tablespoon of truffle cream and then a tablespoon of whipped cream. If desired, decorate with some chopped truffle and a chervil leaf.

Preparation time: 30 minutes
Cooking time: 2 minutes
Difficulty: ☆

Serves four

8 bone marrow pieces, generous 1 oz / 40 g each
generous 3 oz / 100 g caviar
1 tbsp / 15 g flour

For the beet jelly:
4 beets
1 tsp / 5 ml vinegar

a pinch of sugar
1 sheet of gelatin

Today's chefs often see it as their task to satisfy the senses of taste, smell, sight, and touch. This sometimes leads to combinations that require the precision akin to that of a watchmaker. Thus, when you buy the ingredients for this dish you can not make do with any substitutes.

The meticulousness chefs apply in choosing ingredients and raw produce is proof of this precision. This is also the reason that not any caviar can be used for this exquisite trio. Nice and shiny and dark, it should, above all, gently "perfume" the other ingredients. Since the sturgeon is now restricted almost exclusively to the Caspian Sea, there are only a few types of caviar available. Fernando Adría particularly recommends Sevruga caviar, which has slightly finer grains than Ossetra or Beluga,

yet an incomparable flavor. The name "malossol" indicated on some packages does not at all refer to a particular type of caviar; it simply means that this variety has been packed with less salt.

The bone marrow, on the other hand, is a European delicacy, with a texture that is tender and soft. When poached and fried in its own fat, it turns crisp outside and remains tender inside. And to bolster the appearance of this appetizer, Adría has added a dark red jelly made from beets. For this, our chef prefers using medium-sized, dark red beets. And, no matter how surprising this combination first appears, gourmets will always try to combine all three components of this dish on their forks. So, bon appetit!

1. To make the jelly, cook the beets in water with a pinch of sugar and a teaspoon of vinegar for five minutes. Puree in a blender or food processor, stir in the gelatin, and refrigerate.

2. Place the pieces of bone marrow into cold water, bring to a boil and leave to cool in the liquid.

Marrow

3. Drain the marrow pieces carefully, dust with flour, and fry in their own fat.

4. To serve, place three pieces of marrow on each plate, cover completely with caviar, and serve one tablespoon of beet jelly as an accompaniment.

Vegetables with

Preparation time: *30 minutes*
Cooking time: *20 minutes*
Difficulty: ✷

Serves four

2 lb / 1 kg green beans
1 cauliflower
2 lb / 1 kg artichokes
2 lb / 1 kg fava beans
2 lb / 1 kg fresh peas
2 lb / 1 kg fresh porcini mushrooms

2 cloves of garlic
1 bunch of green asparagus
1 bunch of white asparagus
2 slices raw ham (or Prosciutto)
$^1/_2$ cup / 125 ml vegetable oil
$^1/_2$ cup / 125 g flour
1 cup / 250 ml meat broth (such as veal or beef)
salt, pepper to taste

Easily digestible and therefore, in Europe, considered ideally suited for business dinners, this dish reminds our chef, Hilario Arbelaitz, of his mother; it was she who introduced him to the pleasures of cooking at an early age. When preparing this dish, the distinct aromas of each of the ingredients must be preserved. Each will in turn enhance the other, allowing these garden vegetables and wild mushrooms to meld in a most harmonious way.

Porcini, predominantly found in the Basque region, lends this vegetable dish a rustic flavor – a very interesting contrast to the vegetables cooked *al dente*. If no fresh porcini can be found, substitute the more commonly available dried version, which should be soaked in hot water about twenty minutes to soften. Or, alternatively, one could also substitute fresh chanterelles. Regarding the vegetables, since no two of these spring vegetables call for the same cooking time, they must all be prepared separately. The exact composition of vegetables, according to Chef Arbelaitz, is not of any great consequence. What is important is that the main components are peas, green beans, white beans, asparagus, and porcini. Around this central theme you may create your own composition according to what is freshest in the market, as well as your whim and taste. Ideally, the various vegetables chosen should be very fresh, and direct from the garden if possible.

The mushrooms, which tend to toughen up if overcooked and lose their flavor if left to sit for too long, should not be prepared until the last minute. The raw Serrano ham from Spain puts the finishing touch to this dish; if unavailable, one may substitute prosciutto.

If you are preparing this appetizer out of season, spinach and cabbage (use sparingly) may be added.

1. Wash all the vegetables and peel if necessary. Follow the different cooking times meticulously: green beans – eight minutes, cauliflower – ten minutes, artichokes – fifteen minutes, fava beans – three minutes, peas – five minutes, green asparagus – four minutes, white asparagus – ten minutes.

2. Cut the ham into thin strips, fry in oil, add a little flour and fry until crisp.

Porcini Mushrooms

3. Cut the vegetables into 1 in / 2 cm pieces; clean the artichoke down to the heart and cut into pieces as well. Add the vegetables and a little broth to the cooking ham. If fresh, clean the mushrooms with a damp cloth or sponge (not under running water, which will saturate them). If dried, rinse, then soak for 20 minutes in hot water.

4. Slice the mushrooms, fry them in a pan with oil and add them to the vegetable mixture. Slice the garlic; fry in oil until golden brown and add to the vegetables as well. Serve piping hot, garnished, if you wish, with sprigs of chive and chervil leaves.

Red Peppers

Preparation time: *1 hour, 30 minutes*
Cooking time: *1 hour*
Soaking time: 24 hours
Difficulty: ★★

Serves four

generous $^1/_2$ lb / 250 g cod, salted
8 red peppers (see below)
1 onion
3 cloves of garlic
scant $^1/_4$ cup / 50 g fresh bread crumbs
$^2/_3$ cup / 150 ml olive oil

$^2/_3$ cup / 150 ml cream
1 egg
3 sprigs of parsley
a pinch of sugar

On the Spanish side of the Pyrennees mountains, peppers are very popular, especially the so-called Piquillo from the area of Pampelune in Navarra. This is a very fleshy variety that is very hard to find elsewhere. Harvested in September, it is cleaned by hand and then grilled; if it is washed under running water it loses many essential qualities. If desired, this dish can work as a side dish accompanying an entrée instead of an appetizer, with peppers as the main component of the course. Among the peppers you may substitute for the Spanish Piquillos are sweet red bell peppers, or fresh pimientos.

Peppers go particularly well with the strong flavor of cod, which the Spaniards love presenting in a thick sauce made richer with the addition of bread crumbs. Chef Firmin Arrambide recommends serving the sauce separately, as he asserts that this will make the dish more easily digestible.

Cooking is kept to a minimum here to retain the ingredients' freshness: the red peppers, only cooked very briefly, thus do not lose their lovely, bright red color, while the cod stuffing is also cooked for a very short time to prevent it from drying out. The addition of garlic and onion lend the cod a certain lightness of flavor, and make it easily digestible.

This recipe for stuffed peppers served in their own sauce may, of course, also be used with other ingredients. Crab stuffing, minced poultry, or lamb stuffing, or even a delicious potato puree with garlic, for instance, are perfect complements and may be prepared the same way. Likewise, most mushrooms and herbs complement the peppers harmoniously. Indeed, this appetizer may take on innumerable variations.

1. One day ahead, soak the salt cod in water for 24 hours. The next day, to prepare the dish, skewer the eight peppers onto a fork and place them on the grill until their skins turn black. Rinse under cold water, skin, and remove the stems and seeds. Pour olive oil over the peeled peppers, salt them on both sides, and bake in the oven for 15 minutes at 355 °F / 180 °C. Set aside to cool.

2. Peel the onions and cut into strips. Chop the garlic and fry together with the onions in 1 tbsp plus 1 tsp of olive oil, then cook over a low heat for 15 minutes. In the meantime, flake the cod and carefully remove the bones. Add the fish to the onions and garlic and fry for one minute. Take the pan off the heat and add the bread crumbs to bind the stuffing.

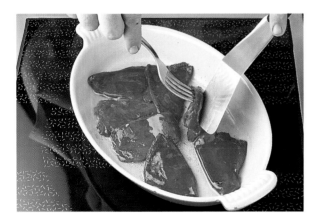

Stuffed with Cod

3. Cut 1 in / 2¹/₂ cm off the wide end of each pepper. Cook these small pieces in ²/₃ cup / 150 ml of cream for 15 minutes, then puree in a blender or food processor and run through a sieve. Season with salt and a pinch of sugar.

4. Use a pastry bag to fill the peppers. Dust with flour and turn in a beaten egg. Fry briefly in a pan with five tablespoons of olive oil. To serve, cover the base of a serving platter with half the pepper sauce, and pour the rest into a gravy boat. Arrange the peppers in the sauce on the platter, and garnish with parsley.

Pigeon Soup with

Preparation time: 1 hour
Cooking time: 1 hour, 30 minutes
Setting time (for pigeons): 8–10 days
Soaking time: 24 hours
Difficulty: ✶✶

Serves four
2 pigeons
7 oz / 200 g green lentils
1 large savoy cabbage
1 onion
1 carrot
1 clove of garlic

1 bouquet garni
3¹/₂ tbsp / 50 g butter
scant ¹/₄ cup / 50 ml crème fraîche
2 tsp / 10 ml Armagnac

The wild pigeons' migration to the south, which can be observed from October to mid-November, triggers a strange disease among humans – the so-called "palombite" (pigeon disease) – all over the southwestern area of France, predominantly in the Basque region. The symptoms of this disease are wild enthusiasm, incessant conversations about the legendary migrating pigeon, and obsessive preparations for the imminent hunt. And starting in the early hours of the morning, passionate hunters camouflaged in pigeon blinds wait for the migration of these magnificent game birds. Sometimes caught in nets, sometimes shot, these pigeons enrich the region's most elegant dinner tables during the hunting season.

The pigeons selected for this dish, according to our chef, Firmin Arrambide, should preferably be young and well-nourished. Thinner birds are better suited for ragouts or salads with porcinis and chanterelles, often crowned with pâté de foie gras. In order to develop their full flavor, the pigeons have to "mature," unplucked, right at the bottom of the refrigerator for eight to ten days. If wild pigeons are unavailable, you might substitute plump, larger squabs.

Our chef recommends serving pigeon in broth with lentils and cabbage, using the breast portion, which is the best part of the bird. The flavor of the pigeon will strongly dominate that of the remaining ingredients; thus, vegetables that on their own can at times play a leading role, here are reduced to the supporting cast. In the Basque region pigeons are also grilled or fried, or cut into small pieces, roasted in a cast iron pot and served with ham; they may also be presented in a red wine sauce.

If you prefer, substitute fresh chestnuts (if in season) for the green lentils when preparing the soup.

1. Soak the green lentils a day ahead. Pluck, draw, and singe the pigeons. Fry in a deep pan for about ten minutes and flambé with Armagnac. Slice off the breast pieces and set aside.

2. Prepare the broth in a saucepan: add some water and a bouquet garni to the pigeon carcasses; simmer over a low flame. Remove the leaves from the cabbage and wash well. Cut into thin strips, bring to a boil in salted water, and keep warm.

Lentils and Cabbage

3. Peel the onion, carrot, and garlic clove and chop all of these finely. Add the drained lentils and 1¹/₂ quarts / 1¹/₂ l of cold water. Cook for about one hour. Puree in a blender or food processor; pass through a sieve. Add a small dab of butter and 3¹/₂ tbsp / 50 ml crème fraîche and season to taste.

4. Form a pyramid of cabbage in the middle of each plate and surround it with an arrangement of thinly sliced pigeon breasts. Serve the soup separately in an accompanying tureen.

Poached Eggs

Preparation time: 10 minutes
Cooking time: 5 minutes
Difficulty: ✭

Serves four

8 very fresh chicken eggs
generous 1 lb / 500 g fresh mushrooms, mixed,
    including button mushrooms, yellow and white
    chanterelles, shiitake
3/4 cup / 200 ml olive oil
scant 1/4 cup / 50 ml light spirit vinegar

1 bunch of chives
salt, coarse
pepper, coarsely ground

Eggs, which pervade every aspect of cooking, are featured in appetizers, main courses, side dishes, and, of course, desserts. Chef Jean Bardet's appetizer with poached eggs requires both a simple and yet at the same time quite complicated procedure: the steps must be exact, though the dish is relatively simple.

The eggs should be absolutely fresh (see the poached eggs recipe on pages 44–45 for a sure-fire way to check their freshness), otherwise the whites will disintegrate when immersed in the simmering water instead of setting around the egg yolk. According to this chef, one should not poach more than four eggs at a time, and the water should not boil but only simmer, to keep the egg whites from toughening. If the eggs are not served immediately, set them aside in cold water to keep them soft. Prepared like this, eggs will sometimes take on bizarre shapes – a process that can be prevented by drying them first on a cloth, which will lend them a more attractive shape.

Mushrooms are an ideal accompaniment. If button mushrooms (also called *champignons de Paris*) are chosen, select mushrooms of firm texture and pure white color – signs of quality and freshness. This variety, famous for its exquisite flavor, is no longer only from Paris. As an alternative, you might try other mushrooms such as chanterelles or shiitake, the perfumed Chinese mushroom, provided they are absolutely fresh. Fresh porcini will also work, although the larger portobellos have too robust a flavor for this delicate dish.

To lend this appetizer a more appealing appearance, Chef Bardet recommends you place the eggs on the plate and cut them in half just before they are served so that the soft egg yolk spreads decoratively across it.

1. Bring eight cups of unsalted water to a simmering boil in a large pot and add vinegar. Crack each egg individually onto a saucer and slide carefully, one after the other, into the simmering water.

2. Simmer them for two to three minutes only, and check by applying light pressure with your finger: The eggs have to stay soft. Place in cold water and set aside.

with Mushrooms

3. Wash and dry the mushrooms; slice evenly. Heat 3$^{1}/_{2}$ tbsp / 50 ml of olive oil in a frying pan, add the sliced mushrooms, and sauté. Season with salt and pepper.

4. Warm the appetizer plates. To serve, place two eggs on each plate and halve, arrange the mushrooms on top, and sprinkle with chopped chives. Pour the remaining oil over the eggs and season with a little coarse salt.

Lasagna with

Preparation time: *2 hours*
Cooking time: *15 minutes*
Difficulty: ★★

Serves four

1 zucchini
1 eggplant
3 tomatoes
$^1/_4$ lb / 120 g Parmesan cheese
$^1/_4$ lb / 120 g butter
$^1/_2$ cup / 120 g flour
$^1/_2$ cup / 120 ml olive oil
2 cloves garlic

1 bunch of basil
1 bunch of rosemary
salt, pepper to taste

For the lasagna dough:
1 generous cup / 250 g semolina flour
3 eggs
1 bunch of smooth-leaved parsley

For the Béchamel sauce:
2 tbs / 30 g butter
2 tbs / 30 g flour
2 egg yolks
generous 3 cups / 750ml whole milk

In Italy no two lasagna dishes are ever the same, since both the filling's color and composition can be infinitely varied, and noodles, particularly with the rising vogue for different colors and tastes, can vary as well. Lasagna recipes are constantly altered and continually delight the gourmet with new flavors. Naturally, however, nobody can prepare this original Italian dish better than an Italian chef. With both a mind for innovation and a sense of the culinary past, a chef such as Guiseppina Beglia may sometimes produce unexpected creations, such as this lasagna made with zucchini and eggplants, or, alternately, with asparagus and peas.

The dough is prepared with parsley, an irreplaceable herb, here used in the smooth-leaved variety, which looks somewhat similar to chervil and goes excellently with this recipe. Always choose parsley that is green and fresh. It has many positive qualities, and is said to be good for improving one's mood.

When all the ingredients have been mixed, the dough should be kneaded for at least a quarter of an hour until it becomes smooth (and easily digestible); this will also make it easier to roll out thinly. The lasagna may be served individually on plates or in bowls, or else in ovenproof dishes intended, family style, for several to eat from. To attain an even heat on the inside and on the sides of the baking dish, lasagna should bake at medium heat, 300–320 º F / 150–160 °C, for a half hour.

The eggplants should be very fresh, deep purple in color, and firm to the touch, without breaks or bruises. With a certain pride, Chef Beglia reminds us that southern Italy, the main producer of eggplants in Europe, is also home to the most tasty varieties, some of which are both small and intensely flavorful. In the United States, although eggplants are available year-round, they are in season in late summer and very early fall.

1. Chop the parsley very finely, combine with three eggs in a blender or food processor, and strain. Pour the flour onto a large pastry board, make a well in the flour, pour in the egg mixture, and mix into the flour. Knead the dough well for approximately 15 minutes and set aside for an hour.

2. Roll out the lasagna dough into thin layers and then cut into rectangles or circles, according to the shape of the baking dish. Boil these in salted water for two minutes; rinse in cold water to stop the cooking process.

Zucchini and Eggplants

3. Thinly slice the eggplant and zucchini and coat lightly with flour; fry and set aside to dry on paper towels. Grease a soufflé mold or ovenproof dish with butter, line with a dough sheet, fill with alternate layers of eggplants, dough sheets, and zucchini. Crush garlic; chop basil and rosemary. Peel, seed, and dice the tomatoes, and fry in a pan with olive oil, adding the crushed garlic, basil, and rosemary. Scatter over the lasagna.

4. Finally, sprinkle with grated Parmesan cheese, cover with Béchamel sauce and slide under the grill for ten minutes before serving, either whole or in pieces, garnished with a healthy basil leaf.

Genoa Style

Preparation time: 50 minutes
Cooking time: 5 minutes
Difficulty: ✴✴

Serves four

⁵/₈ lb / 300 g spinach
2 eggs
2³/₄ oz / 80 g fresh, smooth cottage cheese
¹/₈ lb / 50 g Parmesan cheese (to yield scant ¹/₄ cup /
   50 g grated)
⁵/₈ lb / 300 g borage leaves and flowers
2 bunches of marjoram
salt, pepper to taste

For the nut sauce:
scant ¹/₂ lb / 200 g walnuts
1 tbsp / 15 g pine nuts
1 clove of garlic
1 cup / 250 ml extra virgin olive oil
¹/₂ bunch of parsley

For the dough:
scant 1 cup / 200 g flour
8 egg yolks
scant ¹/₄ cup / 50 ml dry white wine
a pinch of salt

The sheer variety and history of Italian pasta dishes is legendary. Each has its own tradition, its regional origin and its own numerous variants. Such is the case with *pansotti*, from the Italian word for "pot-bellied," presented here by our chef, Giuseppina Beglia. Her version of this triangular ravioli, which was prepared, traditionally, by peasants with a plain cream cheese filling, has certainly undergone a dressing up.

Today's style of gastronomy uses edible flowers to brighten up more and more dishes, much to the delight of both eye and palate. Borage is one of those plants that can charm any dinner table with its hues – like the colors of the French flag, its flowers shine in shades of blue, white, and red. Borage grows wild in damp soil, and has a flavor that resembles that of the cucumber. But the Italians value this plant not for its taste, but mainly for its blaze of color, which enlivens not only any salad, but many other dishes as well.

Smooth cottage cheese, readily available in Europe and increasingly so in the United States, has always been traditionally sold in its whey. Thus packaged it retains its freshness and moisture better than any other comparable produce, though nowadays it is also available without the whey.

Chef Beglia emphasizes that, when preparing the dough of any Italian pasta dish, fresh eggs are of utmost importance. In this case, the dough may be prepared a few days ahead, and kept in plastic wrap in the refrigerator before it is rolled out into thin layers and cut and shaped into the small, triangular *pansotti*.

Finally, the *pansotti* should be cooked briefly in plenty of water so the flavors of its herb and spinach filling are preserved. The typically Mediterranean marjoram will greatly benefit from brief cooking, as too much cooking will flatten its otherwise bouyant, memorable aroma.

1. Grate the Parmesan cheese. Wash the spinach and borage leaves thoroughly. Blanch briefly in salted water and cool in ice-cold water. Drain, squeeze out excess water, and set aside. Crack two eggs into a bowl, add the smooth cottage cheese, and stir in the Parmesan and marjoram.

2. Chop the spinach and borage leaves finely. Prepare the dough with flour, eggs, white wine, and a pinch of salt. Set aside for 15 minutes, then roll out very into thin layers and cut into triangles. Place a small heap of the filling onto each triangle, fold the edges over the middle, and press firmly to seal.

Pansotti with Borage

3. Shell and blanch the walnuts; peel. Crush the walnuts with the pine nuts and the garlic, or chop in the food processor. Add grated Parmesan cheese and whip up the mixture with olive oil and a little salted water to make a sauce. Season with pepper and add chopped parsley.

4. Place the pansotti into a pot of boiling salted water, steep for a few minutes, then drain. To serve, arrange on plates and drizzle with nut sauce, garnishing with borage flowers and leaves.

Fresh Pasta

Preparation time: 1 hour
Cooking time: 10 minutes
Difficulty: ★★

Serves four

For the pasta dough:
generous 1 cup / 250 g fine-ground flour
8 egg yolks
a pinch of salt

For the prawn sauce:
1 dozen prawns
4 zucchini (to yield 3½ oz / 100 g)

4 zucchini flowers
4 tomatoes
1 shallot
generous ³/₈ cup / 100 ml extra virgin olive oil
salt, pepper, hot chili powder to taste

The invention of pasta has been claimed by many cultures, in particular the Italians and the Chinese; still others maintain that they had invented their own version of pasta by the Middle Ages, if not earlier. Regardless of the debate, it is, however, a fact that pasta already adorned Italian menus in the Renaissance period, and that as early as the 15th century noodles were being produced in Naples for commercial distribution and consumption.

This gourmet's treasure deserves as much praise as there are variations – and, considering the inventiveness of great chefs, there will continue to be a host of new creations. The secret of the dough is its admirable simplicity, a basic combination of just water and flour, sometimes with eggs, often with colorings from beets, spinach, or squid, for example. If you prepare the pasta dough in advance, cover it with a damp cloth and keep it in the refrigerator to prevent it from drying out. Then, as our chef, Giuseppina Beglia advises, roll it out just before you cook it, so the dough is supple and easy to work.

Though zucchini is actually a summer vegetable, nowadays it is available all year round. Its skin, with a slightly rough surface and bright green, freckled appearance, should not show any brown marks, as the vegetable is so tender that a bruise will ruin its flavor. The smaller the zucchini, the more tender and flavorful. And if they are are cooked only briefly, their flesh will remain pleasingly *al dente*.

Chef Beglia used the Italian gamberoni for this recipe, a large pink prawn that is found in the gulf of San Remo. Since the availablity of these in the United States is, of course, up to chance, substitute them with any other variety of large prawn, so long as the shellfish are fresh. It is advisable, though laborious, to shell the prawns before preparing them, in order to infuse the flesh with the aroma of the other ingredients.

1. Heap the flour onto a pastry board or marble slab on a solid, flat table, add a pinch of salt and the eggs, and knead well until the dough is soft and elastic. Cover and set aside for an hour, then roll out thinly.

2. Cut the rolled-out dough into approximately 2 in / 5 cm squares and roll these up diagonally over a pencil to make the tubes.

Tubes with Prawns

3. Chop the shallot, dice the zucchini and tomatoes, and shell the prawns. Heat olive oil in a frying pan, add the chopped shallots and diced zucchini and sauté for five minutes. Add the shelled prawns, the diced tomatoes, and zucchini flowers, and season with salt and hot chili powder.

4. Fry all the ingredients for another five minutes, set aside, and keep warm. Cook the pasta rolls in salted water for five minutes, drain, mix with the prawns and vegetables, arrange on plates, and serve immediately.

Risotto with Zucchini

Preparation time: 15 minutes
Cooking time: 20 minutes
Difficulty: ✷✷

Serves four

4 zucchini flowers
³/₄ cup / 180 g rice (such as Carnaroli or Arborio)
20 mussels (such as vongole or blue)
4 red prawns
4 zucchini (to yield generous 3¹/₂ oz / 100 g)
4 tomatoes
1 small leek

1 white onion
2 shallots
1 clove of garlic
generous 1 cup / 250 ml dry white wine
generous 2 cups / 500 ml chicken stock
³/₄ cup / 200 ml extra virgin olive oil
¹/₈ lb Parmesan cheese (to yield scant ¹/₄ cup / 50 g grated)
scant ¹/₈ lb / 50 g butter
1 bunch of parsley
1 sprig of rosemary
salt, pepper to taste

Traditionally, risotto (in Italian the word means "little rice") is mixed with hot stock, fried in fat with chopped onions and then cooked in broth. These days, it is also enriched with numerous ingredients such as seafood, poultry liver, mushrooms, vegetables, or cheese.

In this recipe, as Giuseppina Beglia advises, do not deviate from the instructions when you prepare the rice, or it will not come out with the right consistency. Use a white short-grained variety, like Arborio, or the Italian variety Carnaroli – which Chef Beglia prefers. Do not wash the rice, as the water will rinse the vital starch away. Instead, stir it carefully with a wooden spoon. Once fried with onion and plenty of olive oil, the rice should not be cooked for more than twenty minutes. Towards the end, when the rice is nearly done, add butter and grated Parmesan and cook the mixture over a low heat for a few more minutes.

For the ragout of mussels and prawns, only very fresh seafood should be used. The vongole Chef Beglia prefers for this recipe is a type of mussel predominantly found in the Mediterranean. However, the market may not offer this variety: instead, try substituting cockles or small clams. The only purpose of the white wine in this recipe is to lend the dish a slightly tart flavor, offsetting the presence of the shellfish. It should therefore be used sparingly.

The zucchini flowers are served raw, stuffed with the risotto. Thus large, strong and fleshy flowers should be selected, the male ones being better suited for stuffing although they are certainly more delicate to handle. And bear in mind that the petals wilt very fast, even when covered with a damp cloth, so this part of the preparation should be done quickly, and, if possible, without any interruptions. This warm appetizer, according to Chef Beglia, is particularly popular in the summertime.

1. Chop the onion, shallots, leek, and zucchini, and sauté in a generous pool of olive oil in a deep pot or sauté pan over a low heat for 5–10 minutes. Add the rice, stir with a wooden spoon, and cook for another 3–4 minutes. Add the white wine and cook until the liquid has been absorbed. Grate the Parmesan cheese.

2. Add a cup of hot chicken stock and braise the rice over a high heat while stirring continuously, adding a little more chicken stock gradually. Five minutes before the rice is cooked, bind it with butter and grated Parmesan cheese. Chop the garlic and finely dice the tomatoes.

Flowers and Mussel Ragout

3. In a frying pan lightly pooled with olive oil, place a sprig of rosemary and chopped garlic. Wash the mussels and prawns carefully and shell the tails of the prawns; add into the pan. As soon as the mussels open, add the finely diced tomatoes. Chop the parsley.

4. Pour in the white wine, season, and sprinkle with chopped parsley at the last minute. To serve, after having removed its leaves and stem, fill the calyx of the zucchini flower with risotto. Arrange on plates and garnish with mussel and prawn ragout.

Foie Gras Pudding

Preparation time: 45 minutes
Cooking time: 1 hour
Difficulty: ★★★

Serves four

12 large fresh morels
4 small fresh morels
2 shallots
1 clove of garlic
generous ³/₈ cup / 100 ml cream
generous 5 tbsp / 70 g butter
generous ³/₈ cup / 100 ml Noilly (vermouth)
generous ³/₈ cup / 100 ml veal broth
salt, pepper to taste
half a bunch of chives

For the pudding:
generous ¹/₂ lb / 250 g duck liver (foie gras)
generous 1 cup / 250 ml milk
2 eggs
4 tsp / 20 ml truffle juice
a pinch of nutmeg
a pinch of sugar
salt, fresh-ground pepper to taste

For the stuffing:
generous ¹/₄ lb / 120 g poultry breast
1¹/₂ tbsp / 20 g truffles, chopped
1¹/₂ tbsp / 20 ml truffle juice
¹/₂ cup / 120 ml cream
a pinch of nutmeg
salt, fresh-ground pepper to taste

There are few dishes that enjoy as much worldwide renown and are as unchallenged in their dominance of the dinner table than foie gras. Made of the engorged liver of a specially fed (and fattened) duck or goose, the delicacy is tender, delicious, and dates back to ancient civilizations. The ancient Egyptians practiced the art of raising birds for it, as did the ancient Romans and the Gauls. Some historians maintain that it was introduced to Rome after Gaul had been conquered. Today this outstanding delicacy is primarily – though not exclusively – produced in the southwest of France.

A good foie gras is smooth, round and evenly shaped, with a uniform color and, above all, no bruises. The color will vary depending on the kind of bird it came from, as well as what that bird was fed, and then what the liver is marinated in during its preparation. Foie gras is a carefully regulated product, considered one of the culinary prides of France, and only those sold under the name *foie gras entier* (foie gras in one piece) are guaranteed to contain one hundred per cent genuine foie gras.

In this recipe, our chef, Michel Blanchet, unites foie gras with another classic delicacy, the truffle: the foie gras pudding is seasoned with the juice of this delicious fungus, proving once again that the two are an almost inevitable (and sublime) combination.

The morel, an edible wild mushroom that is related to the truffle, is just as renowned, and in season throughout the spring. It does have one drawback, however, in that the numerous folds and hollows on its honeycomb-like surface collect all kinds of dirt. Thus the cleaning process is rather tedious: a morel must be cleaned very thoroughly in cold water until no traces of dirt remain. The most common type, the *Morchella vulgaris*, will ensure the best result, according to Chef Blanchet. And the bigger the morel, here, the better, since they will be stuffed: if they are big enough, they can easily be filled using a pastry bag. The stuffing should be very well seasoned to contrast with the foie gras.

1. To make the pudding, season the milk with salt, pepper, and nutmeg. Heat, add the raw foie gras (which has been cut into pieces), steep for two minutes, and then puree in the blender or food processor. Add two eggs, the truffle juice, and a pinch of sugar. Season to taste and pass through a fine sieve.

2. For the stuffing, chop the truffles and the poultry breast (which could be goose, duck, or chicken) as finely as possible. Fold the cream into the poultry breast with a wide spatula, add the chopped truffles, truffle juice, and season with salt and pepper. Cut off the stems of the large morels and wash them several times under running water; drain and dry.

with Stuffed Morels

3. Grease four small baking dishes. Spoon in the duck liver mixture and let it steep in a double boiler at 170 °F / 80 °C for 45 minutes. In the meantime, use a pastry bag to fill the morels with the poultry stuffing.

4. Chop the shallots. In a frying pan, sauté the shallots in butter; add the salted and peppered morels and a whole clove of garlic. Add a dash of Noilly and veal broth, cover, and steep for ten minutes. Take the morels out and keep them warm. To make a sauce, add cream, let it thicken, and pass through a fine sieve. To serve, halve the morels, arrange around a mound of pudding; garnish with sauce, chive sprigs and small morels.

Spring Delicacies with

Preparation time: 40 minutes
Cooking time: 20 minutes
Difficulty: ★★★

Serves four

scant 1/2 lb / 200 g puff pastry (see basic recipes)

2 bunches of green asparagus
2 dozen or scant 1 1/2 lb / 700 g langoustines
   (between 2–4 inches / 10 cm)
4 button mushrooms
2 shallots

1 onion
1 carrot
1 bunch of chervil
1 clove of garlic
1 bunch of thyme
1 bay leaf
1 bunch of parsley
1 tbs tomato paste
1 2/3 cups / 400 ml cream
generous 3/8 cup / 100 ml olive oil
1 2/3 cups / 400 ml white wine
salt, pepper to taste

It took many centuries before people knew what to do with asparagus, as this plant that grows underground has confused many a gardener. Although it is pictured on ancient Egyptian frescos, it seems that it was forgotten about for a long time; only at the court of Louis XIV was asparagus rescued from oblivion. During the 19th century, its popularity began to spread worldwide. Asparagus is sold in many varieties, from slender baby asparagus to the much larger, renowned, white asparagus that is ubiquitous in, for instance, the market stalls of Paris. In addition to white or green, it also comes in purple, as, when the tips push through the soil in their search for sunlight, they take on a violet hue. Wild asparagus, which is more rare, is only harvested between mid-May and mid-June.

For this recipe, our chef, Michel Blanchet, opts for green asparagus with fresh, crisp spears and firm tips as an ideal complement for the langoustines. To store the asparagus, wrap it in a damp cloth and store horizontally in the refrigerator.

The maritime component of this recipe is what delights any gourmet from southern Europe: the scampi (prawn) in Italy and the *camarone* in Spain are just as popular as the French langoustine. Take the utmost care when preparing the langoustines as, if cooked too long, the flesh of their tails inevitably turns tough and dry.

The langoustines should be shelled before they are cooked, so the flesh is infused with the dish's aromas. The head, legs, and shells are used to prepare the sauce – which should, incidentally, be well seasoned. At the last minute the sauce is whipped up with butter to provide a tasty finishing touch. The result is a delicious mixture of flavors.

1. Clean the asparagus, place in boiling water until done but still slightly firm, and set aside to cool. Cut the tips to approximately 4 in / 10 cm and the spears into 1 in / 3 cm pieces. Cook the button mushrooms in the same manner.

2. Chop one shallot. Sauté it, and the stems of the mushrooms, in butter, adding the asparagus pieces. Thicken with cream and season. Cut the puff pastry into small diamonds and bake in the oven at 430 °F / 220 °C for approximately 15 minutes. Fill the pastry diamonds with the ragout of mushrooms and asparagus.

Asparagus and Languostines

3. Shell the langoustines while they are still raw, and refrigerate. Prepare a stock from the heads, legs, and shells adding the seasonings indicated. Let the liquid reduce, then strain through cheesecloth or a fine-meshed sieve, and whip up with butter.

4. Sauté the asparagus tips in a frying pan with butter. To serve, arrange the tips in a criss-crossing pattern on each plate, and place the filled puff pastry pieces next to them. Pour the sauce over the langoustines and decorate the composition with chervil leaves.

Cream Soup with

Preparation time: 30 minutes
Cooking time: 40 minutes
Difficulty: ★★

Serves four

4 lb 4 oz / 2 kg mussels
4 lb 4 oz / 2 kg Mediterranean fish, such as rockfish,
    stingray, sea eel, sea robin (also known as
    gurnard)
4 leeks (to yield ⁵/₈ cup / 150 g)
generous 1¹/₂ lb / 750 g tomatoes
4 onions (to yield ⁵/₈ cup / 150 g)
1 clove of garlic
2 shallots

3¹/₂ tbsp / 50 g butter
¹/₈ lb / 50 g Swiss cheese (to yield scant ¹/₈ lb / 50 g
    grated)
1 baguette
1¹/₄ cups / 300 ml crème fraîche
¹/₂ cup / 125 ml olive oil
generous 2 cups / 500 ml sweet white wine
scant ¹/₄ cup / 50 ml pastis (aniseed liqueur)
half a bunch of parsley
¹/₂ bunch fresh fennel (to yield 1 oz / 30 g)
1 bay leaf
1 sprig of thyme
a pinch of saffron filaments
salt, pepper to taste

Whatever else you might think about it, inattentiveness can sometimes leads to surprising results. One day, our chef, the usually meticulous Christian Bouvarel, accidentally added mussels to his usually fish-laden bouillabaisse, and thus inadvertently invented this recipe. It was so successful that it is now a regular item on the menu of Paul Bocuse's restaurant.

Naturally, the quality of the mussels is crucial. The common blue mussel, with its tasty, wonderful orange-yellow flesh, is best suited for this dish. Famous all over the world, the blue mussel is cultivated to keep it free of sand; when arriving at market, it is usually already de-sanded and filtered, thanks to the experience of generations of its farmers. For Chef Bouvarel this is the only type of mussel worth considering, be it from Spain or from the Netherlands, for this reason. Nevertheless, strain the stock once the mussels are cooked and have opened.

(Do not, of course, cook the mussels for too long.) Cook the soup gently over a low heat and round off the flavor by adding crème fraîche.

The Mediterranean fish required for this recipe are basically the same as for a conventional bouillabaisse (if one can call any form of this dish conventional). If you can not find rockfish (also known as scorpion fish), substitute any other fish that catch your eye, such as rosefish or sea bass). The subtle mixture of saffron and pastis, together with a heavy white wine – actually Pouilly-Fuissée in the original recipe – lends the dish a heady, unforgettable presence that will most likely leave no one unmoved. Saffron, incidentally, an aromatic spice that has enjoyed great popularity since the Middle Ages, was first brought to France by Savoyan merchants and has since mainly been grown there in the Rhône valley.

1. Chop the shallots and parsley. Cook the mussels in white wine with the chopped shallots, parsley and 3 tbsp / 50 g of butter until they open. Set aside a few of the cooked mussels for decoration and shell the rest. Gut and scale the fish and chop into large pieces.

2. Chop the onions and cut the leeks into thin strips. Heat the olive oil, add the onions and the saffron filaments, as well as the strips of leek. Steam over a low heat for five minutes.

Mussels and Saffron

3. Chop the tomatoes. To the same pot, add aniseed liqueur, then a little water, wine, mussel stock, fish, tomatoes, and all of the herbs. Cook for 40 minutes and season to taste. Pass the ingredients through a fine sieve to puree the fish as much as possible, then bring to a boil again.

4. Lastly, add the crème fraîche, cook for another two minutes, and pour into a tureen. Grate the cheese and toast the baguette. The grated cheese and the toasted, sliced baguette spread with olive oil and garlic are served separately. Serve the creamy soup with the mussels in soup plates and decorate with the mussels in their shells. Garnish, if desired, with parsley.

Lasagna

Preparation time:	*3 hours*
Cooking time:	*20 minutes*
Difficulty:	★★★

Serves four

4 sea perch filets (see below)

For the dough:
generous 1 lb / 500 g flour
4 egg yolks
2 eggs

1 bunch of spinach
2 tbsp / 10 ml squid ink
¹/₄ cup / 50 g tomato paste
salt

For the basil butter:
generous 2 cups / 500 ml water
1 bunch of basil
1 tbsp / 15 ml roast juice
7 tbsp / 100 g butter

When quizzed on the source for his culinary philosophy, our chef, Carlo Brovelli, tells this story. His uncle went on a trip around the world, and returned with the most important secrets of cooking. These, he passed on to his nephew: treat the products used with respect, follow the cooking times meticulously, and pay attention not only to the role the different flavors play, but how they work together when combined.

Thus is introduced Chef Brovelli's lasagna appetizer, which stands out both because of its inventive dough, and because it combines the principles mentioned above. Pasta ribbons are dyed with the natural essences of squid ink, tomatoes, and spinach and the dish encapsulates all of the chef's skills into a delight for eye and palate. Depending on one's whim and taste, the dough may of course also be dyed with other ingredients to achieve other colors, such as beets or yellow bell peppers.

Naturally, a multitude of lasagna recipes exist in Italy. The most well-known is probably *lasagna alla Bolognese* – that is, with a rich, meaty, tomato and vegetable sauce, but *lasagna al pesto* (with basil) or *lasagna verdi* (with a green sauce) are also very popular. In this case our chef garnishes his lasagna with a fillet of sea perch that has been steamed only briefly so that it does not lose its flavor. This Mediterranean version of the fish is actually an ordinary perch – unlike the genuine sea perch from the North Sea, which is most often used for smoked fillets. If you cannot obtain a Mediterranean perch, substitute sea bass, for instance, or a similar fish.

Reference should also be made to the butter spiced with basil: this aromatic herb thrives in the southern Italian sun. Not surprisingly, the symbol of this sun, *il sole*, adorns the sign of our chef's century-old restaurant, which is situated on one of the most romantic roads in Lombardy.

1. Cook the roast juice with five basil leaves in two cups of water. Reduce to one cup, mix, and strain. Add the remaining chopped basil leaves and butter, whip, and keep warm.

2. Prepare the lasagna dough with flour, eggs, and 4 egg yolks. Puree the spinach. Separate the dough into four equal portions; knead squid ink into the first, tomato paste into the second, spinach puree into the third, and leave the fourth portion uncolored. Keep all under a damp cloth for one hour, then roll out in thin layers. Carefully cut these into long, ribbon-shaped strips.

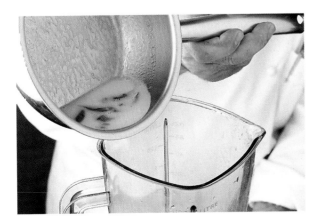

del Sole

3. Place these colorful strips next to each other, adhere together with the remaining egg yolk, cook in salted water, and spread out on a cloth. Season the sea perch filets and steam for three minutes; keep warm.

4. Place a colorful lasagna sheet onto each plate, lay a piece of sea perch fillet on top, pour on the basil butter and cover with another sheet of lasagna. Serve immediately.

Preparation time: 2 hours
Cooking time: 10 minutes
Difficulty: ★★

Serves four

6 eggs
1 bunch of green asparagus
1 carrot
7 oz / 200 g button mushrooms
1 bunch of mustard greens (to yield 3¹/₂ oz / 100 g)
3¹/₂ tbsp / 50 g butter

6¹/₂ tbsp / 100 g truffle butter
salt, pepper to taste

For the ravioli dough
generous 1 cup / 250 g semolina flour
3 egg yolks
1 egg
generous ³/₈ cup / 100 ml extra virgin olive oil

Another family member inspired this next appetizer from Chef Carlo Brovelli – his maternal grandmother Emilia, who passed on to him her idea of culinary simplicity as it was perceived of in Lombardy during the years following the war. And before her, Emilia was preceded by another expert chef, for Chef Brovelli actually represents the fourth consecutive generation of chefs in this venerable restaurant, Il Sole di Ranco, in Ranco. The recipes for the hearty meals prepared here, like this one with ravioli and scrambled eggs, are over half a century old, kept reverently in old school exercise books.

The daisy shape of the ravioli, a symbol of spring, should be either cut out of a daisy-shaped cookie cutter, or composed of circular sections glued together with egg, or even cut carefully with a sharp knife into a flowered shape. Nowadays, one attempts to cook the required vegetables *al dente* for health,

though in earlier days the vegetables would have been cooked for longer.

Asparagus is as important for the preparation and flavor of the dish as for its decoration. Use only very thin, dark green asparagus spears. If these are not available, zucchini flowers cut into thin strips will also provide the right springlike effect. The strong grassy flavor of the mustard greens enhances the flavor and fragrance of the filling. They should, however, be used only sparingly, so as not to throw the other flavors off balance.

Truffle butter rounds off the presentation of these ravioli, but it can easily be substituted with melted butter or even an Italian variety of cheese such as Grana or Pecorino. Whatever you choose, our chef insists that it be absolutely fresh and natural, and, of course, in season.

1. Cut the mustard greens into thin strips. Cook the asparagus until al dente, set aside the tips, and cut the spears into small pieces.
Prepare the ravioli dough, wrap in a damp cloth and refrigerate for an hour and a half. Cut the carrot into long strips, blanch, and set aside.

2. Beat and season the eggs. Heat the butter in a non-stick pan, add the eggs, and stir until they are set.

Daisy Ravioli

3. Combine the mustard greens and asparagus spears with the eggs. Wash the mushrooms and dice finely; fry in olive oil. Roll out the ravioli dough into a thin layer.

4. Fill the ravioli (if possible, cut out in the shape of a daisy) with the egg mixture and simmer gently for ten minutes. Serve three daisies per plate, and decorate with the asparagus tips tied together with the carrot strips. Drizzle with truffle butter, and sprinkle with the diced mushrooms.

Artichoke Crêpes

Preparation time: 1 hour
Cooking time: 35 minutes
Difficulty: ✷✷

Serves four

4 artichokes
16 langoustines
1 cup / 250 ml fish juice
half a bunch of chives
half a bunch of sage
generous ³/₈ cup / 100 g butter

?? oz / 15 ml milk
salt, pepper to taste

For the crêpe batter:
generous 2 cups / 500 ml milk
generous 1 cup / 250 g flour
6¹/₂ tbsp / 100 g sugar
4 eggs
generous ³/₈ cup / 100 g butter
a pinch of salt

In Lombardy, artichokes are used for a multitude of dishes. Related to the wild thistle, the vegetable has been well-known in the Mediterranean area for centuries, and is a popular ingredient not only in risotto, but also in Italian's many traditional pasta dishes. Initially imported from Carthage via Sicily, the Italian artichoke is now mainly grown in and exported from the heart of Italy. In the United States, of course, the artichoke has been cultivated to great success, particularly in California.

The so-called Roman artichoke, an apt accompaniment for meat as well as fish, is somewhat saltier in taste and also more expensive in price. It is grown in the coastal area and resembles the artichoke from Brittany, owing both to its growing in a similar soil quality and containing a similarly low fiber content. For this artichoke appetizer, Chef Carlo Brovelli deliber-

ately casts aside tradition and serves them with crêpes, first surprising the eye and then surprising the palate. If a whole fish is used instead of the langoustines, this dish may be served as a more substantial main course.

Choose langoustines that are medium-sized and very fresh – if possible, still alive. Since they are very delicate, cover them with chopped ice if they are to be kept in the refrigerator for a few hours. Langoustines can be prepared in the oven if you like them crisp, or boiled if you prefer them soft. For this recipe, some will be chopped into small pieces to be added to the artichoke filling, some left in the form of whole tails. To make sure that neither of the two flavors overpowers the other, take care to balance the quantities you're working with.

1. Remove the leaves of the artichokes and clean down to the hearts. Cook these for 30 minutes, then puree in a vegetable press and, if necessary, pass through a sieve. Dilute with a little milk and a small pat of butter.

2. Cook the langoustines over a low heat, preferably in fish broth. Shell the tails and keep them warm.

with Langoustines

3. Cut four of the langoustine tails into thin slices and add to the artichoke puree. Prepare the crêpe mixture, adding the milk slowly to obtain a smooth batter. Melt and brown the butter and stir it into the mixture with a whisk. Pass through a sieve and allow to rest for 15 minutes.

4. Bake the crêpes, place a portion of artichoke puree and a langoustine tail on top, fold the pancake into a parcel and tie up with a blade of chives. Heat briefly in the oven, pour melted sage butter over, and decorate with a langoustine.

Ravioli with Fresh

Preparation time: 1 hour
Cooking time: 8 minutes
Difficulty: ★

Serves four

For the ravioli dough:
generous 1 cup / 250 g semolina flour
1 tbsp / 15 ml oil
3 egg yolks
1 egg
generous 1/2 lb / 250 g spinach
salt to taste

For the filling:
2 zucchini
1 red pepper
1 fennel bulb
1 celery heart
1 bunch mustard greens (7 oz / 200 g)
7 oz / 200 g Ricotta
1/2 cup / 120 g butter
1 bunch of basil
salt, pepper to taste

Particularly in this culinarily adventurous age, when classics are being constantly reinterpreted, there is nothing to prevent a skilled chef from flouting old traditions and filling ravioli with something other than the customary meat, fish or cheese. From Chef Carlo Brovelli, then, comes this suggestion, a vegetarian ravioli filled with a masterly mixture of vegetables cooked *al dente*, balanced by the famous Ricotta cheese.

Spinach, dried well beforehand, lends the dough its green tint. The "starry sky" pattern of the dough – albeit a semolina sky, dotted with green stars, can also be achieved by using Swiss chard leaves. Parsley is not recommended, as it will tint the dough too intensely.

Be careful to adhere strictly to the prescribed cooking instructions of each vegetable, since the individual flavor of each one

must be preserved. And, as Chef Brovelli emphasizes, by no means should one give in to the temptation to use any other vegetables, as this would complicate the recipe unecessarily. One exception, however, are mustard greens, which may certainly be added to this exclusive mixture if you so desire.

Ricotta, a cheese made from cow's or sheep's milk, does not melt when cooked, a characteristic that makes it ideal for fillings, as well as antipasti and pasta dishes. It also adds a strong flavor to the vegetable filling. It should be bought particularly fresh, as it tends to adopt a bitter aftertaste quite quickly – and sometimes gets a bit watery after sitting for a long time – which would spoil the recipe. Chef Brovelli recommends diluting in the blender or food processor with a little milk so it may meld more easily with the vegetable filling.

1. Blanch and chop the spinach. Prepare the ravioli dough with the ingredients indicated and mix it with a portion of the blanched and chopped spinach. Set aside the dough to rest in a damp cloth for an hour and a half, then roll out thinly and cut into wide strips.

2. Cut the zucchini into 1/2 in / 1 cm wide strips, dice, and cook until al dente. Do the same with the other vegetables. Drain everything well and refrigerate.

Vegetable Filling

3. Melt the butter. If using mustard greens, wash and chop them. Mix with the chilled and diced vegetables and the Ricotta cheese, season, and add in melted butter.

4. Cut the dough strips into squares, baste one half with an egg yolk. Prepare the ravioli, spooning a portion of the filling onto each square and covering with another square. Cook in salted water for two minutes, and then arrange four or five on each plate in the shape of a flower. To serve, place one spoonful of diced vegetables in the center of each plate, pour melted butter over, and sprinkle with chopped basil leaves.

Ribbon Noodles with

Preparation time: 1 hour
Cooking time: 10 minutes
Difficulty: ★

Serves four

generous 9 oz / 280 g fresh ribbon noodles
  (trenette; see below)
5 oz / 150 g green beans
generous 3¹/₂ oz / 100 g pine nuts
³/₄ cup / 200 ml extra virgin olive oil
salt

For the pesto:
2 bunches of small-leafed basil
  (to yield generous ¹/₂ lb / 250 g small leaves)
generous 1 cup / 250 ml extra virgin olive oil
¹/₈ lb / 60 g Pecorino (sheep's milk cheese)
1 potato
salt, white pepper to taste

The famous pesto, based on fresh basil and olive oil, originates from Liguria. Yet its reputation has spread nearly across the globe, beginning over the whole of Italy and southern France. Each region claims to have invented this sauce, swearing by its own version of the recipe. The Lombardians, for example, are not at all partial to the pine nuts used in the original recipe. There is, however, one common factor in all the permutations: the use of a mortar to crush the basil by hand, lending it an aromatic, even consistency. Though here too, the process has evolved, with modern chefs now eschewing the traditional technique for the use of a blender or food processor.

The basil should be very fresh; the smaller the leaves, the more tender and tasty they will be. Queen Catherine de Medici is said to have used only the Brazilian Garofanoto variety for her herbal tea, a type also very well-suited for our recipe. Big basil leaves wilt much faster, contrary to what some believe, and do not, in fact, have a better flavor.

The green beans used for the bundled decoration need to be extremely fresh and small. In order to preserve their flavor and the right texture, they are cooked in salted water only until *al dente*. If these are out of season, they may be substituted with small, fresh, white flageolet beans, which have a small dark mark on their base. Though not easily found in U.S. markets, they have a delicate flavor that is well worth the search.

Within a general category ribbon (or flat) noodles come in great varieties, differing from region to region not only in widths, but occasionally, in doughs as well. Prepare this dough with few eggs and, most importantly, roll it out thinly. Cook it in slightly salted water and process it without delay to prevent it from drying out too much.

Finally, this appetizer provides the opportunity to get to know Pecorino, a sheep's milk cheese from Sardinia whose strong flavor mingles in the most delightful way with the extra-virgin olive oil. Of the latter, Chef Carlo Brovelli recommends the olive oil from Liguria – an appropriate component, certainly.

1. Prepare the pasta dough and set aside to rest in a damp cloth for an hour and a half. Roll out very thinly and cut into 1¹/₂ in / 4 cm wide strips. Boil an unpeeled potato in water.

2. Puree the basil leaves, olive oil, cheese, potato, salt and pepper in a blender or food processor. Cook the green beans until al dente, drain and rinse with ice-cold water. Drain and set aside.

Pesto and Green Beans

3. Cook the noodles in salted water until al dente (3–5 minutes), then rinse briefly under cold water. Roast or lightly toast the pine nuts.

4. To serve, arrange the noodles on the plates and arrange the well-seasoned green beans on top. Pour pesto over everything, and sprinkle with roasted pine nuts.

Poached Eggs

Preparation time: 30 minutes
Chilling time: 3 hours
Cooking time: 10 minutes
Difficulty: ☆

Serves four

8 eggs
6 egg yolks
scant ⁷/₈ lb / 400 g hop shoots (or substitute soybean or mung bean sprouts)
generous 2 cups / 500 ml cream

generous 1 cup / 250 ml pale lager beer (Saint-Feuillien from Belgium, if available)
scant ¹/₄ cup / 50 ml white whine vinegar
1 tbsp / 15 g mild prepared mustard
1 bunch of chervil
salt, pepper to taste

Eggs have the virtually unchallenged position of being utilized in every realm of cooking, from appetizer to dessert. Sweet or savory, they contribute to innumerable gastronomic masterpieces. One of the great egg-producing countries in Europe is Belgium, with a production figure of more than three billion eggs a year. The nutritional value of eggs is extraordinary; the egg is practically the only natural product containing vitamin D as well as vitamins A, E and K, thus providing exceptionally balanced and nourishing nutrition.

Eggs, importantly, should always be consumed fresh. One way to test their freshness is to put them in cold water. A fresh egg lies horizontally at the bottom of the bowl, whereas a less fresh one stands up vertically, or even floats to the surface. For the preparation of poached eggs, extremely fresh eggs are naturally required. These should be refrigerated beforehand for a few hours, so that the egg white coagulates better when cooked. Trim any irregular edges before serving.

Hop shoots are an interesting Belgian specialty, unfortunately only available from mid-March to the end of April, and rare in the United States. They are said to have medicinal healing powers; the French poet Rabelais swore by their aphrodisiac effect. The best shoots are firm and crisp. They have to be washed several times under running water, since they grow underground. If hop shoots are not available, they may be substituted with soybean or mung bean sprouts, though since quite delicate, these can be cooked only for about a minute.

Saint-Feuillien beer, a pale lager, is very common in Belgium and harmonizes well with the hop shoots. If it is unavailable, other beers, preferably pale lagers, may be used for the sauce.

1. Wash the hop shoots well and remove the hard part of the shoots. Reduce ²/₃ cup / 150 ml of beer in a pot by a quarter. Add cream, bring to a boil again, and season with salt and pepper. Add the drained hop shoots, cook for another five minutes, then take them out and set the liquid aside. If using soybean or mung bean sprouts, cook for only one minute.

2. Bring ¹/₂ cup / 100 ml of water and a ¹/₄ cup / 50 ml of vinegar to a boil in a pot. In the meantime, crack eight eggs into eight small bowls. Gently slide one egg after the other into the boiling vinegar water. Cook them for two minutes; then take out and set aside in lukewarm water.

in Beer Sauce

3. In a bowl, blend six egg yolks with 7 tbsp / 100 ml of pale lager, beat until frothy, and then whisk briskly over a low heat until a creamy sauce develops. Add the stock from the hop shoots and 1 tsp / 5 g of mustard, and season with salt and pepper. Pass the sauce through a sieve.

4. To serve, arrange the hop sprouts on the plate in the shape of a nest. Dry the poached eggs and trim off the rough edges. Place one egg on each nest, pour the sauce around it, and garnish with chervil leaves.

Celeriac Ravioli

Preparation time: 1 hour
Cooking time: 10 minutes
Difficulty: ★★

Serves four

generous 2 lb / 1 kg celeriac
generous 1 oz / 40 g black truffle
1 bunch celery (to yield celery leaves)
scant ³/₄ lb / 350 g goose liver (foie gras)
³/₄ cup / 200 ml truffle juice
³/₄ cup / 200 ml concentrated vegetable broth

¹/₂ cup / 125 g potato flour
¹/₄ cup / 60 g butter
2 tbsp / 30 ml lemon juice
salt, pepper to taste

Some people say that Savoy, that historical region straddling southeastern France and northwestern Italy, is the birthplace of the ravioli recipe. Originally, these were made in the form of small balls made of green vegetables and eggs. Today, when one pictures ravioli, one tends to imagine the later Italian version: square pockets, usually made from semolina-floured pasta dough, filled with vegetables, or cheese, or meat, and flavored with herbs. Our specialty here comes from southeastern France and is highly esteemed in the area around Nice and on Corsica, though the Romans in the Rhône valley and other cities also claim to have a right to it. Our Belgian chef, Jean-Pierre Bruneau, inspired by this method of preparation, here introduces his own very original version.

The most important novelty is the use of celeriac, or root celery, which is mainly available in winter. The bulb selected should be heavy, firm, and white, with no blemishes. To preserve its color, it must be washed in vinegar water as soon as it is peeled and then cut into regular thin slices. The so-called mandolin, a kitchen tool common in many European kitchens, will do the trick. These slices are then cut, with a cookie cutter if possible, into circles; for the sake of presentation they should all be the same size. Gluing the celeriac slices together using the potato flour requires concentration and great care, since these ravioli are very fragile. For this reason they must also be steamed instead of boiled to prevent them from disintegrating.

For easy processing, the goose liver should be kneaded until soft and pressed through a pastry bag without a nozzle, then left in plastic wrap to set again. Prepared this way, it may be cut into beautifully even slices.

1. Press the goose liver through a nozzle-less pastry bag to shape into a roll with a diameter of approximately 1¹/₂ in / 3 cm. Cut into thin slices. Peel the celeriac, slice thinly, and cut out circles of about 2 in / 4 cm in diameter. Blanch in boiling water, to which salt and lemon juice have been added, for 3–4 minutes; briefly rinse with cold water.

2. Cut the truffles into thin slices and then into circles of about 1–1¹/₂ in / 3 cm in diameter. Place each goose liver circle between two truffle slices. In the meantime, drain the celeriac slices on paper toweling. Heat the truffle juice with the vegetable broth.

with Truffles

3. Place one piece of the goose liver and truffle combination between two celeriac slices. Dust the edges of the celeriac slices with potato flour to stick them together. Steam the ravioli in a suitable pot for two minutes.

4. Whip the truffle sauce with a whisk, adding small pats of butter, and season to taste. Whip up the sauce once more in a blender just before it is served. Serve the ravioli in soup plates, pour the sauce over, and decorate with a few lightly fried celery leaves.

Tripe Florentines

Preparation time: 25 minutes
Cooking time: 15 minutes
Difficulty: ★★

Serves four

generous ¹/₂ lb / 250 g cooked tripe sausage
generous ¹/₂ lb / 250 g smoked tripe sausage
4 whole leaves green lettuce
1 Jerusalem artichoke (Topinambur), 7 oz / 200 g
2 bunches of spinach, 14 oz / 400 g
2 tbsp / 30 ml balsamic vinegar

2 tsp / 10 ml white wine or must
1 tbsp / 15 ml heavy cream
generous ³/₄ cup / 200 g butter
4 bunches of smooth-leaved parsley
salt, pepper to taste

After the end of the Second World War, root or tuberous vegetables like the jerusalem artichoke (known in France as *topinambur*, named after a native Brazilian tribe) and the rutabaga (also called swede) fell into disfavor, and since then have played a more minor part in cuisine than in eras past. But their flavors and nutritional qualities should not simply be forgotten. On the 50th anniversary of the Allied landing in Normandy, this dish, created by Chef Michel Bruneau, was served to the greatest statesmen of the world.

The Jerusalem artichoke originated in North America, and was brought to France. There, it was often fried, or incorporated into salads or dishes served with creamy sauces. Its taste resembles that of the artichoke; its nutrients include the very valuable inullin, a carbohydrate similar to starch.

Two types of tripe sausage compete for our favor here: the one from Brittany is large and fat, consisting of rumen pieces stuffed into each other, and is either cooked or smoked and then cut into round pieces. The other variety from Normandy is comprised of rumen pieces that are finely chopped before being stuffed into the sausage skin. Both varieties have their own supporters and detractors; the choice, here, is up to you.

Regarding the spinach, cook it as briefly as possible before serving to preserve its aroma and green color. The butter sauce can be prepared either with white wine or with must. If you boil it down a little, you will reduce the acetic acid and enhance the flavor, but this should only be done in moderation. According to our chef, this warm appetizer is most popular in summer. If it is to be served as a main course, the quantity of the ingredients simply has to be increased adequately; the ingredients themselves are hearty enough.

1. Peel the jerusalem artichoke, dice three-quarters of it, and slice the rest to use as the garnish. Strip the spinach leaves off their stalks. Bring the artichoke and spinach leaves to a boil; keep warm. Blanch the lettuce leaves. Skin and slice the tripe sausage and retain the skin.

2. To prepare the butter sauce, chop the parsley; boil the sausage skins with the parsley in white wine (or must) until the liquid is reduced. In a different saucepan reduce the balsamic vinegar. In the meantime, sauté the diced artichoke in butter.

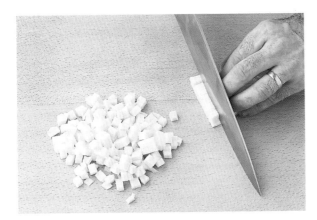

with Topinambur

3. Heat small glass or porcelain bowls in a double boiler. Grease the warm bowls with butter, put one sausage slice in each one, place a lettuce leaf on top, fill up with the spinach and jerusalem artichoke mixture, and cover with another sausage slice.

4. Finally, whip up the prepared white wine or must sauce with butter, add heavy cream, and strain through a funnel-shaped sieve. Keep warm in a double boiler. Arrange the sausage florentines on plates, pour over the butter sauce and a small quantity of the balsamic vinegar; decorate with parsley leaves and a few slices of jerusalem artichoke.

Warm Oysters with

Preparation time: 25 minutes
Cooking time: 30 minutes
Difficulty: ★★

Serves four

20 oysters
2 apples (e.g. Rennet or Granny Smith)
2 shallots
³/₄ cup / 200 ml Calvados
generous ³/₈ cup / 100 ml Pommeau
generous 2 tbsp / 40 ml heavy cream

¹/₂ cup / 125 g coarse salt (see below)
fresh-ground pepper to taste

Oysters have been a loved and esteemed part of culinary history since time immemorial, used and prepared in many different ways. The ancient Greeks ground oyster shells into a powder, which they consumed as an aphrodisiac. Iron-rich and packed with vitamins, this "fish," as it is sometimes called by professional gastronomes, can be enjoyed raw, cooked or baked. The many methods of preparating oysters are often based on very old traditions, as is the choice of oyster used. The large oysters found in the open sea, for example, with their slightly nutty flavor, are often used in warm dishes.

Chef Michel Bruneau recommends either Granny Smith or Rennet apples for this dish; depending on your preference, both may be used in ample quantities and, due to their slightly tart, sharp taste, go very well with oysters. In terms of size, the smaller the apples the better, as they will contain a greater concentration of fruit acid. Pommeau, a mixture of Calvados and fresh apple cider fermented in vats, goes very well with fish and seafood and also refines all sorts of apple-based desserts. In our recipe, the sauce – but not the oysters – may be prepared a day in advance.

The salt is dyed with green aqueous plants, preferably seaweed, to emphasize the maritime character of this dish even more. As an alternative, fresh parsley can also be used. Just before you slide the oysters under the grill, sprinkle them with fresh-ground pepper to round off their iodine flavor.

1. Open the oysters, drain, and reserve the juice. Shell, then wash the shells well and set them aside. Peel and seed the apples, cut into eighths, then cut a small quantity into extremely thin (julienne) strips and set aside. Chop the shallots.

2. Place the large apple pieces in a saucepan, add Calvados, Pommeau, and the chopped shallots. Bring to a boil and reduce to three-quarters of the original volume. Stir in heavy cream and boil again over a low heat to bind the sauce. Add the oyster juice and strain by passing everything through a fine sieve.

Flavors from the Orchard

3. Place one oyster into each shell and top with a few of the julienned apple strips. Add pepper, cover with sauce, and grill gently in the oven. In the meantime, mix the coarse salt with seaweed or parsley in a blender or food processor until the salt is dyed green.

4. Using a suitable mold, shape the dyed salt into five "pedestals" per plate. Place one oyster au gratin on each of these pedestals. Decorate the plates with seaweed or parsley as desired and serve promptly.

Leek Tidbits in a

Preparation time: 1 hour
Cooking time: 20 minutes
Difficulty: ★★

Serves four

6.6 lb / 3 kg leeks
generous 2 lb / 1 kg tomatoes
juice of 1 lemon
4 egg yolks
1 tbsp / 15 g coarse prepared mustard
generous ³/₈ cup / 100 g butter

1 tbsp / 15 ml olive oil
1 bunch of basil
salt, white pepper to taste
2 tbsp / 30 g green peppercorns from a jar

Of Nero, the cruel and bloodthirsty emperor, the world was left with a generally bad impression. But few know that the ruler loved leek dishes, believing the vegetable would improve a warrior's courage as well as an orator's voice. He thus strove to promote the cultivation of this vegetable. There are, of course, those who flatly reject leeks, and it may well require delicious dishes like this one, from Chef Alain Burnel, to change their minds.

If possible, the leeks selected for this appetizer should be very fresh and medium-sized (the larger plants are hollow and hard). The green part of the stalk can be reserved for a different purpose, such as a soup or a side dish. The white part of the stalk will be peeled, cooked until *al dente* (since overcooked leeks tend to disintegrate) and then peeled once more.

The success of this recipe depends to a great extent on the frothy cream, refined with traditional European mustard and green peppercorns, to complement the leeks. By traditional mustard, one means the coarse mustard that still contains small bits of the crushed mustard seeds; in the U.S., this is sometimes called country mustard. The name *Moutarde de Dijon* (Dijon mustard) does not actually refer to its geographical origin – mustard, in fact, did not originate in Dijon – but rather to a manufacturing method that began in the 14th century, when the vinegar-makers of the Duc de Bourgogne – who lived in the town of Dijon – were granted the relevant license.

In Chef Alain Burnel's composition, the strong flavors come from the mustard and leeks, while the other ingredients have more gentle flavors. Preparation of the frothy cream requires a good deal of care and sensitivity: at first, pour only a little water onto the egg yolks, gently whip to a froth in a double boiler, and never be in a hurry, especially not when you stir in the mustard. This should be added last, when the sauce has already been taken off the stove.

1. Peel the leeks; reserve the green parts of the stems for other uses. Cook the white sections in water with a little butter and lemon juice for 20 minutes. Peel the leek pieces again and keep them warm in their stock.

2. Dice the tomatoes finely, add chopped basil butter, and pan-fry while continuously stirring in small amounts of olive oil.

Frothy Mustard Cream

3. Gently whip the egg yolks and a little water until creamy, at first directly on the stove, then in a double boiler. Add mustard after the sauce is off the stove. Brush the leek pieces with butter.

4. Spread one tablespoon of the tomato mixture over the center of each plate, and arrange the leek pieces on top. Surround with a generous pour of sauce; sprinkle with a few green peppercorns and serve at room temperature.

Tomato Tarts in Olive

Preparation time: 1 hour
Baking time: 15 minutes
Difficulty: ★

Serves four

14 oz / 400 g puff pastry (see basic recipes)
5^1/$_2$ lb / 2^1/$_2$ kg tomatoes
3 sprigs of lavender
4 oz / 100 g fresh mozzarella
generous ^{3}/$_8$ cup / 100 ml olive oil
salt, pepper to taste

For the decoration:
4 small cherry tomatoes
half a bunch of chives

In the past, olive oil was not as lauded as it is now, said to raise one's cholesterol levels and contain too much fat. Nutritionists, if they recommended it at all, did so only reluctantly. But these days, pure, extra-virgin olive oil is highly touted, and enjoys the reputation of being one of the sun's true gifts. Master chefs like Ducasse and Troisgros are especially partial to it; this appetizer, from Chef Alain Burnel, celebrates it well.

French master chefs get their oil from Maussane-les-Alpilles, a little village near Baux-de-Provence in the magnificent Provence district in the south of France. The region's oil mills are famous all over the world. Each process – from selecting the olives to the actual milling – is repeated four times, carried out with utmost care according to the old Provençal traditions. Following these time-tested methods, this area produces a most extraordinary olive oil with a delicate flavor.

But olive oil alone is not enough; the tomatoes selected have to be firm, not too watery, very fresh, and, of course, very tasty. The so-called Roma tomatoes combine all these qualities, particularly during the sunny months of July and August when they are in season. Otherwise, use vine-ripened globe or beefsteak tomatoes. After the tomatoes are peeled they should be dried thoroughly before being marinated in olive oil – from Maussane, if at all possible, according to our chef.

Lavender lends the olive oil an authentic Provençal touch, evoking an image of the huge lavender fields that stretch like a mauve carpet all the way to the horizon. In this recipe, the lavender sprigs (with their flowers) are marinated in olive oil and placed in the sun; if one is lucky enough to live in a sunny region, forty-eight hours are usually enough.

1. Peel and seed the tomatoes. Dry well, cut out rounds, and dry again with paper towels. Bake in a 430 °F / 220 °C oven for 12 minutes.

2. Pour olive oil over the tomatoes, salt them, and set them aside to cool. Slice the fresh Mozzarella into strips. Marinate the lavender in olive oil and leave to steep.

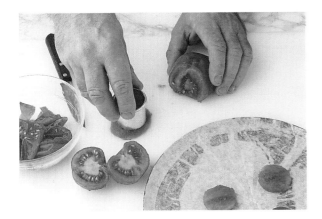

Oil and Lavender

3. Fill small baking molds with one layer of tomatoes, one layer of Mozzarella, another layer of tomatoes, and so on. Roll out the puff pastry and cut it to fit the baking molds.

4. Cover the filled baking molds with puff pastry and bake for 15 minutes. Cool and turn over onto the plates. Sprinkle a few drops of olive oil and a few lavender flowers around the tart, and garnish it with chive sprigs and a cherry tomato centerpiece. Serve at room temperature.

Calves' Brains with Marinated

Preparation time: 1 hour
Marinating time: 1 hour
Soaking time: up to 24 hours
Cooking time: 15 minutes
Difficulty: ☆

Serves four

generous 1 lb / 500 g veal brains
14 oz / 400 g fresh boletus mushrooms
1 bouquet garni
juice of 1 lemon

1 egg
generous ³/₈ cup / 100 g bread crumbs
2 bacon strips (to yield 1 tbsp / 15 g coarsely
   chopped)
1 lb / 450 g assorted green lettuces
1 bunch of chives (to yield 1 generous tbsp / 15 g
   chopped)
2 tomatoes (to yield 2 tbsp / 30 g diced)
generous ³/₈ cup / 100 ml vinegar
3 cups / 750 ml meat broth
salt, pepper to taste

Brains, one of the most delicious types of offal, have a high phosphorus content. They must always be fresh when bought and should be prepared and eaten soon after. There are many different methods of preparation, of which the most successful one is probably pan-frying, which results in a perfect contrast of crunchy outside and tender inside.

Though quite a lot of time and effort are involved in preparing calves' brains, the result is well worth it. To start, soak the brains in salted vinegar water for up to twenty-four hours to wash out any remaining blood, and to facilitate removing the thin membranes that cover and connect them. Then poach them

in broth. Set them aside in the broth to cool, which will make them easier to slice.

Boletus mushrooms, which taste best when they are young, stand out for their noble, nut-laced flavor. Although marinated (or dried) boletus are also available in the market, you should ideally buy them fresh, marinating them yourself. For this purpose, pour olive oil heated to 210 °F / 100 °C over the well-dried, quartered mushrooms. Then add a few seasonal herbs and set the marinade aside to cool. This appetizer should be served hot, and consumed immediately.

1. Soak the brains in a mixture of cold vinegar and salted water overnight, or, if more convenient, a full day. Then rinse well under running water and remove the veins and membranes.

2. Cook the brains in broth with the bouquet garni, set aside to cool, and cut into ¹/₂ in / 1 cm thick slices. Wash and drain the lettuce, break up into loose leaves, and combine to make a salad of assorted leaves.

Boletus Mushrooms

3. Coat the brain slices with bread crumbs and whisked egg and fry in butter until the outer surface is crisp. Season the lettuce salad with salt, pepper, lemon juice, and the olive oil from the mushroom marinade. Chop the chives and dice the tomatoes.

4. Fry the bacon strips in butter and add to the salad. To serve, arrange a ring of salad on each plate. Spoon the marinated mushrooms into the center, place the fried slices of brains on top, and sprinkle with a little vinegar as well as the chopped chives and diced tomatoes.

Sardine Fritters

Preparation time: 30 minutes
Cooking time: 5 minutes
Difficulty: ★

Serves four

10¹/₂ lb oz / 300 g sardines

For the batter:
scant ¹/₄ cup / 50 g flour
scant ¹/₄ cup / 50 g cornstarch
1 tsp / 5 g baking powder
assorted fresh herbs, chopped

For the citrus vinegar:
generous ³/₈ cup / 100 ml fresh orange juice
2 tsp / 10 ml sherry vinegar
2 tsp / 10 ml whine vinegar
1²/₃ cups / 400 ml olive oil
salt, pepper to taste

For the decoration:
6 oz / 150 g mixed lettuces
4 tomatoes

The way sardines are packed together in a can unintentionally reflects the typical behavior of these fish, which crowd together, moving through the water in giant, shimmering shoals. This recipe, however, requires the fresh, uncanned variety of sardines, preferably from the Mediterranean. Their size is also relevant: legend has it, after all, that it was a giant sardine that obstructed the harbor of Marseilles, and though a sardine that large is certainly a myth, they do grow as large as six inches (fifteen centimeters) long. For our purposes, however, we will use smaller specimens – even very small sardinelles – for this dish.

Fresh sardines, mostly available in the summer months, are firm and shiny. They must be handled with care since the delicate flesh breaks easily. Pre-gutted sardines are a lot tricker to handle as they often collapse. When gutting sardines and removing their backbones, take care not to pull the two fillets apart: the fish must always stay in one piece.

Of all the sardine recipes known in the Mediterranean region, the one presented here, by our chef, Jacques Cagna, is a particular delight because it makes a most elegant warm appetizer. The sardines, fried in a thin coat of batter and arranged like the radiating spires of a dome, provide a delicious contrast to the fresh salad. The tart citrus vinegar rounds off the flavor harmoniously.

The salad of mixed seasonal lettuces should, of course, be as fresh, crisp, and colorful as possible.

1. Scale, gut, and dehead the sardines, then open the fish from the back to remove the backbones. To prepare the batter, mix the flour with water, cornstarch, baking powder and, chopped herbs.

2. Puree the tomatoes. For the citrus vinegar, squeeze the juice from one orange and add to the two types of vinegar and the olive oil. Season with salt and pepper, and whisk well.

with Citrus Vinegar

3. Heat the deep-fat fryer to 355 °F / 180 °C. Hold the sardine by the tail, dip it into the batter and deep-fry in hot fat for a few minutes. Drain on paper towels.

4. To serve, place a small portion of salad dressed with citrus vinegar in the center of each plate, arrange the sardines on top in a radiating shape, and garnish the plates with chives and a few drops of tomato puree.

Fresh Mackerel Fillets

Preparation time: 25 minutes
Cooking time: 6 minutes
Difficulty: ★★

Serves four

5/8 lb / 300 g fresh mackerel
generous 1 oz / 40 g dried seaweed
2 scant tbsp / 25 g sesame seeds
2 cucumbers (to yield 7 oz / 200 g chopped)
scant 1/4 cup / 50 g flour
generous 3/8 cup / 100 g butter
1 egg

1 tbsp cream
generous 1 cup / 250 ml whole milk
2/3 cup / 150 ml olive oil
1/2 cup / 125 ml vinaigrette (see below)
salt, pepper to taste

For the blini:
flour
egg
milk
cream
seaweed

According to our chef, Jacques Cagna, whose self-titled restaurant is located in Paris, the very best place to eat a half-cooked mackerel is where it was caught. Not very surprising, since no matter what kind of fish is prepared this way, it must of course be absolutely fresh. The mackerel in particular, which has a reputation for being a very fatty type of fish that does not keep fresh for long, should be consumed immediately after being quickly, lightly fried.

Mackerel travel in large shoals and are generally caught in trawl nets, though sometimes taken by rod. Found along the whole Atlantic coast and in the Mediterranean, the fish has a different nickname in every region, from kingfish (king mackerel) to jack. Some gourmets, particularly in Normandy, prefer small, young mackerel – these are perhaps the best-suited for this recipe. You quickly find out how little time you need to get the mackerel, coated in sesame seeds and resting on a bed of cucumber, ready to serve.

For centuries, cucumber had the reputation of being hard to digest. But in fact cucumber is a light vegetable containing a large amount of water; it should be somewhat dehydrated with coarse salt before consumption so it becomes tender and can be consumed without hesitation. It is interesting that the cucumber is just as popular in Scandinavia as it is in southern Europe, where the Greeks enjoy using it to prepare wonderful, refreshing appetizers. Here the cucumber imparts its freshness to the half-raw fish served in this recipe.

1. To prepare the blini, blend flour, egg, whole milk, cream, and blanched, chopped seaweed in a bowl. Fill small baking molds of 2 in / 5 cm in diameter and 1/2 in / 1 cm in height to the rim with the mixture, and cook over a low heat.

2. Fillet the mackerel, carefully remove the bones, dip the skin side into sesame seeds, and cover.

on Seaweed Blini

3. Heat the olive oil in a frying pan and brown the mackerel fillets on both sides, making sure that the sesame seeds do not burn. Prepare a vinaigrette of olive oil, vinegar, salt, and pepper.

4. Peel, hollow out and grate the cucumbers, then sauté in butter. To serve, put a blin in the center of each plate, cover with cucumber, and set the fillets on top. Surround with a pour of vinaigrette.

Loch Fyne Mussels

Preparation time: 35 minutes
Cooking time: 10 minutes
Chilling time: approximately 1 hour
Difficulty: ✶✶

Serves four

3 lb / 1 1/2 kg mussels (see below)

For the salmon filling
14 oz / 400 g salmon fillet
1 shallot
2 large egg whites
generous 1 cup / 250 ml cream

1 oz / 15 ml cognac (or brandy)
a pinch of cayenne pepper
salt, pepper to taste

For the sauce:
4 tsp / 20 g Keta caviar (see below)
4 tsp / 20 g butter
generous 1 cup / 250 ml cream
2/3 cup / 150 ml mussel juice
2 tbsp / 30 ml white wine
quarter bunch of chives (to yield 1 tbsp / 15 g chopped)
1 shallot
salt, pepper to taste

Our chef Stewart Cameron, from Scotland, bases this appetizer on the renowned mussels farmed in the Loch Fyne area on Scotland's west coast. Loch Fyne is one of those rare examples of a haven for saltwater and freshwater fish alike, and this recipe, combining salmon roe and mussels, reflects that quality. As opposed to the larger versions of the mollusc from Spain or the Mediterranean Bouchot mussels, here Chef Cameron calls for medium-sized mussels. And in honor of the old adage that a good mussel is either open or closed, these are opened, filled, and then tied shut to cook. Finally, they are served open, adorned with globes of salmon roe.

The trick in this recipe lies in filling the mussel shells as full as possible. For this reason, remove the thin membrane-like skin inside the shells before spooning in the filling. You have probably never tied up a mussel to keep it closed before, but without this precautionary measure the recipe can not be prepared correctly. As the filling should not be too stiff, it is important not to add too much egg white.

Keta caviar is a cured salmon roe imported from Norway. Though Chef Cameron often uses it as an integral component of his recipes (see the following recipe for one example), here it is actually used only for decoration. Since its flavor goes so well with the other ingredients, you can certainly be generous when you sprinkle it over the mussels.

As far as any substitutions or additions, Chef Cameron relates that, after many failed attempts at using oysters in this recipe, he must advise against it. Other than that, any variations in the combination making up the filling are welcome, even if it is only to enjoy more fully the multitude of both saltwater and freshwater delicacies from Loch Fyne.

1. To prepare the filling, chop the shallot. Combine the salmon with cognac, chopped shallot, egg whites, and cayenne pepper; puree. Refrigerate for approximately 15 minutes, add cream, and refrigerate once more.

2. Wash the mussels thoroughly and cook them briefly over a high heat until they open up. Shell and set aside the flesh. Fill half the mussel shells with the salmon filling.

with Salmon Filling

3. Place the mussel flesh back into the shells, on top of the filling. Close both halves of the shells and tie them up. Poach the mussels for about five minutes, as this will be enough to cook the filling.

4. Remove the strings and the top half of the shell, and arrange the filled mussels in a star pattern on each plate. For the sauce, sauté a teaspoon of chopped shallots in butter, add the white wine, and reduce to half the amount. Then add the mussel juice and reduce once more. Stir in the cream and strain. Sprinkle with chopped chives and Keta caviar.

Salmon Roulade

Preparation time: 1 hour
Cooking time: 20 minutes
Difficulty: ★★

Serves four

4 large scallops
1¼ lb / 600 g salmon fillet
generous 1 cup / 250 ml fish stock
1 bunch of dill (or chives)

For the sauce:
2 tsp / 10 g Keta caviar (see below)
2 shallots
scant ½ lb / 220 g butter
generous 1 cup / 250 ml heavy cream
½ cup / 120 ml white wine

In the clear waters of the Tay River in the northwest of Scotland live a host of fish, crustaceans and shellfish of incomparable quality. To symbolize their harmonious coexistence, our chef, Stewart Cameron, has created an appetizer based on salmon and scallops. The result is a harmony of aromas, enhanced by the delicate flavor of Keta caviar. In Cameron's experience, Scottish salmon is superior to any other variety, and certainly the French concur. For Scottish salmon was the first fish, and what is more, the first foreign fish, to be awarded the distinguished *label rouge*, the red ribbon of French cuisine.

This recipe requires very fresh salmon, with meat that is firm to the touch and of an even orange-pink hue. The rest is a matter of patience, involving, if your fishmonger has not already done it, gutting, de-boning and removing blood spots and other blemishes. The accompanying scallops should be bought, if possible, alive, if not extremely fresh; these also should be thoroughly cleaned and checked for blemishes. Chef Cameron also points out that this is another recipe where substitutions or additions would greatly diminish its impact, since scallops create such a perfect harmony with the salmon that there is no room for another partner.

Finally, the Keta caviar is, due to fishing laws (it must be imported from Norway) the only non-Scottish product in this recipe. Actually cured salmon roe, it plays an important, integral role in the butter sauce. If you are partial to its taste, as Cameron is, you can use Keta caviar as well as an accompanying element in numerous fish or seafood dishes.

1. If not already done, carefully bone the salmon and cut fillets into pieces about the size of tournedos, measuring a bit more than a 5¼ oz / 150 g.

2. Open the scallops, remove the flesh from the shells and clean thoroughly under running water.

with Scallops

3. Wrap the salmon around the flesh of the scallops to fashion small bundles, and fasten together with wooden skewers. Cook, covered, in fish stock over a low heat for a few minutes. Take out the bundles and reduce the stock to half its volume.

4. Sauté the chopped shallots in butter, add white wine and reduce to half the amount. Then add fish stock and heavy cream, bring to a boil again, season to taste and strain. While the sauce is still hot, add the remaining butter and the Keta caviar. Decorate with a dill sprig or chives, if desired.

Mezzeluna with

Preparation time: 2 hours
Cooking time: 20 minutes
Difficulty: ★★

Serves four

For the ravioli dough:
1¼ cups / 300 g flour
3 eggs
half a bunch of spinach
  (to yield generous 1 oz / 40 g)

For the sauce:
1 eggplant
2 zucchini

generous ³/₈ cup / 100 ml cream
generous ³/₈ cup / 100 g butter
half a bunch of thyme
salt to taste

For the filling:
scant ½ lb / 200 g fish (such as halibut, sole, cod)
3½ oz / 100 g Ricotta
1 shallot
½ cup / 120 ml white wine
½ tbsp / 10 g butter
half a bunch of parsley
salt, pepper to taste

There exist innumerable Italian pasta dishes, many of which have whimsical, memorable names. A mixture of green spinach-dyed noodles and golden-yellow egg noodles, for instance, is called *paglia e fieno*, or hay and straw. In the case of this appetizer from our inventive chef Marco Cavalucci, green and yellow ravioli are shaped like half-moons, thus aptly named *mezzeluna*. Adapted by our chef to the taste of the time, this traditional recipe has conquered a widespread public.

Ricotta, a fresh sheep's milk cheese of remarkable versatility, provides an ideal addition to the filling made of Adriatic fish. Raw or cooked, it works well in a wide array of combinations, from salads to appetizers, from main courses to desserts.

As Chef Cavalucci emphasizes, the choice of fish must never be left to chance: whatever is used and in whatever combina-

tion, be it halibut, sole, or cod, for instance, it should all hail from the same maritime region and have certain common qualities. The delicate character and fine structure of the three fish mentioned means they will work well together, and harmonize perfectly with the spices used here. You could, of course, also use ocean perch or monkfish, but under no circumstances should you use salmon or goatfish, as their flavor is too strong for this appetizer.

The vegetable sauce, laced with thyme, lends the dish a certain lightness. If you wish, substitute other ingredients for the zucchini and eggplant, such as yellow peppers, boletus mushrooms, or even lentils. Let the old kitchen adage, "It should look good, taste good, and be easy to digest," guide you.

1. Chop the shallot and parsley. Clean and cut the fish into pieces; steam in butter with the chopped shallots. Add white wine and reduce. Add the parsley and set aside to cool. Set a small portion aside for garnishing. Stir in Ricotta, salt and pepper, and puree the mixture in a blender or food processor. Blanch and chop the spinach.

2. Prepare the ravioli dough and dye some of it with the spinach. Allow to sit for an hour. Roll out the dough and cut out small rounds. Spoon the fish filling onto these, fold in half, and shape into half-moons.

Vegetables and Thyme

3. Dice the eggplant and zucchini finely, season with salt and thyme, and fry in 3¹/₂ tbsp / 50 g of butter. Keep half warm, add the cream to the other half, and cook until done.

4. Cook the ravioli in salted water (until al dente), drain, and add the remaining butter. Puree and strain the cooked vegetables. Pour this sauce onto pre-warmed plates. Arrange the ravioli on top in the shape of a flower, alternating between green and yellow half-moons. Place the pieces of fish and the rest of the diced vegetables in the center as a garnish.

Sheep's Milk Cheese Ravioli

Preparation time: 1 hour 15 minutes
Cooking time: 40 minutes
Difficulty: ★★

Serves four

For the pepper cream:
2 yellow peppers
1 shallot
scant ¼ cup / 50 ml cream
2 tbsp / 30 g butter
salt to taste

For the filling:
7 oz / 200 g Ricotta
7 oz / 200 g aged sheep's milk cheese
2 egg yolks
½ tsp / 3 g grated nutmeg
1 bunch of parsley
salt, pepper to taste

For the ravioli dough:
1¼ cups / 300 g flour
3 eggs

For the decoration:
1 red pepper

Once again, credit is due to Marco Cavalucci, for reminding us that filled pasta comes in countless varieties, the only limits being the chef's creativity. Certainly, the art of preparing ravioli allows the imagination to go unfettered, and yet requires extraordinary culinary skills.

Chef Cavalucci provides a typical Italian example, here using two different kinds of sheep's milk cheese that are equally popular on the peninsula. One is Ricotta, a two- to three-day-old sheep's milk cheese from the Emilia-Romagna region, recognizable by its smooth consistency. The other one is a classic cheese made from curdled sheep's milk, which matures for several months, if not for over a year, by which point it assumes a considerably stronger character. These two cheeses harmonize very well, provided the latter has not exceeded its maturity and, as a result, exudes too strong an aroma. Ravioli

may of course also be prepared with other types of sheep's milk cheese, even with *pecorino di fossa* – its name referring to its three-month-long maturation process, which takes place in a hole in the ground. The variety of flavors, which may all be combined with each other, thus provide innumerable options for ravioli fillings.

On the other hand, however, one should take into account the mildness of the peppers, for the contrast between this vegetable's sweet flavor and the filling's strong taste is what will render this recipe a solid success. Among all the different color varieties of the sweet bell pepper, our chef recommends choosing the yellow variety, which is tender and juicy with a glossy, smooth skin.

1. To prepare the yellow pepper cream, chop the shallot and then fry it in butter. Finely dice the peppers, then add to the shallot with some water and salt; cook until soft. Puree in the blender or food processor, then strain and add the cream. Cook again until the sauce is smooth and creamy, then let it sit in a warm place.

2. Melt the different types of cheese in a double boiler and then stir in the other ingredients.

with Yellow Pepper Cream

3. Prepare the ravioli dough from flour and eggs, form into a ball, and set aside to rest for one hour. Roll out the dough into two sheets of similar size. Place little balls of the filling onto the one sheet and cover with the other. Cut into traditional square ravioli with a pastry cutter, then cook in plenty of water. Cut the red pepper into long, fine strips.

4. Briefly fry the ravioli and the strips of red pepper in butter. Cover the center of the pre-warmed plates with the pepper cream, arrange the ravioli on top, and decorate with the red pepper strips.

Preparation time: 45 minutes
Cooking time: 20 minutes
Difficulty: ☆

Serves four

For the pasta dough:
1¼ cups / 300 g semolina flour
1 egg
1 pinch salt
⅛ cup water

For the sauce:
3½ oz / 100 g smoked bacon
4 tsp / 20 ml balsamic vinegar
⅛ lb / 50 g Parmesan cheese, grated
⅛ lb / 50 g butter
2 tbsp / 30 ml meat broth
salt, pepper to taste

There are entire books devoted to the etymology and origin of the names of Italy's myriad pasta dishes. Suffice to say, for Chef Marco Cavalucci, the *strozzapretti* presented here pay homage to the anticlerical forces operating in the Emilia-Romagna in the past, an element that will remind any Italian of his or her history classes. On the other hand, the name simply stands for hand-rolled tagliatelle, that is, noodles that are generally served as a main course and refined with a sauce made from this region's finest ingredients.

The bacon, for example, which, unlike pancetta, is cured with smoke, is one of the classic specialities of this region; but there is nothing like the typical balsamic vinegar that dominates the flavor of the whole dish. This "must," made from Trebbiano grapes, is in reality not really a vinegar at all. It should by no means be substituted with any other similar products, since none will match in flavor. As our chef notes, if you absolutely have to, you may use red wine vinegar instead, but if you do, you should at least have a guilty conscience about it. The genuine *aceto balsamico di modena*, as it is called, has an incomparable gentle aroma; this precious liquid enchants any dish, but must only be used in small quantities.

This appetizer is an expression of subtle, imaginative gastronomy. Our chef has created a most harmonious union between the products of the friendly countryside of Emilia (with the matchless balsamic vinegar) and those of the harsher neighboring region of Romagna (with its *strozzapretti*). We hope that he will continue this tasty, vital tradition for a long time.

1. Knead flour, egg, water, and salt on a board until the dough is smooth and workable. Roll it out with a rolling pin to a thickness of a ¼ in / ½ cm and cut into long, approximately ½ in / 1 cm wide strips.

2. Roll these strips by hand into about 4 in / 10 cm long round noodles.

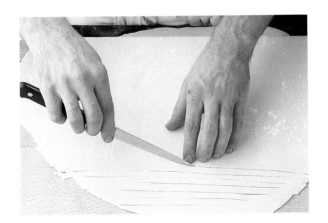

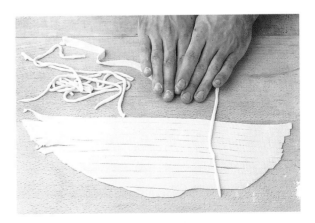

Balsamic Vinegar

3. Cut the bacon into strips. Fry in a pan, drain and add balsamic vinegar. Add the stock. Cook the noodles in plenty of salted water and drain. Grate the Parmesan.

4. Toss the noodles, adding a bit of butter, in the sauce. Add the grated Parmesan cheese and mix well. To serve, arrange on plates and sprinkle with a little balsamic vinegar.

Scallops in Lemon

Preparation time: 40 minutes
Cooking time: 30 minutes
Difficulty: ✶

Serves four

1 dozen large scallops
2 large carrots
4 celery stalks
2 large zucchini
1 large cucumber
1 white leek stalk

1 medium-sized onion
1 clove of garlic
1 lemon
1 lime
quarter bunch of thyme (to yield 3 springs, to be
    sprinkled with lemon juice)
half a bunch of lemon balm (to yield 6 leaves)
$^1/_4$ cup vanilla beans
$^2/_3$ cup / 150 ml dry white wine
2 tbsp / 30 g butter
salt, fresh-ground pepper to taste

Our chef, Francis Chaveau, has taken a traditional recipe of scallops in sauce and extended upon it in a quite surprising way – he adds a contrast of crisp vegetable spaghetti as well as the flavors of vanilla and lemon.

Select only large, fresh scallops for this appetizer, if possible without the red coral found in some types. The scallops should be poached in simmering water for a very short time only, so that they remain tender and tasty.

The distinct aroma of vanilla does, in fact, go very well with fish and other seafood; nevertheless it should be used sparingly so it does not conceal the scallops' own flavor and thus throw off the harmony of the whole dish. As Chef Chaveau explains,

the vanilla is meant only to add a touch of freshness and depth to this appetizer.

The same applies to the lemon balm, an aromatic herb that comes in many varieties. Most types are imported from the Antilles or from Southeast Asia, though the herb is now also grown in many home and local gardens. Lemon balm was introduced into European (and then American) cooking fairly recently, but a different type of balm has long been valued by pharmacists as a digestive aid. Lemon balm should also be used sparingly, as it has a very intense flavor.

Finally, if you prefer, you might substitute some crustaceans, such as crayfish or lobster, for the scallops.

1. Peel one carrot, two celery stalks and the cucumber, and cut into long spaghetti-shaped strips. Proceed similarly with the green peel of the zucchini. Briefly cook all vegetables separately and rinse under cold water; combine.

2. Chop the second carrot and the remaining celery finely together with the leek, onion, and garlic, put in a large pot, pour over white wine and water. Add the whiskers of the scallops, a little lemon balm and thyme, and cook everything for 30 minutes. Scoop off the foam, strain, add a vanilla bean to the sauce, and set aside to steep.

and Vanilla Froth

3. Open the scallops and wash thoroughly. Shell, slice in half, and poach in the sauce without bringing it to a boil. Remove the vanilla bean and the scallops. Cut the lemon and lime peels into thin strips, blanch, and leave to set.

4. Whip the sauce with the butter until creamy, add lemon juice, and season. To serve, arrange six slices of the scallop flesh in the center of each soup plate and cover with the sauce. Top with the vegetable spaghetti and lemon peel, and garnish with a few vanilla beans and the thyme leaves sprinkled with lemon juice.

Scampi Risotto with Boletus

Preparation time: 30 minutes
Cooking time: 45 minutes
Difficulty: ★

Serves four

12 prawns, scant $^1/_8$ lb / 50g each
scant $^7/_8$ cup / 200 g Italian Arborio rice
10$^1/_2$ oz / 300 g fresh boletus mushrooms
4 violet artichokes
1 large onion (to yield generous $^1/_8$ cup / 40 g chopped)
1 oz / 30 g Provence black truffles
scant $^1/_4$ cup / 50 ml truffle juice
1 cup / 250 ml extra virgin olive oil

4 whole, large leaves of basil
$^1/_4$ cup / 50 g butter
$^1/_4$ lb / 50 g Parmesan cheese
salt, fresh-ground pepper to taste

For the scampi stock:
1 carrot (to yield generous 1 oz / 40 g chopped)
1 onion (to yield 1 generous 1 oz / 40 g chopped)
1 celery stalk (to yield generous 1 oz / 40 g chopped)
1 clove of garlic
1 sprig of thyme
$^2/_3$ cup / 150 ml white wine

Here, courtesy of Chef Francis Chauveau, we are introduced to various specialties – truffles from Provence in the south of France, risotto from Italy, and scampi from the Mediterranean – combined to make a Mediterranean treasure.

Risotto alla milanaise is famous all over the world. It is traditionally prepared from a variety of rice, Nano Vialone, that is renowned south of the Alps, but unfortunately very difficult to find in shops. Carnaroli, on the other hand, another popular type, is more common; even more common still is Arborio, now a fixture in American gourmet shops. The latter is what Chauveau has chosen.

Since Arborio rice's thick grains contain a high starch content, the rice should not be washed before it is cooked. Instead it is fried in olive oil with chopped onions, and then dark brown, light-veined truffles – mashed with a fork ahead of time – are added. While cooking the rice, add scampi stock (made from prawns) regularly to prevent the rice from drying out: Chef Chauveau recommends crushing the prawn heads before cooking to lend the stock even more flavor. Should prawns be unavailable, use langoustines or northern lobsters. To ensure the dish's creamy consistency, the rice should be stirred gently with a wooden spoon. The result will be a gorgeous risotto in which the boletus mushrooms act like a soft counterpoint to the shrimp's firmer flesh.

1. Mash the truffles with a fork to soften them. Chop the onions. Fry with the rice in olive oil until golden, then add the mashed truffles and braise. For the scampi stock, shell the prawn tails, cut lengthwise into two pieces, and remove the guts. Crush the heads and fry together with the vegetable mixture mentioned above. Add a dash of white wine and water, cook for 30 minutes and strain.

2. Pour the scampi stock over the rice. Cook for 18 minutes, repeatedly adding a little stock while stirring gently with a wooden spoon. Add the truffle juice and, if necessary, more stock. Stir in butter and a little olive oil to render the rice soft and creamy.

Mushrooms and Truffle Essence

3. Remove the leaves of the artichokes, cut the hearts and stems into slices. Clean the boletus mushrooms and slice as well. Fry the artichokes and mushrooms separately. Cut four long, pointed strips from a chunk of Parmesan cheese. Strip leaves off the basil, and fry the basil leaves in oil. Fry the scampi briefly, but over a high heat.

4. To serve, spread a layer of risotto over the entire plate, then arrange the boletus and artichokes on top. Heap the scampi in the center, and decorate with cheese strips and basil leaves.

Green Asparagus with

Preparation time: 20 minutes
Cooking time: 10 minutes
Difficulty: ☆

Serves four

3 bunches green, white, or violet asparagus (to yield 32 good spears)
1/4 cup / 60 g coarse salt (to add to the cooking water)
2 fresh, firm eggplants (to yield 5/8 lb / 300 g chopped)
1/8 cup / 30 g coarse salt (to add to the cooking water)

To season the eggplants:
1 tbsp / 30 ml olive oil
1 clove of garlic
half a bunch of dill or fennel
2 oz / 60 g black olives

For the sauce:
1/3 cup / 80 g butter
scant 1/4 cup / 50 ml water
1 tsp / 5 g green aniseed
juice and grated peel of 1 lemon
1/2 cup / 125 ml olive oil
salt, pepper to taste

This appetizer, from Chef Jacques Chibois, combines three gastronomic specialties from the area surrounding Cannes in the south of France – asparagus, eggplants, and black olives. The combined colors of these ingredients will appeal to the eye as much as their blending flavors please the palate.

Chef Chibois recommends green or white asparagus – particularly the violet type, with tips that have blushed purple from being exposed to the sun for a few hours, giving them a slightly stronger flavor. If you must store the asparagus for a few days before preparing the dish, Chibois advocates wrapping it in a damp cloth and refrigerating it in a horizontal position. It will be cooked in water to which coarse sea salt has been added: this salt contains more iodine, which will keep the spears tender and supple. The best eggplants to use are firm

with a smooth, shiny skin; they should also be as young as possible (and therefore of a smaller size and with fewer seeds) to reduce the amount of time they need to be cooked. The olives, of course, should be small and juicy: look for the so-called Nice olives, which have to be blanched to rid them of the brine in which they are preserved, but which have a superior, redolent flavor.

Take care when preparing the butter sauce, as, being very delicate, it can easily curdle if labored over for too long. Finally, this recipe would be incomplete without making reference to the green aniseed (not to be mistaken for star anise) employed here, whose subtle, typically southern flavor plays an important role in this appetizer.

1. Peel the asparagus, tie into bundles, and cut the bottoms to the same length. Add coarse salt and asparagus to boiling water and cook, uncovered, for ten minutes. Rinse with hot water and keep warm.

2. Skin the eggplants and cut them into cubes of approximately 1/2 in / 1 cm. Cut the skin into thin strips, cook in salted water, and immediately rinse under cold water to stop the cooking process. Soak the eggplant cubes in water for 15 minutes, then cook in boiling water for five minutes; rinse under cold water and drain for an hour.

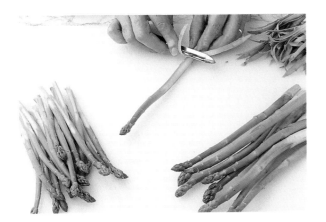

Olives and Aniseed

3. Place the cubed eggplant in a non-stick frying pan with olive oil, garlic, salt, pepper, and half the black olives, and brown briefly. Seed the other half of the olives, cut into eighths, and blanch twice.

4. Boil up the aniseed in water, add butter and olive oil as well as grated lemon peel, a dash of lemon juice, salt and pepper. Lastly, add the other half of the olives to the sauce. Arrange the eggplants, sprinkled with lemon juice to keep their color, on the plates, place asparagus on top, and pour the sauce over. Decorate with olives and small sprigs of dill.

Vegetable Ravioli

Preparation time: 1 hour
Cooking time: 10 minutes
Difficulty: ★★

Serves four

For the ravioli dough:
generous 1 cup / 250 g flour
1 egg
4 egg yolks
a pinch of salt
1/4 cup / 50 ml peanut oil

For the filling:
5 oz / 140 g button mushrooms
1/4 lb / 120 g carrots

1/8 lb / 60 g celeriac
2 shallots (to yield 1 oz / 30 g chopped)
7 oz / 200 g spinach
3 1/2 tbsp / 50 g butter

For the sauce:
1 shallot (to yield 1 tbsp / 15 g chopped)
1 cup / 250 ml white wine
2 tsp / 10 ml Noilly (vermouth)
generous 1 cup / 250 ml cream
3 1/2 tbsp / 50 g butter
1/2 oz / 15 g dried morels, or 1/4 lb / 120 g fresh
    morels
1 bunch of chervil
salt, pepper to taste

One of Chef Jacques Chibois' fondest childhood memories is the immense pleasure of being allowed to accompany his mother when she collected mushrooms. Here he presents an appetizer in which mushrooms play important roles. The button mushrooms star in the filling, and the noble morels star in the sauce.

The morel, an extraordinary edible fungus, has a conical shape and honeycombed surface that requires very thorough cleaning, since all kinds of dirt collect in its myriad indentations. But the mushroom's incomparable flavor justifies such efforts. If possible, purchase morels that are fresh, not dried. The water, in which the cleaned mushrooms must be soaked, can be reserved and used as a delicious addition to other sauces. If you do have to use dried morels, bear in mind that they will regain their original shape after being soaked twice in water,

and allowed to dry in between soakings.

Make sure you do not leave any of the prescribed ingredients out of the vegetable filling, least of all the spinach. Whether you prepare the filling by hand, in the blender, or in the food processor, it should wind up thick enough to give the ravioli a certain firmness. It is also advisable to prepare the ravioli quickly, before the dough has a chance to dry out. If a little olive oil is added to the cooking water, the ravioli dough will be even tastier.

Finally, should morels be unavailable, the sauce may also be prepared with button mushrooms, provided they are firm and white. But, as our chef cautions, naturally the result will not be quite as memorable.

1. Clean, chop, and cook the spinach. Very finely chop the button mushrooms. Clean and peel the carrots, clean the celeriac, and peel the shallots. Brown everything, including half the shallots, in butter over a medium heat, stirring continuously. Add the spinach. Spread out the filling on a plate and set aside to cool and dry.

2. Mix the ingredients for the ravioli dough to an even consistency. Refrigerate for two hours. Then roll out the dough as thinly as possible and cut out circles of about 3 1/2 in / 9 cm in diameter with an appropriately sized and shaped cookie cutter.

with Morels

3. Place one teaspoon of filling onto each circle of ravioli dough. Moisten the edges with a little egg yolk or water, fold in half, and press well to seal. Cook the ravioli in boiling salted water with a little olive oil until done, then drain and keep warm.

4. Steam the other half of the chopped shallots in the white wine. Reduce the liquid to three-quarters of its original volume. Add the quartered morels, season, and cook for three to four minutes. Stir in the butter, vermouth, and cream with a whisk. Pour the morel sauce onto the plates, arrange the ravioli on top, and decorate with chervil leaves.

Fried Whiting and

Preparation time:	1 hour
Cooking time:	25 minutes
Difficulty:	★★★

Serves four

generous ¹/₂ lb / 250 g whiting fillet
4 langoustines
1¹/₃ yards / 1 m sausage skin (pork)
³/₄ cup / 200 ml cream
¹/₄ lb / 50 g butter
1 bunch of chervil
salt, pepper to taste

For the sausage filling:
(to yield generous ¹/₄ lb / 125 g)
¹/₈ cup / 30 g flour

1 egg yolk
generous ¹/₄ cup / 65 ml whole milk
5 tsp / 25 g butter
¹/₂ tsp / 3 g ground nutmeg
salt, pepper to taste

For the sauce:
langoustine heads, claws, and shells
generous ¹/₂ cup / 125 g butter
1 shallot
1 tbsp / 15 ml cream
1 bunch of celery (for leaves)
half a bunch of thyme
2 bay leaves
half a bunch of parsley

Traditionally, Europeans associate seafood and crustaceans with a rich, glorious feast. The langoustine crowns it all. This pride of Brittany's fishing harbors is lovingly called "the little lobster from Norway" or even "Mademoiselle Langoustine." It is predominantly found in the cold waters off Iceland, Scotland, and Ireland, often sold alive by fishmongers. If living langoustines are unavailable, firm bodies and shiny eyes are an indication of freshness. In France, the crustacean's oblong body is often referred to as *coffre*, which means a treasure chest, and indeed, this chest bears a truly rich treasure.

Sausage skins, available at most butchers, must be handled gently, as they break very easily. For the sausage filling our

chef, Serge Courville, recommends whiting, praising its numerous qualities: it is not fatty, it is fairly economical, and above all it is rich in minerals. When trawled in giant nets, these fish are unfortunately often squashed together, so, before you choose one, make sure its belly has not collapsed. The light, shiny whiting is far tastier and more tender than the common blue whiting. Other products of the sea, such as red mullet, pike, pike-perch, or even shellfish such as scallops are also suitable for this recipe. When preparing the filling, it is important not to knead the mixture too much – the cream could turn to butter. It is, however, perfectly feasible to prepare the filling the previous evening. Langoustines, if unavailable, may be substituted with lobster or crayfish.

1. Clean and section the tails from the langoustines; gently shell. Fry briefly in butter and slice thinly. Fillet and bone the whiting, and puree in the blender or food processor.

2. To prepare the filling, mix ¹/₂ cup / 125 g of butter, 3¹/₂ tbsp / 50 g of flour, and ¹/₄ cup / 60 ml of milk; bring to a boil, add the egg yolk, and refrigerate. Mix after chilling with the fish puree. Puree everything again while adding ¹/₂ cup / 125 ml of whipping cream. Pass through a fine sieve and season to taste.

Langoustine Sausage

3. Combine the langoustine meat with the filling mixture; use a pastry bag to fill the sausage skins, then poach the sausages in water heated to 175 °F / 80 °C. Crush the heads, claws, and shells of the langoustines. Cook in water with one chopped shallot and the herbs for 15 minutes and then strain.

4. Reduce the liquid and thicken with a little cream. Add half a cup of butter, season to taste, and keep warm. Score the sausages, fry in a non-stick frying pan first, and then gently grill in the oven. Serve the fried sausages with rice and decorate with chervil leaves.

Duck Liver Foie

Preparation time: 45 minutes
Marinating time: 24 hours
Cooking time: 35 minutes
Difficulty: ★★

Serves four

1 generous lb / 500 g duck liver (foie gras)
4 tsp / 20 g goose fat
1¼ lbs / 600 g white grapes
2 carrots
1 onion

generous ⅜ cup / 100 ml white wine
3½ tbsp / 50 ml port
generous ⅜ cup / 100 ml poultry broth
salt, pepper to taste

For centuries, grapes were viewed as good enough for making wine, but certainly not for the table – hardly anyone would have considered eating them. Only under the very cultured French King Francis I, who reigned from 1515–1547, did table grapes come to fame.

Succulent, crisp and sweet, table grapes in France are harvested between July and October, with one of the largest cultivation areas in the southwest of France. From that region comes the type Chasselas de Moissac, a grape so distinguished it is regulated by France's *Appellation d'Origine Contrôlée*. A particularly thin-skinned and delicious variety grows on the estates of the famous Tarn-et-Garonne monastery and is harvested from mid-August right through to November.

Our chefs, Bernard and Jean Cousseau, call for a marinade of white wine and port, but if a good port is unavailable, you can marinate the grapes instead in white wine from Sancerre or Jurançon; the character and flavor of these two wines are very similar.

If you prefer apples to grapes for this side dish, the Cousseaus recommends the European Rennet apples, whose firm, succulent flesh goes superbly with foie gras, or, with similar qualities, Granny Smith apples. Whichever you use, these should be peeled, seeded, and sliced thinly. Sprinkled with sugar, they are then baked in a hot oven for thirty seconds before being draped over the duck liver and garnished with a little sauce.

Fresh foie gras from grain-fed, free-range ducks, a welcome alternative to the classic foie gras, is by far the best for this recipe. The liver should be firm and smooth, without blemishes or bruises. It will remains nice and tender when baked in goose fat. Braise it in a covered pan and only take off the lid right at the end to caramelize lightly the surface of the liver.

1. Wash, skin, and seed the grapes. Place in a glass bowl, cover in white wine and port. Cover the bowl and refrigerate for 24 hours. Clean the liver thoroughly and cut off any pieces that might have touched the gall.

2. Wash and peel the carrots. Cut, with the onion, into thin slices and place in an ovenproof dish. Place the entire liver over the carrots and onions, add the goose fat and cover with aluminum foil. Bake in the oven at 355° F / 180 °C for 25–30 minutes.

Gras with Grapes

3. Set the liver aside. Spoon out the fat from the pot and replace with the mixture of white wine and port that served as a marinade for the grapes and the poultry broth. Reduce to about half the liquid over a medium heat.

4. Strain the sauce and heat again for three to four minutes. Cut the liver into large slices, arrange on plates, and cover with sauce. To serve, arrange the marinated grapes in an attractive pattern next to the slices of liver.

Snail Näpfchen

Preparation time: 30 minutes
Cooking time: 1 hour, 30 minutes
Difficulty: ✹✹

Serves four

4 dozen snails
1 shallot
2 cloves of garlic
$^3/_4$ cup / 200 ml broth
$^1/_3$ cup / 80 g butter
$^1/_2$ cup / 125 ml cream

5 cloves
1 bouquet garni composed of parsley, thyme, bay
    leaf, celery leaves
1 bunch of smooth-leaved parsley

For the Näpfchen:
2 carrots
2 onions
2 zucchini
$^5/_8$ lb / 150 g button mushrooms
$^1/_4$ cup / 50 g butter

Näpfchen is an old German term for small, pan-shaped containers made of clay or porcelain. In time the word took on another meaning, and now also refers to small meals that have been either prepared in such pans or at least give that impression. The common feature of these dishes is the combination of different ingredients. Our recipe here, a *Näpfchen* without a bottom, provides a good example.

If you can find them, look for snails from Bourgogne, which are the most renowned of the edible snails, with their yellowish-spiraled shell, even dark-colored body, and firm and juicy flesh.

Chef Richard Coutanceau designed this recipe to enhance the snails' own flavor by adding aromatic herbs, yet at the same time preserve the tender, springlike flavors of the zucchini, carrots, and button mushrooms that accompany the dish. The finishing touch is a parsley sauce in a garlic cream base, which hearkens back to the old, 17th century tradition of seasoning poultry dishes with a parsley-based sauce. The snails will have to be washed several times in vinegar water before they are cooked in broth. Ultimately, they are taken out of their shells and the bottom tip of the body is cut off; only then are they ready for consumption.

Chef Coutanceau cautions that building a *Näpfchen* from zucchini is a matter of patience. The easiest method is to cut the zucchini into thin half-moons, and carefully arrange them along the inside walls of a form.

1. Strip the leaves off parsley sprigs and boil in a large pot of salted water for five minutes. Drain, cool, and puree in a blender or food processor. Cook the snails in the broth together with the bouquet garni, the cloves and the butter for approximately an hour and a half. Take the snails out of their shells and make sure to cut off the bottom tips of their bodies.

2. Halve one zucchini lengthwise. Cut the halves into very thin half-moon slices and cook briefly in a large pot of boiling water. Rinse under cold water and drain. Grease the inside of a ring-shaped form with butter. Stand the zucchini slices, overlapping each other, along the inside wall of the ring.

with Parsley Cream

3. Chop the carrots, the second zucchini, the button mushrooms, and the onions. Boil the carrots in salted water for five minutes, rinse under cold water and drain. Sauté the mushrooms and onions in butter. Boil up the cream. Add the peeled garlic, cook for 15 minutes, and puree.

4. Heat a small quantity of the snail stock in a saucepan. Add the pureed parsley, a little butter, and half a tablespoon of garlic cream. Steam the snails and the chopped shallot in this mixture and add the vegetables. To serve, transfer the zucchini rings onto pre-warmed plates, fill with snails and vegetables, and pour over with the parsley sauce.

Snails in a

Preparation time: 45 minutes
Cooking time: 20 minutes
Difficulty: ★★

Serves four

generous 1 lb / 500 g fresh or canned snails
generous ¹/₂ lb / 250 g button mushrooms
generous ¹/₂ lb / 250 g champignon de Paris, oyster
   or chanterelle mushrooms
6 shallots
1 clove of garlic

6 tomatoes (to yield generous ³/₈ cup / 100 g
   pureed)
generous 2 cups / 500 ml dry white wine
generous 2 cups / 500 ml cream
1 bouquet garni
1 bunch of parsley
salt, pepper to taste

For the puff pastry hat:
(see basic recipes)

While enjoying a meal in Paul Bocuse's restaurant, our chef, Jean Crotet, wagered that he could create a snail dish that would be easier to digest than the traditional version laden with garlic butter. Here, then, is his recipe.

Snails are particularly popular in France, so it is not surprising that Crotet strongly recommends the large specimen from the Bourgogne (known as *Helix pomatia linné*) despite all the other varieties on the market. This species has a light-brown shell with black stripes. The smaller variety (*Helix aspersa*) will most likely be easier to get hold of, particularly in U.S. markets, and is also very well-suited for this recipe. If you prefer, you may also use canned snails, as they at least have the advantage of having been produced under hygienic conditions. The other essential ingredients for this appetizer include the mushrooms that used to be grown in the deserted mines around

Paris (which explains their name, *champignon de Paris*). These must be light and firm and have round closed heads. If not available, oyster mushrooms or chanterelles are equally suitable. A good dry white wine, possibly from the Bourgogne, would be very well worth using for the preparation of the mushrooms.

Once the prepared mixture has been ladeled into ovenproof soup bowls or tureens, these are covered with puff pastry hats that spill over the rims of the bowls to produce a highly decorative, fanciful impression. Before the puff pastry is used, it must have been refrigerated for at least an hour and a half to prevent it from absorbing the flavors of the other ingredients when baked. The crispness of the puff pastry and the freshness of the other ingredients require that this appetizer is served immediately after it is prepared and, of course, then consumed immediately.

1. Wash the mushrooms and cut them into ¹/₂ in / 1 cm cubes. Chop the parsley, shallots, and garlic finely.

2. Steam the shallots and garlic, add a dash of white wine and the bouquet garni, and reduce to three-quarters of the volume. Add the mushrooms with salt and pepper. Cover the pot and bring to a boil. Add the cream, bring to a boil again, and set aside.

Puff Pastry Hat

3. Take the snails out of their juice and place in the soup bowls or tureens. Puree the tomatoes. Spoon the pureed tomatoes, herbs, and cream over the snails.

4. After preparing and then chilling the puff pastry dough for an hour and a half, roll it out and place enough over the filled soup bowls to amply cover and drape over the sides. Brush the pastry dough with egg yolk and bake in a pre-heated oven at 390 °F / 200 °C for 10–15 minutes. Serve immediately.

Smoked Salmon

Preparation time: 30 minutes
Cooking time: 5 minutes
Difficulty: ☆

Serves four

generous 1¹/₄ lbs / 600 g smoked salmon
generous ⁵/₈ lb / 320 g small new potatoes
2 bunches of watercress
³/₄ cup / 200 ml cream
¹/₃ cup / 80 ml olive oil
salt, pepper to taste

After closely studying salmon smoking methods in Denmark, Chef Jean Crotet decided to develop a technique according to his own ideas. With extensive experience gathered in his gastronomic homeland, the Bourgogne, he achieved excellent results using vines and juniper berries in the smoking process, thus imparting a much more delicate flavor to the smoked salmon. With the necessary equipment you may try out this method at home. Store the vines to be used in the smoking in a very humid place so that, by retaining moisture, they produce as much smoke as possible.

The best salmon has always been and will always be that from Scotland. Its ideal weight is between nine and eleven pounds (four and five kilograms), its flesh is not excessively fatty and it has the typical pink coloring one wants. It must be noted that the color will vary slightly depending on the type of wood used for smoking. The Scots mostly use oak, while the French prefer beech. In any case, once the salmon has been smoked, it must be left to cure for at least a day.

Chef Crotet insists that the watercress puree in this recipe should never be substituted with anything else, as no other green vegetable will complement the salmon as well as watercress does.

For an accompaniment, new potatoes, with their small size and thin skins, are ideal. Heated and arranged like a bed for the slices of salmon, their primary purpose in this recipe is to warm up the fish without overheating it, as the salmon must not get hot or else it will turn dry and stringy.

1. Wash the watercress and cook in salted water for two to three minutes. Drain and cool. Wrap in a towel and squeeze to remove any excess water. Then puree the watercress, strain, and set aside.

2. Wash, peel, and cut the potatoes into paper-thin slices. Cook in salted water for no more than five minutes; the potatoes should remain fairly firm. Place the potato slices into ²/₃ cup / 150 ml cream and season lightly with salt and pepper.

with Watercress

3. Heat the watercress puree, add the olive oil and the rest of the cream and season.

4. Spread out the potatoes with the sauce over three-quarters of each plate. Cover the remaining quarter with watercress. Arrange the salmon in waves on top of the potatoes and serve immediately.

Bulgur Wheat

Preparation time: 45 minutes
Cooking time: 2 hours
Difficulty: ★★

Serves four

generous 1 cup / 250 g coarse bulgur wheat
5¼ oz / 150 g snails
1 slice smoked ham
⅝ lb / 300 g boletus mushrooms
2 large white onions
2 bunches of watercress
1 bouquet garni
1 poultry stock cube
1 tbsp / 15 ml cream
½ cup / 125 ml olive oil

generous 2 cups / 500 ml white wine
2 tbsp / 30 g butter
salt, pepper to taste

For the veal broth:
scant ⅞ lb / 400 g fatty veal
2 tomatoes
1 onion
1 carrot
1 celery stalk
1 bouquet garni
1 tbsp / 15 ml port
¾ cup / 200 ml white wine
¼ cup / 50 g butter

For the snail butter:
2 carrots
2 onions, studded with cloves
generous ⅜ cup / 100 g butter
2 cloves of garlic
half a bunch of smooth-leaved parsley (to yield scant ¼ cup / 50 g chopped)

Bulgur, a Mediterranean staple, is a coarsely ground wheat with a nutty flavor, certainly well-known in Europe and the U.S. to vegetarians but gaining in renown among gourmets as well. In comparison with the classic Mediterranean *pil-pil*, bulgur is coarser semolina made from dried, chopped-up wheat.

Often prepared like risotto (though, since bulgur cooks faster than rice, it must be carefully watched), the bulgur grains are poured into very hot oil to swell up; a steamed onion is then added, and gradually stock is poured on. It must be absorbed totally by the bulgur. And, importantly, the grains should be stirred with a wooden spoon, which no self-respecting Italian cook would do without, as anything harsher might damage the grains. Our chef, Michel Del Burgo, moreover recommends adding olive oil throughout the entire cooking process.

If you prefer, rice can be used as a substitute for bulgur, so long as you lengthen the cooking time accordingly; or, to be adventurous, try spelt, another grain offered in health food stores that would provide a suitable alternative.

Since on its own, the bulgur would probably be a bit bland, Chef Burgo refines the dish with produce from his homeland, such as snails and boletus mushrooms from the southwest of France, and smoked ham (which can well bear comparison with Bayonne ham) from the mountains of that region. If these regional specialties are unavailable in U.S. markets, try substituting another variety of snail of similar size, and, possibly, pancetta or Bayonne ham.

1. To prepare the veal broth, chop the vegetables; fry the veal pieces (as fatty as possible) in a frying pan. Add the bouquet garni and the vegetables and pour on a dash of white wine and port. Reduce the broth, cover the meat and vegetables with water, and cook for about two hours. Just before serving, pass the broth through a sieve and whip it up with butter.

2. Cook the snails in a stock made of water, wine, carrots, onions studded with garlic and a bouquet garni, until just tender. Knead the butter with parsley and finely chopped garlic, season with salt and pepper and refrigerate. Cut ham into strips and the boletus into ½ in / 1 cm cubes.

with Snails

3. Finely chop an onion; sauté in olive oil, add bulgur wheat, and cover with veal broth. Cook over a low heat for 20–25 minutes, stirring continuously, and add broth (and a bit of olive oil) regularly. Cook the watercress leaves in salted water, allow to cool, and squeeze dry in a towel. Then strain or puree and set aside.

4. Add some butter to the cooked bulgur and stir gently with a wooden spoon. Add watercress, and lastly the cream and seasoning. Fry the snails briefly in garlic butter and parsley. Add the boletus and ham strips and brown lightly. To serve, mound the bulgur and top with the boletus and ham; pool with remaining broth.

Anchovy

Preparation time: 45 minutes
Cooking time: 20 minutes
Difficulty: ★★

Serves four

1 lb / 450 g fresh anchovies (approximately 80 fish)
8 medium-sized potatoes
20 large tomatoes
2 large onions
1 bouquet garni
generous 1 oz / 40 g black olives
2 tsp / 10 ml sherry vinegar

¹/₂ cup / 125 ml olive oil
half a bunch of chives (to yield 2 tbsp chopped)
1 bunch of basil
salt, pepper to taste

For the dressing:
¹/₂ cup / 125 ml olive oil
4 tsp / 20 ml lemon juice
4 large pieces of cod liver
salt, pepper to taste

Chef Michel Del Burgo, representing the French region of Languedoc-Roussillon, once prepared an enormous anchovy gâteau at an official reception in Barcelona. The recipe is set out here, albeit in much smaller proportions, and provides a rare opportunity to appreciate the delicate, unforgettable flavor of fresh anchovies.

The Europeans know only one type of anchovy, as a true anchovy hails from the Mediterranean region, while there are countless other fishes labeled anchovies that are not, in fact, the real thing. Anchovies, which belong to the herring family, travel in the summer months in big shoals, swimming just beneath the surface of the sea. They spend the winter breeding at the bottom of the ocean. The fishermen of the Mediterranean lure them at night with their searchlights and catch them by

their thousands in fine-meshed trawling nets. The harbor of Sete, a particularly rich site for the fish, is the main center for the anchovy trade.

When fresh, anchovies are roughly four to five inches (ten to fifteen centimeters) long, with shiny eyes and stiff and fragile bodies. Once the head is removed, filleting and removing the relatively big bones is easy. For this recipe, which centers around an olive oil and lemon juice dressing, cod liver is an important ingredient. If the liver is well prepared and passed through a sieve, it will make a delicious, even, creamy sauce. For the base of the tarts, slightly floury potatoes (such as Idaho) are just as suitable as new potatoes. And, if fresh anchovies are unavailable, small sardines will do as well, although their flavor is not quite as pronounced.

1. Gut and clean the anchovies as described above and wash thoroughly. Arrange on a stainless steel plate in a rosette, using a ring of approximately 5 in / 15 cm in diameter. Skin, seed, and coarsely chop the tomatoes. Chop the onions finely and fry in olive oil. Add the tomatoes and bouquet garni, season, and reduce the liquid a little.

2. Cook and peel the potatoes. Mash with a fork to form the bases of the tarts. Add a little olive oil, sherry vinegar, salt, pepper, and chopped chives. Warm this mixture in a bowl. Seed the black olives and chop into small pieces.

Tarts

3. For the vinaigrette, mix olive oil and lemon juice. Mash the cod liver pieces with a fork, add the sauce, season, and pass through a fine sieve. Add the olive pieces and the chopped basil leaves to the tomatoes and season to taste.

4. Use the same rings as for the anchovy rosettes and spoon in a $^1/_2$ in / 1 cm thick layer of potatoes, followed by an equally thick layer of tomatoes. In the meantime, bake the anchovy rosettes under the grill and place them on top of the tarts with the help of a spatula. Serve decorated with chives and basil leaves, and dribbled with the sauce.

Lamb Sweetbreads

Preparation time: 1 hour
Cooking time: 10 minutes
Difficulty: ★★

Serves four

generous 1 lb / 500 g lamb sweetbreads
1 bunch of young carrots
1 bunch of green asparagus (to yield 12 spears)
6 purple artichokes
1 zucchini
$2^3/_4$ oz / 80 g young peas
$3^1/_2$ oz / 100 g small, fresh fava beans
1 bunch of chives
juice of 1 lemon
$^1/_8$ cup / 25 g flour

For the vinaigrette:
3 shallots (to yield scant $^1/_3$ cup / 80 g)
generous 1 cup / 250 ml balsamic vinegar
generous $^3/_8$ cup / 100 ml olive oil

For the veal broth:
generous $^1/_2$ lb / 250 g veal (soup bone, etc.)
1 tomato
2 carrots
2 onions
1 bouquet garni
$^2/_3$ cup / 150 ml white wine
$^1/_3$ cup / 80 ml port
$^1/_4$ cup / 50 g butter
half a bunch of chervil
half a bunch of chives
salt, pepper to taste

Chef Michel Del Burgo was in Flamanville in northern France when he discovered the exquisite flavor of lamb sweetbreads, although his homeland, the Basque region, has a similar specialty called *atxuria*. In both cases the sweetbreads are from lamb that are quite young – no older than nine or ten weeks, and no heavier than twenty or twenty-two pounds (a generous kilo).

Offal should always be prepared and consumed immediately. The sweetbreads are first placed into ice-cold water and then cleaned thoroughly. Before being fried briefly over a high heat, the thin skin surrounding them must be removed.

The vegetables chosen for this dish are well-known and loved amongst the Basques, from the fava beans (known in Europe as broad beans), to the artichokes. Fava beans in particular are a Basque favorite, used in soups and ragouts or as a raw ingredient in salads.

Always make sure all the vegetables are fresh and, whenever possible, cook them only until *al dente*. This applies above all to the peas, which ought to be prepared first. Chef Del Burgo always finds fresh vegetables in the markets of his hometown of Carcassonne. But increasing varieties of fresh vegetables are generally available at any time of the year, and sometimes there is even a surprising selection of new types of produce.

1. Remove the artichoke leaves and partially sever the stems. Sprinkle the hearts with lemon juice, cover, and cook in salted water with a little lemon juice and flour. Remove the fine hairs (the choke) after cooking. Peel the carrots and retain the greens. Cook all the vegetables separately in salted water, then leave to cool.

2. For the veal broth, brown the meat pieces, add the bouquet garni and the vegetables, then pour on the white wine and port. Reduce the liquid, add water and cook; pass through a fine sieve. For the vinaigrette, sauté the shallots in olive oil, add the balsamic vinegar, reduce, add the veal broth and reduce again.

with Fresh Vegetables

3. Blanch the sweetbreads and set aside to cool, then pan-fry in butter and oil until golden brown. Chop shallots and chives. Add the chopped shallots, a little broth, olive oil, the chives, chervil leaves and the juice of a lemon to the reduced vinaigrette and season.

4. Heat the vegetables in butter again, adding the fava beans and peas at the last minute. Serve the vegetable mixture with the sweetbreads on plates, sprinkled with vinaigrette and garnished with fresh herbs.

Frogs' Legs in a

Preparation time: 20 minutes
Cooking time: 15 minutes
Difficulty: ☆

Serves four

1¼ lbs / 600 g frogs' legs
2 cloves of garlic (to yield 1 oz / 30 g) chopped finely)
2 shallots (to yield 1 oz / 30 g chopped finely)
1 bunch of chives
1 quart / approximately 1 l poultry broth

generous 3 cups / 750 ml cream
3½ tbsp / 50 g butter
salt, pepper to taste

In today's gastronomy, sauces play a crucial role. You recognize the true talent of a great chef by the finesse of his or her sauce and its harmony with the other ingredients of the dish. Sauces also distinctly reflect the character of a region. At times, certain ingredients, such as garlic and crème fraîche may, in fact, reveal the geographic origin of a sauce.

The banks of the little Erdre river, a tributary of the Loire, have always provided an ideal habitat for amphibians. Chef Joseph Delphin and his son Jean-Louis are therefore in a quandary, since most of the frogs marketed in Europe come not from Europe, but – due to animal protection laws – from Asia. (Also see the recipe on pages 104–105 for more information.) As Chef Delphin says, it's up to you whether or not you serve the Asian imports, or use the rarer European frogs. Of the latter, there are three main types: the common frog (*rana esculenta*), the grass frog (*rana temporaria*) and the agile frog (*rana dalmatina*). They all have distinctively firm and shiny flesh.

Frogs' legs should be cooked (but not overcooked, as this will toughen them) in a sauce with garlic; the sauce is then used for the preparation of the poultry cream. Salt is only added at the end of the cooking time; the small pinch added in the beginning is only meant to combine the various ingredients. The more finely the garlic, shallots, and chives are chopped, the more their aromatic flavors will be absorbed in the sauce.

1. Many markets sell ready-to-serve frogs' legs already on skewers. Clean these and cut off the bottom section of the legs.

2. Blanch the frogs' legs in broth, bring to a boil, and take them off the heat immediately.

Creamy Poultry Sauce

3. Very finely chop garlic, shallots, and chives. Heat 3 generous tbsp / 150 g of butter, add the chopped garlic and shallots, and sauté for a few minutes. Add the drained frogs' legs and reheat so that the flavors of garlic and shallots can be absorbed. Stir, using a wooden spoon (a metal one might damage the frogs' legs).

4. Lift out the frogs' legs, add two ladles of broth to the sauce, gradually swirl in the cream, and season to taste again. Finally, add the chopped chives, and serve hot.

Scrambled Eggs in Waffle Pastry

Preparation time: 20 minutes
Cooking time: 5–7 minutes
Difficulty: ✳

Serves four

8 eggs
2 sea urchins
generous 1oz / 40 g truffles
4 tsp / 20 g butter
1/3 cup / 80 ml heavy cream
3 sprigs of chervil (to yield 1 tsp / 5 g chopped)
6 sheets phyllo dough, or 3/4 lb / 350 g puff pastry
  (see basic recipes)
pepper to taste

For the sea urchin sauce:
1 tsp / 5 g sea urchin flesh
2 tsp / 10 g butter
generous 3/8 cup / 100 ml cream
juice of 1 lemon
1/2 bunch cilantro

For the tomato puree:
5 1/4 oz / 150 g tomatoes
1 bouquet garni
2 shallots
2 cloves of garlic
salt, pepper to garlic

During the open season for sea urchins from early May to the end of August, sophisticated dishes often appear on menus in Japan, Europe, and the United States to take advantage of this marine delicacy. To balance their extremely pronounced iodine flavor, sea urchins are here served with scrambled eggs and truffles; the concoction, from Chef Phillippe Dorange, will certainly delight your guests.

There are three types of edible sea urchins available: green, black, and purple. The latter should be given preference. This type lives on the bottom of the sea at a depth of some one hundred yards (one hundred meters), and is caught in cast-out fishing nets that are weighted down to comb the seabed as they drag across it. The only edible part of a sea urchin is the flesh inside the shell, where five "tongues" form a star shape around the very complex mouth opening. These so-called tongues are actually sex organs, and within them are contained minute, delicious eggs. After a complicated metamorphosis the eggs produce a new sea urchin, a miniature version of the adult. Since, as it has been proven, sea urchins can breed only in their natural environment, there are no farmed sea urchins for sale, and they remain a delicacy. When purchasing them, black, shiny spikes clinging tightly to the shell are the safest indication of freshness.

Never prepare scrambled eggs in a hurry, as any chef will tell you, or they will become tough. Instead, stir them gently with a wooden spoon and add the heavy cream right at the last minute. Use only very fresh eggs to obtain an even, creamy consistency.

1. Crack the eggs into a bowl. Chop the truffles, mix with the eggs, and set aside. Open the sea urchin, take the eggs out, and preserve the liquid. Wash the shells.

2. To prepare the sauce, pour the sea urchin liquid into a saucepan, add a dash of lemon juice, a little butter, and chopped, fresh cilantro. Heat up and bind with the eggs of the sea urchins. Whip with a whisk and pass through a sieve. Fold in the whipped cream. Prepare the tomato puree in a blender or food processor with the above ingredients.

with Sea Urchins and Truffles

3. Using a wooden spoon, prepare the scrambled eggs in a pan in melted butter. Season with salt and pepper, add heavy cream right at the end, and remove the mixture from the stove.

4. Spoon the scrambled eggs either into the sea urchin shells or into phyllo or puff pastry molds. Place the lukewarm eggs of the sea urchins on top. Spread a tablespoon of tomato puree in the center of each soup plate, arrange the shells or pastry molds on top and pour the sauce around them. Decorate with chopped truffles and chervil leaves.

Leipziger Medley

Preparation time: 30 minutes
Soaking time (optional): three hours
Cooking time: 30 minutes
Difficulty: ★ ★

Serves four

12 river crayfish
generous ¹/₂ lb / 250 g veal sweetbread
5¹/₄ oz / 150 g fresh morel mushrooms
generous 2 lbs / 1 kg spring vegetables (such as
    spring leeks, peas, carrots,
green and white asparagus, rutabaga, kohlrabi,
    celery stalks)
7 oz / 200 g butter
1 bouquet garni
1 tsp / 5 g nutmeg

salt, pepper to taste
4 puff pastry cookies (see basic recipes)

For the crayfish sauce (to yield ³/₄ cup / 200 ml):
crayfish carcasses
generous 1 cup / 250 ml chicken broth
4 tsp / 20 ml white wine
2 tsp / 10 ml brandy
2 tbsp / 30 ml cream
2 tsp / 10 ml grape seed oil
2 shallots
4 tsp / 20 g butter
4 tsp / 20 g tomato puree
1 bay leaf
1 clove
4 peppercorns
salt, pepper to taste

For the champagne sauce (to yield ³/₄ cup / 200 ml):
(see basic recipes)

This recipe might well go down in German history, created by Chef Lothar Eiermann on October 3, 1990, when Germany became unified once again. The original title, *Leipziger Allerlei*, refers to a recipe from post-war Leipzig in the former German Democratic Republic, when even vegetables like carrots, asparagus, and peas were hard to come by. According to vague records, the original recipe also contained, somewhat surprisingly, veal sweetbreads and crayfish. Thus, here is our chef's own new version of this post-war recipe.

As Eiermann insists, veal sweetbreads, crayfish, and morels do not tolerate being substituted, so immediately set aside any intention to substitute one or another of these with more common produce. Also, the success of this recipe depends on the quality of the veal sweetbreads, which should, if at all possible, come from very young (preferably suckling) calves only. These should be no bigger than a man's fist and have an even color without blemishes or bruising. If still containing blood, they should be placed in cold water for a few hours and then cooked in one piece. Since the skin covering the sweetbread acts as a protection against excessive heat exposure, Eiermann recommends removing it only after cooking. Finally, follow the instructions carefully when preparing the crayfish sauce.

1. Clean the veal sweetbreads, and cook in seasoned water until pink. For the champagne sauce, add shallot, bay leaf, and pepper to the sweetbread stock and reduce to half the amount. Stir in cream and reduce again. Strain through a cloth, add Noilly (vermouth) and bring to a boil again. Stir in crème fraîche and butter. Lastly add champagne and season. Clean the morels and blanch with the vegetables.

2. Fry the crayfish carcasses over a high heat, add shallots, bay leaf, clove and pepper and fry again. Stir in the tomato puree and flambé with brandy. Add white wine and broth and reduce to half the volume. Finally stir in the cream and strain everything through a cloth. Whip up with butter and season to taste.

with Vegetables

3. Skin and slice the veal sweetbread, dust with flour, and fry in a bit of butter until golden brown. Sauté the morels, salt them lightly and mix with the bouquet garni.

4. Sauté the crayfish tails in butter. Proceed similarly with the various types of vegetables, then add the crayfish sauce. Cover the plates with the light sauce. Arrange vegetables, sweetbread, crayfish, and morels on top and decorate with a puff pastry cookie.

Breaded Calf's

Preparation time: 25 minutes
Cooking time: 3 hours
Difficulty: ★★

Serves four

For the calf's head pieces:
1 calf's head
1 egg
generous $^3/_8$ cup / 100 g dry bread crumbs
2 tbsp / 30 g flour
scant $^1/_4$ cup / 50 g melted butter
salt, pepper to taste

For the crayfish:
1 dozen crayfish
scant $^1/_4$ cup / 50 g butter
1 cup / 250 ml vegetable stock

For the asparagus salad:
1 bunch of green asparagus (to yield 1 dozen
    spears)
$3^1/_2$ oz / 100 g morels
1 tomato
4 tsp / 20 ml olive oil
4 tsp / 20 ml grape seed vinegar
4 tsp / 20 ml champagne vinegar
a pinch of sugar
1 bunch of chives
salt, pepper to taste

According to gastronomes, the fact that dishes centered around the delicately flavored calf's head are less popular in Germany than in neighboring European countries, such as France, is a mystery. Suffice to say that German chefs have a mandate to be imaginative and creative, in order to produce dishes that have undeniable gastronomic appeal.

Chef Lothar Eiermann, up to the challenge, thus had the idea of combining calf's head and crayfish in one dish. Germans are particularly fond of the crayfish found in Bavaria's freshwaters, where they thrive despite difficult environmental conditions. However, these are rarely imported, so, in general, any red river crayfish will prove suitable for this appetizer. What is more, every part of this crustacean can be made use of, from the tail with its tender and tasty flesh to the carcass, which is used to prepare the sauce.

As to obtaining a high-quality calf's head, Chef Eiermann is extremely demanding. After selecting the head (from a calf five to six months old), he prefers trimming and preparing it himself. If this task is too unappealing, however, you may instead have the butcher handle it. Since the head in and of itself does not bear a very strong flavor, various sauces, such as the crayfish sauce and the asparagus sauce, take on an important role in this appetizer. If asparagus is unavailable, or simply out of season, replace it with carrots, pureed into a sauce; if morels cannot be found, these may be substituted with other wild mushrooms.

1. Cut the calf's head into pieces of roughly 1 in / 2 cm square. Season with salt and pepper and turn in egg, flour, and bread crumbs. Cook the crayfish in a strong vegetable stock for three minutes, rinse under cold water, and take apart. Save the broth and set it aside.

2. Cook the asparagus spears in water with salt and a pinch of sugar until just barely cooked (al dente). Rinse them under cold water to stop the cooking process, cut off the tips, and cut the spears into small pieces. Reduce the asparagus stock to a third of its volume and add to the vinegar and oil mixture. Skin, seed, and dice the tomato. Chop the chives, add everything to the vinaigrette, and mix well.

Head with Crayfish

3. Deep-fry the breaded calf's head pieces in melted butter. Clean the morels well, steam them in butter, and add them to the asparagus salad.

4. Reduce the crayfish broth to half its volume and whip up with a little butter. To serve, arrange a bed of asparagus salad on each plate. Place the calf's head pieces and the crayfish flesh on top, decorate with asparagus tips, and sprinkle with a little crayfish butter.

Frogs' Legs Soup

Preparation time: 30 minutes
Cooking time: 25 minutes
Difficulty: ★★

Serves four

generous 2 lb / 1 kg frogs' legs
1 bunch of watercress
1 large carrot
generous ³/₈ cup / 100 ml whipping cream
scant ¹/₄ lb / 50 g butter
¹/₂ cup / 125 ml olive oil
salt, pepper to taste

To cook the frogs' legs:
generous 3 cups / 750 ml beef stock
generous 2 cups / 500 ml cream

For the sauce:
bones from the frogs' legs
3 shallots (to yield ¹/₃ cup / 80 g chopped)
1 clove of garlic (to yield 4 tsp / 20 g chopped)
1 cup / 250 ml dry white wine

For the roux:
1 tbsp / 15 g flour
1 tbsp / 15 g butter
generous 1 cup / 250 ml whole milk

The area between the French Jura and the Beaujolais vineyards used to be the stronghold of the Bourbon dynasty. This region, with its numerous crystal-clear lakes and rivers, is home to a diversity of creatures – among them, carp, pike, teal duck, snipe, and, of course, frogs.

While it is now quite difficult to find frogs' legs in Germany, as frogs are now a protected species, in our chef's homeland of France they are still a sought-after delicacy. Our chef, Jean Fleury, prefers not to use any very large specimens, or excessively muscular thighs, as American bullfrogs often have, for this appetizer. In addition, he recommends paying close attention to the cooking time, as overcooking will toughen frogs'

legs quickly. After cooking, the frogs' legs are boned and the bones used to prepare the sauce. This time-consuming process lends the dish a uniquely harmonious flavor.

The watercress used here, another treasure from the water (hence it is known is some regions as "water garlic") lends the dish a slightly acid and sharp taste, which harmoniously balances the frog meat's full flavor. In the past, watercress was said to have healing powers and was used in many medicinal mixtures; today it is still regarded by some as a surefire aid in digestion. Make sure this plant is fresh when you buy it, as it tends to wilt fast and then lose both flavor and nutrition. If watercress is unavailable, try substituting it with sorrel.

1. Gently poach the frogs' legs in a mixture of beef stock and cream. Bone the cooked pieces and reserve the bones for the preparation of the sauce.

2. To prepare the sauce, chop the shallots and garlic, and fry the bones in a saucepan together with them; add white wine and reduce the liquid. Pour on the cooking liquid of the frogs' legs and cook for approximately 15 minutes.

with Watercress

3. Strain the sauce and bind it with the prepared roux. Dice the carrot finely and cook only briefly to keep it crisp.

4. To serve, place a spoonful of carrots in the middle of each soup plate. Arrange the frogs' legs around the carrots in a star shape and pour the sauce over them. Top with whipped cream and decorate with watercress leaves.

Duck Liver Pie

Preparation time: 45 minutes
Cooking time: 35 minutes
Difficulty: ★★

Serves four

⁵/₈ lb / 300 g duck liver (foie gras)
4 oz / 120 g truffles
generous 2 lb / 1 kg puff pastry (see basic recipes)
2 savoy cabbages
2 egg yolks
¹/₂ cup / 125 gflour
¹/₄ cup / 50 g butter
salt, pepper to taste

For the sauce:
generous 3 oz / 100 g truffles
generous ³/₈ cup / 100 ml truffle juice
generous ³/₈ cup / 100 ml Madeira
generous 2 cups / 500 ml veal broth
¹/₄ cup / 50 g butter

Our recipe is inspired by a dish, "sea perch in puff pastry," that Paul Bocuse offers in his restaurant to the delight of his guests. In his recipe and in this one from Chef Jean Fleury, different flavors are harmoniously combined; here, Fleury combines foie gras, truffles, and savoy cabbage baked in one of a chef's most reliable allies, a puff pastry.

Foie gras is attained by force-feeding ducks or geese twice a day for three weeks until they are fattened to their maximum weight. But, as Fleury points out, the biggest livers are not always the best, because they disintegrate more easily during preparation. And although one would think that truffles, being an expensive, specialty item, would be of consistent quality, quite the opposite is usually the case: there are innumerable types of the most varied quality. Make sure your truffles are not bruised, wormy, or excessively dirty. When cutting them use either an electric carving knife or a mandolin, which is perfectly suited for slicing the very firm flesh.

To keep up with these noble ingredients, the savoy cabbage should be nice and fresh as well as firm and heavy. Remove the outer leaves, then blanch and prepare the rest as usual. In spring, green asparagus tips can substitute for the savoy cabbage, as their subtle bitterness will contrast well with the tender flavor of the duck liver.

When the puff pastry turns a golden brown in the oven, the pie will be done.

1. Slice the duck liver. Season with salt and pepper, coat with flour and brown in a non-stick pan. Drain on paper towels. Blanch the savoy cabbage leaves, rinse under cold water, cook in butter over a low heat and leave to cool.

2. Roll out the puff pastry and line a baking mold of approximately 10 in / 25 cm in diameter and 4 in / 10 cm in height. Fill with alternate layers of cabbage, liver, and truffle slices, ending with a layer of cabbage.

with Truffles

3. Cover with puff pastry, brush with egg yolk and bake in the oven at approximately 390 °F / 200 °C for about 35 minutes.

4. To prepare the sauce, sauté the chopped truffles in a pan, add Madeira and truffle juice, and reduce the liquid. Add the veal broth and season. Stir in butter and whisk until creamy. Take the pie out of the oven, cut with an electric knife, and serve with the sauce.

Fish Tarts with

Preparation time: 45 minutes
Cooking time: 40 minutes
Difficulty: ★★★

Serves four

2 dozen mussels
1 pollack
1 large potatoe (such as Idaho or Yukon Gold)
6 cloves of garlic
6 egg yolks
generous 3/8 cup / 100 ml olive oil
1/2 lb 250 g puff pastry (see basic recipes)
salt, pepper to taste

For the fish stock:
2 lb / 1 kg fish bones
2 onions
6 cloves of garlic
2 shallots
3 leeks (to yield generous 3 oz / 100 g of the white section)
3 celery stalks
peel of 2 oranges
scant 1 1/2 cups / 350 ml dry white wine
1/4 lb / 50 g butter
half a bunch of thyme
1 bay leaf
half a bunch of smooth-leaved parsley
pepper to taste

Here, Dutch chef Constant Fonk transforms the classic fish soup into a simple, yet inventive appetizer, where potatoes, a Dutch staple, substitute for bread croutons. Small puff pastry biscuits decorate the finished dish and provide a pleasant contrast to the melt-in-the-mouth fish tarts.

The success of this recipe depends to a large extent on the refined flavors of the fish stock, and on how long the pollack is cooked in it. If pollack is unavailable, other whitefish like monkfish or ocean perch are good alternatives. The mussels serve as an accompaniment: if possible search for Holland's so-called Zeeland mussels, which are the typical species of the local mussel production, and are presently experiencing a huge boom in the export business. Since they are relatively big, they are thus a bit more difficult to handle. But, on the other hand,

Dutch mussel farmers ensure that they are sand-free. French Bouchot mussels are also excellent in this dish, but they first have to be cleaned in salted water for an hour and a half. If you prefer, substitute these imported versions for a native North American mussel; just make sure you clean the shellfish thoroughly.

The potato must be thinly sliced and blanched before it is used for the tarts. As Chef Fonk relates, the tart molds he used were originally used for spice cookies, a specialty with jam filling that was predominantly baked in convents.

This appetizer must be served very hot. It will impress the gourmet with its pleasant presentation as well as its superb flavor.

1. Soak and clean the fish bones, soften in butter, and add white wine. Reduce the liquid, then pour on water again. Add the ingredients for the fish stock and cook for 25 minutes. Pass through a sieve and poach the pollack in this stock.

2. Boil the potato. Prepare the aïoli sauce in a blender, starting with the egg yolks, then adding five teaspoons of boiled potato, six crushed cloves of garlic, and olive oil. Bind the fish stock with half of this sauce. Open the mussels, place one piece of mussel flesh into each half, fill with aïoli sauce and grill in the oven.

Mussels and Sauce

3. Cut the raw potato into thin slices and blanch. Cover the base of the tart molds with a slice of potato and fill three-quarters full with the cooked pollack flesh.

4. Fill up the molds with the aïoli sauce and slide under a hot grill for three minutes. Prepare the puff pastry if you have not already done so. Shape the puff pastry into crescent moons and bake in the oven for 20 minutes, initially at 390 °F / 200 °C, later reducing the heat to 355 °F / 180 °C, until golden brown. Serve the tarts, as pictured, in deep plates in a pool of sauce with the mussels and a puff pastry

Goatfish Tarts with

Preparation time: 1 hour
Cooking time: 20 minutes
Difficulty: ★★

Serves four

1½ lb / 1.2 kg goatfish
1¾ lb / 800 g spinach
4 tomatoes
2 onions
2 cloves of garlic
1 bunch of flowering thyme

1 bunch of basil
1 bunch of rosemary
1 bouquet garni
¾ cup + 1 tbsp / 200 g butter
generous 1 cup / 250 ml fish stock
½ cup / 125 ml olive oil
salt, pepper to taste

The beard-like growths on the goatfish's bottom lip gave it its nickname in Europe, "bearded barbel." It is also known as a red barbel or a red mullet. There are two types, living in rock cliffs and sandy seabeds; both are extremely tasty though, unfortunately, very bony as well. Once committed to cooking with it, chefs are committed to its thorough preparation. Choose the largest specimens you can find, fillet them cautiously (or have your fishmonger do it instead), and patiently remove any remaining bones. And, as one chef suggested, use the time you spend filleting your goatfish to reflect on the fact that many of the finer details of gastronomy are, unfortunately, lost in the English language. In French, for instance, there is the term for a knife used solely to fillet fish (*couteau à filets de sole*), and in German, there is a separate word for fishbones (*gräte*).

In Provence, such tarts or various au gratin dishes used to be baked on round plates of clay or stoneware (also known as *tian*). In our recipe, the goatfish rests on a tart of spinach and finely chopped tomato, which brings out the typical Provençal character of this dish. To this end, the spinach is blanched briefly, softened in butter, and only salted right at the end.

Goatfish easily dry out when cooked or baked, so it is important to prepare the tarts in the order indicated. If the fish is placed on the spinach and tomato mixture and baked in a 355° F / 180 °C oven for a maximum of three minutes, it will not dry out. This appetizer should be served immediately.

1. Wash the spinach and remove the stalks. Dip the leaves, a few at a time, into boiling salted water for five seconds each, rinse them under cold water, drain, and squeeze out any excess water. Then sauté the spinach in butter and season to taste.

2. Skin and seed the tomatoes and chop them very finely. Chop the onions (to yield about one-twelfth the quantity of the tomatoes) and sauté in butter and olive oil. Add tomatoes and garlic (one clove of garlic for every 2 lb / 1 kg of raw tomatoes) and lastly the bouquet garni, salt, and pepper. Cook until all the liquid has evaporated.

Spinach and Tomatoes

3. Reduce the fish stock to three-quarters of its volume and add the chopped tomatoes, thyme, and basil (1 cup / 250 ml of fish stock, 3¹/₂ oz / 100 g of tomatoes and three pinches of thyme and basil per generous ³/₄ cup / 200 g of butter). Butter the round tart molds of approximately 3 in / 8 cm in diameter.

4. Place the rings on baking paper, spoon in a layer of spinach and spread 1 tbsp / 15 g of tomato puree over it. Cut the goatfish fillets into ¹/₄ in / 1 cm thick strips, brush with oil, season with salt and pepper, and sprinkle with rosemary. Bake the tarts under the grill or in a very hot oven for no more than three minutes.

Black Salsify with

Preparation time: *45 minutes*
Soaking time: *12 hours*
Cooking time: *1 hour, 30 minutes*
Difficulty: *★*

Serves four

8.8 lb / 4 kg black salsify
7 oz / 200 g black radish
1 lemon
one dozen fresh walnuts
1 tbsp / 15 g paprika

scant ¹/₂ cup / 120 g flour
scant 1 cup / 200 ml olive oil
quarter bunch of marjoram
salt to taste

For the hollandaise sauce:
(see basic recipes)

Our chef, Phillippe Groult, enjoys crusading against culinary prejudices. Here he fights for the black salsify. This quite unappetizing-looking vegetable, also known as oyster root in the United States, makes an excellent accompaniment to meat dishes. The smoother the surface and firmer the flesh of these highly absorbent roots, the greater the freshness. For this appetizer, choose salsify that is about as thick as a thumb, as any thinner and it would not prepare well.

Opinions vary as to how long salsify should be cooked for. At any rate, it is first soaked in cold water with two heaping tablespoons (thirty grams) of flour and some lemon juice for one hour. Smaller pieces will require a shorter cooking period.

Fresh walnuts, here soaked overnight before being cooked, are available from October until March. Their flavor goes very well with black radish, which is very popular in Eastern Europe but virtually scorned (for no good reason) in the west. This bulbous root vegetable is high in vitamin C and as easy to prepare as carrots. Red radishes are easier to get hold of, particularly in the U.S., and may be used instead.

This dish is always accompanied by a hollandaise sauce enriched with unsweetened almond milk cream, which rounds off the flavor of the salsify. The paprika, on the other hand, moderates the sharpness of the radish. This appetizer should be served lukewarm.

1. The night before, soak the walnuts, still in their shells, in sugar water. The day of preparation, begin by washing the salsify under running water, peel, and cut into 5 in / 12 cm pieces. Soak in water with one teaspoon of flour per cup, and add the juice of one lemon. Bring to a boil. Cook accordingly: salsify with a diameter of approximately ¹/₂ in / 1 cm needs to be cooked for one hour and ten minutes; thicker salsify should be cooked for slightly longer.

2. Whip up the hollandaise sauce over a low heat with egg yolks and four ladles of water. Warm the butter, gradually stir into the sauce, season, and add cayenne pepper and four drops of almond milk.

Fresh Walnuts

3. Drain the salsify on a cloth, dip in olive oil, and dust the ends of the spears with paprika. Shell the pre-soaked nuts. Peel the black radish, slice thinly and place in cold water.

4. Pour 3 tbsp / 45 g of hollandaise sauce onto each plate and arrange the salsify in an attractive pattern on top. Decorate with three radish slices and three walnuts per plate, dust with paprika, and scatter a few marjoram leaves over the arrangement.

Frog Leg

Preparation time: 1 hour, 15 minutes
Cooking time: 30 minutes
Difficulty: ★★★

Serves four

scant 3¼ lb / 1¼ kg frogs' legs
5¼ oz / 150 g pike fillets
¾ lb / 350 g spinach
3 shallots
1 clove of garlic
juice of 1 lemon

2 egg whites
generous 2 cups / 500 ml cream
⅝ cup / 150 g butter
1⅔ cups / 400 ml Riesling wine
1 tbsp / 15 g roux (see below)
1 bunch of chives
salt, pepper to taste

A virtuoso of the kitchen devised this mousseline more than forty years ago, when frogs' legs were still a ubiquitous item. They remain sought after in France, so our chef, Marc Haeberlin, brings this classic back to light.

For this dish, Chef Haeberlin prefers the freshwater pike, particularly one with a shiny greenish coloring on its back, a hammer-shaped mouth, silver fins, and tender flesh. Avoid older specimens, which sometimes exude a strong muddy smell, after having lived in dirty muddy waters for a long time. Otherwise, wash the fish in vinegar water. Pike-perch may also be used, but it has less protein than pike does, so should only be a second choice. It is interesting to note that great efforts are being made to reintroduce larger numbers of this famous greedy predator to many rivers.

Like the pike, the frogs' legs are salted before and after they are pureed. The salt binds the mixture and makes it even and creamy. The eggs and the cream are added in small amounts, and need to be very cold during these stages.

Before filling the tart molds, brush their insides with butter, then chill and butter again just before filling them. Ideally, the filled molds should be left for a few hours before they are cooked.

1. Sauté the chopped shallots in butter and add half the frogs' legs. Pour the Riesling over, season with salt and pepper, and cook, covered, for ten minutes. Take the frogs' legs out, strain the stock, reheat, and reduce to half the volume. Add half the cream, butter and roux to the sauce, whip with a whisk until creamy and season with salt, pepper and lemon juice.

2. Bone the other half of the frogs' legs when still raw. Bone the cooked frogs' legs as well and set aside. Blanch the spinach in boiling salted water for five minutes, drain in a sieve and thoroughly squeeze out (by hand) any excess water.

Mousseline

3. To prepare the mousse, combine the raw meat of the frogs' legs and the flesh of the pike with two egg whites and puree this mixture in a blender or food processor. Gradually add the same amount of cream. Season with salt and pepper as soon as the mousse is creamy. Spoon the mixture into a bowl and set aside. Sauté the garlic in 3 tbsp / 50 g of butter, add the spinach, salt and pepper, and leave to steep for five minutes.

4. Fill the mousse into a pastry bag and cover the base of the molds with it. Place the cooked frogs' legs on top, fill the molds with mousse, and place in a double boiler. Cook in the oven at 355 °F / 180 °C for 15 minutes. Serve in shallow bowls, with the mousse in the center, surrounded by a pour of sauce and an arrangement of spinach, and garnish with chopped chives and chive sprigs.

Goose Liver Toast

Preparation time: 30 minutes
Cooking time: 15 minutes
Difficulty: ★

Serves four

1 goose liver (foie gras)
8 slices rye bread
2 Golden Delicious apples
1 onion
¹/₄ cup / 50 g butter
generous ³/₈ cup / 100 ml alcoholic cider

4 tsp / 20 ml Calvados
⁵/₈ cup / 150 ml veal broth
scant ¹/₄ cup / 50 ml light gravy (see basic recipes)
¹/₄ cup / 50 g flour
salt, pepper to taste

For any connoisseur and gourmet, foie gras is the epitome of French gastronomy. It should be firm to the touch and smooth at the same time, it should not look bruised or smell unpleasant. If you press your finger on it, the indentation should disappear on its own.

Our chef, Michel Haquin, would rather not address the often-repeated question of whether foie gras from a goose is better than that from a duck. For this recipe, he prefers goose liver, as its slightly tangy flavor goes better with this toast. But, as the story goes, the Belgians still have a bone to pick with geese. Long ago, the inhabitants of Visé on the Meuse slaughtered and ate all their geese, to punish the birds for not having warned them prior to an attack on the town, unlike the legendary geese of Rome, which made much noise before an attack on the Capital.

Such exquisite ingredients naturally require appropriate preparation. Brown the foie gras quickly in a non-stick pan without any fat or oil, and handle it gently, as this tender liver disintegrates very easily. The Golden Delicious apples make a good succulent accompaniment, preventing the liver from drying out while being prepared. Other types of apples with firm flesh, such as sharp-flavored Granny Smiths, may be used as an alternative, though they will not be as sweet.

This appetizer should be served very hot. It cannot be kept, but this need, as our chef confesses, is hardly likely to arise.

1. Peel the apples and cut the peels into straw-thin strips. Cut one peeled apple into 24 thin slices.

2. Cut the other apple into eight slices, spread them out on a baking tray, and dry in the oven at 355 °F / 180 °C. Deep-fry the apple strips at 320 °F / 160 °C and drain on paper towels. Brown the waste pieces of the apples with the chopped onion, pour on cider and Calvados. Add the veal broth and the light gravy and season with salt and pepper.

with Apples

3. Cook the gravy over a low heat for ten minutes. Fry the apple slices in melted butter. Cut the crust off the bread and brown the slices in butter. Slice the goose liver, season, dust with flour and fry on each side for one minute. Place on paper towels.

4. Pour the gravy through a fine sieve and add a little butter. Arrange six apple pieces on the first slice of bread, place a slice of liver on top, and cover with a slice of bread. Top with the peel strips and the very thin apple slices, sprinkle a little gravy around the toast, and decorate with smooth-leaved parsley as desired.

Paul Heathcote's

Preparation time: 1 hour 30 minutes
Soaking time: 12 hours
Cooking time: 3 hours,
                      45 minutes
Difficulty: ★★★

Serves four

1 lb / 450 g veal (or lamb) sweetbreads
1³/₄ cups / 450 ml pig's blood
sausage skin (enough for about 20 sausage slices)
2 large potatoes
1 onion
8 cocktail onions

scant ¹/₄ cup / 50 g dried Navy beans (or dried
   black-eyed peas)
4 carrots (to yield scant ¹/₄ cup / 50 g cut)
scant ¹/₄ cup / 50 g oats
scant ¹/₄ cup / 50 g raisins
generous 1 cup / 250 ml light veal broth
generous ³/₈ cup / 100 ml white grape vinegar
¹/₂ cup / 125 ml olive oil
scant ¹/₂ lb / 200 g butter
1 sprig of rosemary
1 sprig of thyme
3 bay leaves
salt, pepper

Paul Heathcote, of England, created this very personal version of black pudding at the request of a French restaurant in the Champagne region. They had originally envisaged a recipe based on caviar, truffles or foie gras. Many a famous British chef has since included this recipe on his menu, and its success remains unrivalled.

Chef Heathcote deviates from the old tradition of mixing fat cubes into the black pudding, substituting them with raisins marinated in vinegar. Fresh yet slightly congealed pig's blood is ideal for the preparation of this dish. It requires concentration and care, as the blood must not boil, but should curdle, in a double boiler. Heat the water in the double boiler to exactly 180 °F / 82 °C to attain the required 167 °F / 75 °C in the sausage itself. In Britain, oats and black pudding are old friends.

The various flavors of these ingredients are harmoniously enhanced by thyme and rosemary and especially by the bay leaves, which are crushed to develop a stronger aroma.

Veal sweetbreads, fresh and in immaculate condition, take the lead role – fried in a pan to sweat out as much juice as possible. Lamb sweetbreads may be used as an alternative.

For the mashed potatoes, we use a floury, and thus absorbent, type of potato. Of some one thousand different types possible, our chef recommends the Maris Piper, which is very popular in Britain, though there are certainly other varieties available in the U.S. that will work as well. For the beans, substitute black-eyed peas if Navy beans are unavailable; either variety will have to be soaked and then pre-cooked.

1. The night before, soak the dried beans in a large pot of cold water. On the day of preparation, slow-cook the rinsed beans for three hours. Blanch the sweetbreads in boiling water for one minute. Remove the skin membrane. Chop the sweetbread and fry the pieces in olive oil until golden brown. Marinate the raisins and a bay leaf in enough vinegar for it to be totally absorbed. Steam the raisins over a low heat without caramelizing them; the vinegar in them should evaporate.

2. Heat the pig's blood in a double boiler, stirring continually, until it curdles. Pick thyme and rosemary leaves off the sprigs. Mix all the ingredients indicated (onion, oats, veal sweetbread, raisins and herbs) with the blood and season to taste.

Black Pudding

3. Fill sausage skins with this mixture and poach in a double boiler at exactly 180 °F / 82 °C for 40 minutes. Cook the beans as well as the carrots and the cocktail onions in veal broth with crushed bay leaves for half an hour. Take out some of the vegetables and pass the rest through a sieve.

4. Cook the potatoes in their jackets, then skin and mash them with a fork. Add butter, salt, and pepper. To serve, slice the cooled blood sausages, fry in olive oil, and place on top of the mashed potatoes. Reheat the retained vegetables in the sauce and spoon around the mashed potatoes.

Smoked Haddock

Preparation time: *30 minutes*
Soaking time: *1 hour*
Cooking time: *10 minutes*
Difficulty: ★

Serves four

4 smoked haddock fillets / generous ¹/₂ lb / 250 g
7 oz / 200 g young peas, extra fine
1 head of lettuce
2 large carrots
2 eggs

1 tbsp / 15 g capers
³/₄ cup / 200 g butter
juice of 1 lemon
vegetable oil for deep-frying
1 tbsp butter / 15 g
1 bunch of chives
pepper to taste

For poaching:
4 bay leaves
2 cups / 500 ml whole milk
pepper to taste

With an endless coastline and seemingly limitless stock of riches from the sea, Norway has developed many methods to preserve whatever can not be consumed immediately. Norwegians are, therefore, consummate experts in the art of smoking, salting, and drying fish. They are very partial to smoked fillets of haddock, a cousin of cod that is found predominantly in the North Sea and along the Norwegian coast, mainly in the strait of Skagerrak. Haddock, by the way, is also extremely popular in Great Britain.

After having been salted and smoked with juniper or pine wood, which lends a typical orange hue to the fish, haddock lasts for about a week. For easy handling, as our chef Eyvind Hellstrøm advises, do not remove the skins of the fillets until you are ready to flake the flesh. The steps are: soak the fillets in milk, skin them, flake the flesh, season, and prepare them uncooked.

The crisp texture of the young, extra fine peas used in this appetizer provides a pleasant contrast to the soft haddock; their sweet flavor harmonizes well with the fish's strong, salty taste. If you prefer, try another variation, using pasta or mustard sauce as a side dish. And, if you prefer a less pronounced flavor, substitute the smoked haddock with halibut, salmon, or smoked cod.

1. Soak the smoked haddock fillets (still in their skins) in milk, add bay leaves and peppercorns, and poach lightly. Boil the eggs until hard, leave to cool, and chop.

2. Boil the peas and the lettuce leaves in salted water, leave to cool. Cut the carrots into thin strips and sauté in oil. Heat the peas and the lettuce leaves in a saucepan with butter.

with Young Peas

3. Drain the haddock fillets, skin carefully and flake, then arrange on pre-warmed plates.

4. Chop the chives and the eggs. Stir butter and a little water into the sauce and whip until creamy. Add the chives, capers, lemon juice, and chopped eggs. Pour the finished sauce over the fish and serve at once.

"Klippfisk"

Preparation time: 30 minutes
Soaking time: 48 hours
Cooking time: 10 minutes
Difficulty: ★★

Serves four

generous ¹/₂ lb / 250 g dried salt cod
7 oz / 200 g potatoes
1 packet of brek pastry (see below)
1 clove of garlic
³/₄ cup / 200 ml olive oil
generous ³/₈ cup / 100 ml whole milk

¹/₄ cup / 50 g melted butter
1 bunch of basil
salt, cayenne pepper to taste

For the sauce and the garnish:
1 green pepper
4 large tomatoes
1 clove of garlic
2 onions
1 dozen black olives
generous ³/₈ cup / 100 ml olive oil
generous ³/₈ cup / 100 ml fish stock

Dried cod pickled in coarse salt is not only popular in Norway but all over Europe, especially in Spain and Portugal, which actually import a large portion of what Scandinavia produces. Our recipe for crisp fish tarts with bacalao sauce (*bacalao* is the Spanish term for dried and salted cod) unites connoisseurs from both Nordic and southern European countries. Cod is mainly found in the cold waters of the North Atlantic; in winter, fishermen catch it in large fish traps in the Norwegian fjords. The big commercial trawlers, carrying up to a thousand tons (tonnes) of fish, are naturally operating on a totally different scale.

Our chef Eyvind Hellstrøm is an expert in his field. He prefers to use air-dried cod, which contains more moisture and has therefore a smoother texture, and to retain its flavor he processes the fish puree as soon as it is cooked. Fish, potatoes, and milk blend well when they are all the same temperature. This mixture, with basil added, is shaped into small tarts and wrapped in brek or puff pastry, as desired; the former is a Tunisian specialty that has found its way into many other cuisines, as its delicate, flaky layers are ideal for many different dishes. Puff pastry, on the other hand, will give the tarts a slightly heavier feel. The spicy olive puree lends this dish a Mediterranean touch, and brings out the full flavor of the fish.

Bacalao sauce originates from Spain: this delicious blend of olive oil, onions, garlic, and tomatoes with a little added cod and piquant spices will certainly delight your guests. And, if you prefer, try using salted stringray instead, which, despite its smoother flesh and higher gelatin content, is similar in flavor and may be prepared the same way.

1. Steep the dried cod for 48 hours. Peel the garlic, blanch three times, puree, and set aside for the fish filling. Poach 5¹/₄ oz / 150 g of dried cod in milk, peel and cook the potatoes, and blend everything with the garlic puree. Season with salt and cayenne pepper.

2. Spread out layers of brek pastry or puff pastry rolled paper-thin (see basic recipes to prepare), place some fish mixture and a basil leaf on top, fold up and shape into little parcels.

3. Fry the parcels in butter and olive oil until golden brown. Blanch the pepper, skin; slice the tomatoes. Chop the onion finely and sauté in olive oil. Make a puree of black olives, garlic, and olive oil.

4. To prepare the bacalao sauce, sauté onions, tomatoes, and garlic in olive oil. Add the fish stock and the remaining 3¹/₂ oz / 100 g dried cod and reduce the liquid. Puree and season to taste. Serve three to a plate, ringed with sauce and garnished with garlic, olive paste, basil leaves, and tomato.

Ribbon Noodles with

Preparation time: 30 minutes
Setting time: 1 hour
Cooking time: 20 minutes
Difficulty: ★

Serves four

generous 1 lb / 500 g mussels (venus mussels,
   if available)
4 zucchini
1 shallot
1 clove of garlic
generous $^3/_8$ cup / 100 ml extra-virgin olive oil
1 bunch of smooth-leaved parsley

For the pasta dough:
$^5/_8$ lb / 300 g fine-ground semolina flour
2 tbsp / 30 ml water
generous $^3/_8$ cup / 100 ml extra virgin olive oil

Homemade pasta is a traditional part of nearly every Italian's daily diet. It is rich in protein and highly valued by athletes for its high carbohydrate level. In this recipe our chef, Alfonso Iaccarino, combines the thin ribbon noodles known as linguini with traditional vegetables cooked in olive oil. The appetizer is enriched with a special kind of mussel from the Bay of Naples. Known as venus mussels, these molluscs have yellow and brown striped shells, and are of medium size. They are generally consumed alive, like oysters, or else just cooked briefly to preserve the mild iodine flavor of its flesh. If such mussels are not available, substitute with medium-sized blue mussels.

Interestingly, the dough for the linguini noodles is made from finely ground semolina, and does not use eggs. If the water remains clear (and thus, free of starch) while the noodles are being cooked, you will know that you have prepared them perfectly.

The sauce that is prepared together with the noodles is based on zucchini, shallots, and, of course, extra-virgin olive oil. The zucchini is a common ingredient in Mediterranean dishes; choose ones that are ripe, tender, and green with a diameter of about about an inch (two centimeters). Shallots, on the other hand, are very rare in southern Italy, a fact that induced Chef Iaccarino to grow French shallots himself, on his own farm.

1. Chop the shallot finely, slice the zucchini thinly, and sauté both in olive oil over medium heat for 15 minutes. Prepare the dough by mixing semolina with water and olive oil, knead well, and leave to set for one hour.

2. Sauté the garlic in olive oil and remove from the pan. Add the mussels to this oil and fry over a high heat until they open. Roll out the pasta dough, cut into thin strips, and cook in salted water until al dente. Drain, rinse under cold water and keep warm.

Mussels and Zucchini

3. Finely chop the parsley. Add the zucchini slices, the finely chopped shallot, and equally finely chopped parsley to the mussels in the pan.

4. Reheat and season again. Add the noodles, mix everything well, and serve immediately.

Sheep's Milk Cheese Ravioli

Preparation time: 40 minutes
Chilling time: 1 hour
Cooking time: 1 hour (2 days in advance), 10 minutes

Difficulty: ★★

Serves four

For the filling:
generous ¹/₂ lb / 250 g Caciotta sheep's milk cheese (see below)
1 egg yolk
1 sprig of marjoram

For the tomato sauce:
generous 1 lb / 500 g tomatoes
1 bunch of medium-leaf basil
1 clove of garlic
generous ³/₈ cup / 100 ml olive oil

For the ravioli dough:
1²/₃ cups / 400 g semolina flour
generous ³/₈ cup / 100 ml olive oil
2 tbsp / 30 ml water
a pinch of salt

For this recipe, our chef, Alfonso Iaacarino, swears by San Marzano tomatoes, the only ones he would ever use. Shiny, deep red, cylindrical and about three inches (eight centimeters) long, these tomatoes ripen in August, and Italians all over the country go through the yearly ritual of preserving their beloved tomatoes so they can enjoy them throughout the year. It was Alfonso Iaccarino's grandfather, Don Alfonso, who taught his grandson to treat this extraordinary fruit with respect.

Of course, San Marzanos are not always available everywhere – even in the cornucopia of a gourmet produce stand at the height of the season, they can be hard to find. Instead, one may have to make do with another types of tomatoes, such as Roma or a small variety of globe, so long as they are nice and red with a fully matured flavor, and were not grown in a hothouse, but rather had the chance to mature outside, on the vine.

Tomatoes should be cooked in their skins, as this will hold them together and preserve their flavor. If prepared two days in advance, the sauce will assume the desired dark, rich color associated with an outstanding tomato sauce. The ravioli dough, on the other hand, should be prepared on the same day the appetizer will be served, and should then be left to "sweat" in an open wooden bowl in the refrigerator for about an hour.

As for the cheese, preference is given to products from the region of Campania, such as Caciotta, a traditional sheep's milk cheese. This is another instance where availability may be limited. So, if Caciotta is not available, you may substitute it with Panegio cheese from northern Italy, or simply a ripe Brie. Accompanied by olive oil, basil, and marjoram, this appetizer is redolent with the flavors of Mediterranean cooking.

1. To prepare the ravioli dough, heap the flour into a pyramid, make a well in the middle, add olive oil, water, and salt, and knead well. Shape the dough into a ball and refrigerate for one hour.

2. Prepare the filling by combining the cheese with the chopped marjoram and an egg yolk.

with Tomatoes and Basil

3. Roll out the ravioli dough, cut out hearts with a cookie cutter, fill with the cheese mixture, and seal well. Cook in salted water for two minutes.

4. To make the sauce, sauté garlic in a pan with olive oil. Chop tomatoes. Mash the garlic, add the tomatoes, and fry over a high heat for five minutes. Arrange the ravioli on plates, pour the sauce over, and decorate with basil leaves.

Garlic Soup with

Preparation time: 30 minutes
Cooking time: 20 minutes
Difficulty: ★

Serves four

generous 1 lb / 500 g small blue mussels
generous 1 lb / 500 g fresh garlic
generous 1 lb / 500 g potatoes
1 bunch of fresh sage
generous ³/₈ cup / 100 ml extra-virgin olive oil
generous 1 cup / 250 ml white wine

generous 3 cups / 750 ml whole milk
salt, pepper

In the ancient world, the healing powers of garlic were well known. In those days it was used to rid the body of parasites and ward off infections and colds, but it was also said to be hard to digest. Today, garlic is grown in Europe on a large scale predominantly in southern Italy and in the southwest of France, mainly cultivated in Saint-Clar in the Gers region. Although normally used as a flavoring, to spice sauces and meat, fish, or poultry dishes, garlic plays the leading role in this recipe.

When garlic is prepared together with potatoes and milk, it is easier to digest. Chef Alfonso Iaccarino, who grows his garlic, amongst other crops, on his own farm, suggests using young, fresh garlic of medium size that is harvested from May to September and that is not excessively strong in taste.

Very fresh garlic should dry for a few days before being used. It dries best in plaits, (and is sold that way in Saint-Clar) and hung in an airy room at the right temperature. Old garlic, on the other hand, often absorbs an earthy taste, and is not recommended; kept in the refrigerator for too long, even fresh garlic will lose some of its flavor.

So-called winter potatoes, such as round whites or Yukon gold, are best suited to ensure the creamy consistency of the soup, as they are well-suited to boiling. To round off their flavor, you can use rosemary, marjoram, or sage, which also serves as a lovely garnish. Despite its bitter aftertaste, sage is widely used in the whole Mediterranean region for its spicy aroma.

1. Peel and dice the potatoes. Sauté with the garlic over a low heat.

2. Cover the potatoes with a mixture of white wine and whole milk and bring to a boil.

Sage and Mussels

3. Cook the potatoes over a low heat for 20 minutes, then blend and strain. Season to taste and keep warm.

4. Wash the mussels, steam them, and shell. Serve the soup in deep plates, sink mussels into the liquid, and garnish with fresh herbs, such as sage, rosemary, or marjoram.

Goatfish in Pastry Coats with

Preparation time: 45 minutes
Cooking time: 20 minutes
Difficulty: ★

Serves four

2 goatfish
1 packet of brek pastry sheets or ¹/₂ lb / 250 g puff
    pastry dough (see basic recipes)
2 globe tomatoes
1 large tomato (to yield 1 tbsp / 15 g tomato puree)
1 red pepper
1 green pepper
1 yellow pepper

1 egg yolk
4 cloves of garlic
2 shallots
4 leaves of green lettuce
3¹/₂ oz / 100 g green olives
4 tbsp / 50 g rice
2 tbsp / 30 ml champagne vinegar
3 tbsp / 50 ml olive oil
1 tbsp / 15 g white sugar
1 tbsp / 15 g grated ginger
1 tbsp / 15 g tapioca starch
generous ³/₈ cup / 100 ml chicken stock
salt, pepper

According to our chef, André Jaeger, it is said that there is no better goatfish (otherwise known as red barbel or red mullet) than the goatfish from Bandol, a little fishing harbour on the French Mediterranean coast that also happens to be home to a wonderful wine. But, as Jaeger notes, the goatfish found in Norway and off the Canadian coast, and even in Switzerland, are also highly esteemed.

Goatfish in general seem to be the subject of frequent debate, and the editors do not want to get involved in the argument of whether red barbels caught in rocky waters are better than those living on muddy seabeds. The latter, however, are red-brown and their flavor is less distinct. Whether from rocky waters or muddy seabeds, goatfish are often used in the famous bouillabaisse. Tender and fragile, they must be handled with great care, in particular when they are filleted and freed from their masses of bones.

Do not cook goatfish for more than seven minutes or it may lose its tender flavor. Aware of this, our chef wraps his in a coat made of either Tunisian brek pastry dough, or puff pastry, to protect them against the oven's strong heat. And he lays the fillets skin side up inside the pastry to provide even more protection.

Since Chef Jaeger has spent much time in Asia, it is not surprising that his sweet pepper sauce conveys a strong eastern influence that Europeans might not be accustomed to, with ginger root and tapioca starch. Other ingredients used in the recipe, however, will be more common to a western palate, from the egg yolk used to seal the pastry sheets together to the nice big lettuce leaves with strong ribs used as an inner wrapper for this fish.

1. First cook the rice and wash the lettuce. Fillet the goatfish and carefully remove all the bones. Spread out the brek sheets or roll out the puff pastry into very thin layers. Place a lettuce leaf and a tablespoon of rice onto each square.

2. Salt the fillets and place them, skin side up, on top of the rice. Brush the pastry edges with egg yolk and seal. Bake in the oven at 480 °F / 250 °C for seven minutes.

Asian Sweet Pepper Sauce

3. Quarter the peppers, remove the middle section and seeds, peel the rest and cut into ¹/₄ in / ¹/₂ cm wide strips. Peel the garlic and the shallots, cut into small slices and blanch in boiling water. Heat olive oil in a frying pan, add peppers, garlic and shallots and fry over a high heat. Puree one tomato.

4. Stir the tomato puree into the mixture, and leave to steep. Skin, seed, and chop the other tomatoes. Add these to the pan, pour on the chicken stock, cover, and braise over a low heat for five minutes. Seed and halve the olives and add them to the pan. Blend the tapioca starch with vinegar and add as well. Season with ground ginger, sugar, and salt.

Oxtail Soup with

Preparation time: 25 minutes
Chilling time: 12 hours
Cooking time: 50 minutes
Difficulty: ★★

Serves four

2²/₃ oz / 80 g black truffles
7 oz / 200 g beef (to be minced)
14 oz / 400 g beef cheek
14 oz / 400 g oxtail
5 carrots (to yield 7 oz / 200 g))
3 onions (to yield 3¹/₂ oz / 100 g))

1 leek stalk
1 celery stalk
2 tbsp / 30 ml sherry vinegar
4 tbsp / 65 ml truffle juice
1 generous lb / 500 g puff pastry
  (see Basic Recipes)
3 egg yolks
generous ³/₈ cup / 100 g butter
quarter bunch of thyme
1 bay leaf
quarter bunch of parsley
salt, pepper to taste

This venerable soup has been on the menu of Paul Bocuse's famous restaurant in Collognes-au-Mont-d'Or since 1975, and it is still greeted with great enthusiasm. Here, Chef Roger Jaloux presents its preparation.

Contrary to what some believe, the size of a truffle has actually no influence on its quality. The most famous truffles are found around Aups in Provence and in the Ardèche region. Collecting truffles can be a difficult undertaking: the pigs trained to dig out truffles, so-called "truffle pigs," also enjoy eating them; the dogs who sometimes take their place have been known to dig too enthusiastically; rain is another factor. There are even merchants, like the preeminent Messrs Dumont and Guyon, who have specialized exclusively in truffles; they have been supplying the world's top restaurants for more than twenty years. If you want to buy truffles yourself, beware of street vendors, and never buy truffles that have not been thoroughly cleaned: often

the dirt clinging to them can weigh more than the truffles. Truffles are best preserved in an air-tight container with uncooked rice to absorb the moisture. As a bonus, when the rice is cooked, it will have absorbed the rich aroma of the truffles.

Puff pastry should never be baked for more than twenty minutes. Chef Jaloux recommends that the pastry and the soup be prepared a day ahead of time, and stored in a cool place overnight. This precautionary measure gives the pastry a firmer structure, and prevents it from collapsing in the oven or possibly sinking into the soup.

The soup itself does not require great cooking skills. Beef cheek and oxtail ensure its delicious flavor. For some reason that is incomprehensible to the editors, this refined delicacy is also called, rather rustically, a "shepherd's soup."

1. One day ahead of time, prepare the puff pastry; let it chill overnight; you may also want to prepare the soup a day ahead as well. Begin preparing the appetizer by cleaning the truffles thoroughly and slicing them thinly.

2. Cook broth from the beef and oxtail pieces (for 20 minutes). At the same time dice the vegetables and fry them in butter. Then dice the cooked meat finely.

Puff Pastry Hat

3. Spoon the cooled meat and the fried vegetables into soup bowls and mix. Place one tablespoon of truffles on top.

4. Fill the soup bowls with broth and season. Cover with a sheet of puff pastry, brush with egg yolk, and bake in the oven at 390 °F / 200 °C for 20 minutes.

Mashed Potatoes

Preparation time: 20 minutes
Cooking time: 15 minutes
Difficulty: ✶✶

Serves four

7 oz / 200 g mussels
2 small squid or octopus
4 langoustines
2 scallops
1³/₄ lb / 800 g Charlotte or new potatoes, boiled
2 shallots

1 bunch of chives
generous ³/₈ cup / 100 ml light cream
scant ¹/₄ cup / 50 ml olive oil
generous 1 cup / 250 ml melted butter
generous ³/₈ cup / 100 ml balsamic vinegar
1¹/₄ cups / 300 ml white wine
salt, pepper to taste

Charlotte potatoes, which have been on the European market for about ten years, have the advantage of being both very tasty and very firm. In the U.S., if they are not available, other types of early potatoes will do, sold under the general term new potatoes, or early round whites. Early potatoes are harvested when they are still very tender, before they have fully ripened, whereas ripe potatoes are harvested in August. Both types retain their flavor when they are cooked. Since it would be a pity to puree potatoes of such quality in a blender or food processor – and risk obliterating their flavor – one should use instead a good old-fashioned potato masher. In this recipe, Chef Patrick Jeffroy substitutes milk with cream and olive oil.

All the seafood should still be alive or at least extremely fresh when bought; the mussels will be closed if they are fresh.

Prepare the shellfish at the last minute, especially the mussels, which must be kept in their stock to prevent them from drying out. Be careful not to cook the other seafood a second time when you finally heat it up in melted butter, otherwise it will become tough and dry. It is, of course, a matter of personal taste whether to use other types of seafood such as oysters or venus mussels as well.

The octopus with its elongated body and eight tentacles covered with suckers, also joins this happy mix of fruits of the sea, substituted, if you prefer, by squid instead, which has ten tentacles instead, two being longer than the rest. Both belong to the mollusc family and are famous for their hearty flavor. There are several types, differing from each other in the size of their bodies and the length of their tentacles.

1. Chop the shallot. Scrub the mussels, wash several times in clear water, drain and cook in white wine with the chopped shallot. Remove from the stove as soon as the mussels open. Shell the mussels and reserve some of the shells for decoration.

2. Gut and skin the octopus or squid. Wash it carefully in clear water, dry, and slice the body into rings. Place the langoustines into boiling salted water and take them out as soon as the water starts boiling again. Cool and shell the tails.

with Seafood

3. Mash the boiled potatoes with a potato masher, adding olive oil and light cream. Using a pastry bag, pipe the puree onto plates in the shape of a ring. Cook the octopus or squid flesh in the mussel stock for two minutes.

4. Sauté the langoustines and scallops briefly. Heat the seafood in melted butter, but do not cook. Remove and arrange on the mashed potatoes. Season the melted butter to taste and pour over the seafood. Sprinkle with chopped chives and a little balsamic vinegar.

Scrambled Eggs

Preparation time: 30 minutes
Cooking time: 10 minutes
Difficulty: ★

Serves four

half a dozen eggs
1 lb 5 oz / 600 g frogs' legs
1 shallot
2 tbsp / 30 g butter
³/₄ cup / 200 ml Alsatian Riesling (white wine)
scant ¹/₄ cup / 50 ml Noilly Prat (vermouth)

scant ¹/₄ cup / 50 ml cream
1 bunch of parsley
1 bunch of sorrel
salt, pepper to taste

This recipe provides an elegant contrast between melt-in-your-mouth scrambled eggs, succulent frogs' legs, and the spicy flavors of Riesling and fresh sorrel.

The eggs used for this dish must be absolutely fresh; their size is irrelevant. A common rule of thumb in the kitchen is that a fresh egg placed in a glass of water will not rise to the surface. Scrambled eggs should always be prepared over a very low heat, or even in a double boiler; under no circumstances should they fry. Avoid lumps by continually stirring with a wooden spoon. The result is an evenly combined, creamy mixture that should be consumed immediately before it becomes stiff.

The days when frogs were so plentiful they could be caught in virtually any river are long gone; in fact frogs' legs are difficult to get hold of in many countries. But in France, our chef Émile Jung does not face this problem, and thus has presented this dish with enthusiasm.

Wine-lovers are familiar with the seven special quality wines from Alsace, one of them being Riesling. Be it from Riquewihr or from Ribeauvillé, it is always offered in its typical long-necked bottle, which is also called the "Alsatian flute". This fruity white wine refines many sauces and also harmonizes wonderfully with vermouth, another ingredient of this dish. The vermouth, however, must be used sparingly, as its slightly bitter taste should only support the other flavors, and not dominate them.

1. Chop the shallot. Salt and pepper the frogs' legs and place them in a pot. Add the shallot, the Riesling, and vermouth, and then heat.

2. As soon as the liquid has reached a boil, cover with greaseproof paper cut to size and then cook for five minutes. Take out the frogs' legs, reduce, add cream, and then strain the sauce. Bone the frogs' legs.

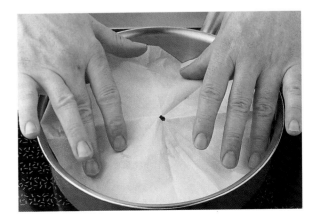

with Frogs' Legs

3. Whisk the eggs, and season with salt and pepper. Stir continually with a wooden spoon in a double boiler or on a low flame until set. While stirring, add half the butter to make a creamy mixture.

4. Chop the parsley. Add the boned frogs' legs, then the sorrel, the chopped parsley and the rest of the butter. Mix well, serve in soup plates, and sprinkle with sauce, garnished with sorrel leaves.

Maultaschen with Rabbit

Preparation time: 1 hour 30 minutes
Cooking time: 15 minutes
Difficulty: ✶✶

Serves four

backs of 2 rabbits, including kidneys and liver
heads of 2 rabbits
5$^{1}/_{4}$ oz / 150 g vegetable brunoise of celery, carrots,
    leeks
2 shallots
generous $^{3}/_{8}$ cup / 100 ml rabbit or vegetable stock
$^{1}/_{4}$ cup / 50 ml vegetable oil
$^{1}/_{4}$ cup / 50 g butter
half a bunch of thyme

half a bunch of rosemary
salt, pepper to taste

For the carrot sauce:
7 oz / 200 g carrots
leaves from the carrot tops
2 shallots
$^{3}/_{4}$ cup / 200 ml rabbit or vegetable stock
$^{1}/_{4}$ cup / 50 g crème fraîche
$^{1}/_{4}$ cup / 50 g butter
scant $^{1}/_{4}$ cup / 50 ml white wine

For the pasta dough:
3 small eggs
generous 1 cup / 250 g flour
pinch of salt

In southern Germany, people love *Maultaschen*: pasta pockets that look like giant ravioli with open edges. This very filling dish originating from Swabia is most often served with a broth or with mixed salads. The version presented here by Chef Dieter Kaufmann is lighter and easier to digest. The rabbit meat used is low in fat and calories, but high in protein. Free-range rabbits fed on barley and other grains are ideal for this purpose. When you select a rabbit, make sure its legs are still soft to the touch, as this is an indication of freshness.

With a chef's sense of humor, the carrots in this dish are served with a nod to the famous Bugs Bunny cartoons. Young fresh carrots are ideal; they go very well with this dish and are available throughout the year. The Mediterranean herbs suggested by Dieter Kaufmann should only be used in moderation so as not to mask the vegetables' own flavors.

Instead of decorating with carrot leaves, you may of course garnish with other vegetables or herbs, such as leeks, chervil, or smooth-leaved parsley. It is mainly the color contrast that is important, so feel free to experiment. Finally, note that this dish is not only suitable as an appetizer, but could also liven up a family supper.

1. Prepare the pasta dough ahead of time. To prepare the dish, begin by finely cutting the vegetables for the brunoise, and chopping the shallots. Fillet the rabbit backs and fry the meat in butter along with the kidneys and livers. Add the rabbit heads, with 5$^{1}/_{4}$ oz / 150 g of finely cut vegetables and chopped shallots. Add a dash of the stock and cook for 15 minutes. Remove the rabbit brains and tongues.

2. Roll out the previously prepared pasta dough into sheets. Decorate half of them with carrot greens or other herbs, cut them into rectangles, cook in rapidly boiling salted water and rinse under cold water to stop the cooking process.

Meat in Carrot Butter

3. To prepare the carrot sauce, sauté chopped shallots and diced carrots in butter. Add the crème fraîche and the stock and cook for about ten minutes. Then mix and strain. Mix the white wine and the carrot greens with the sauce.

4. Cut each of the rabbit fillets into three pieces. Place one pasta rectangle onto each plate, top with rabbit meat, a piece of tongue, brains, kidney, and liver, sprinkle with stock, cover with another sheet of pasta and surround with the carrot sauce.

Chèvre in Courgette Slices with

Preparation time: 30 minutes
Cooking time: 2 minutes
Difficulty: ☆

Serves four

2 chèvres (goat's milk cheeses), such as Picodon
  (see below)
2 zucchini
4 ripe tomatoes
1 sprig of thyme
1 bunch of basil
2 tbsp / 30 ml vegetable bouillon

scant ¼ cup / 50 ml balsamic vinegar
2 tbsp / 30 ml extra-virgin olive oil
salt, pepper to taste

Many of Dieter and Elvira Kaufmann's German guests have never heard of Picodon before, and have no idea what to expect when they order this light, surprising appetizer with its strong Mediterranean character.

Actually, Picodon is one of the many outstanding varieties of goat's milk cheeses that are known generally as chèvres and are becoming increasingly popular in many kitchens. This soft variety, produced in southern France in the Vivarais region around Tricastin, needs two to three weeks to mature. During this time it develops its piquant flavor. It is recognizable by its round, tartlet shape, and the mottled, blue-gray coloring of its rind.

Since Picodon is a Mediterranean cheese, it tends to be combined with aromas from Provence – in this case, ripe tomatoes and fresh basil. The zucchinis (in French they are known as *courgettes*) should be extremely fresh, a vibrant green with yellow flecks, and both medium-sized and firm, so they can be sliced very thinly and cooked as briefly as possible. Zucchinis are very low in calories and balance out the rich cheese (which is 45% fat).

Dieter Kaufmann serves this appetizer lukewarm and only mentions the words "goat's milk" once his guests have eaten their fill. If Picodon is unavailable, there are countless other types of chèvres, such as the classic types from Central France – Pouligny Saint-Pièrre, or Valençay. The zucchinis may also be substituted with cucumbers: in this case, just sauté them together with the cheese instead of cooking them first.

1. Cut the zucchini into long thin slices. Slice, salt, and pepper the goat's milk cheese.

2. Skin, seed, and dice the tomatoes and mix them with finely chopped thyme and basil leaves. Spread this mixture over the cheese slices.

Tomato and Basil Vinaigrette

3. Wrap the cheese with zucchini slices. Prepare a vinaigrette from the remaining ingredients.

4. Fry the cheese wraps briefly in a pan with olive oil and then bake in a very hot oven for one minute. Arrange on pre-warmed plates, surround them with a sprinkling of the vinaigrette, and decorate with basil leaves.

Preparation time: 25 minutes
Cooking time: 5 minutes
Difficulty: ★

Serves four

1 bunch of stinging nettles (without flowers)
4 quail eggs
4 cups / 1 l chicken broth
half a bunch of chives (to yield 4 tbsp / 80 g
   chopped)
a pinch of aniseed powder
a pinch of fennel powder
salt, pepper to taste

For the roux:
1 tbsp / 15 g flour
1 tbsp / 15 g butter

Chef Örjan Klein, from Sweden, fashioned this dish to remind his guests that stinging nettles have a high iron content and are good for one's health. He was raised on this understanding, since his grandmother Hildur used to take him along when she went to collect stinging nettles for her delicious soup. Collecting these nettles is quite a complicated affair, and gloves are a must. But our chef is partial to this stinging nettle soup, and claims it is well worth the trouble. So, come early spring, he treats his guests to this delight. The appetizer has become so popular that the daily consumption amounts to more than three gallons (some fifteen liters), which of course, necessitates a whole army of people to gather the nettles, and many pairs of gloves.

In the past soups were the obligatory first course of each meal. In Sweden yellow pea soup was particularly popular. This filling soup, prepared with pork and bacon, was always served on a Thursday evening since, according to Catholic tradition, Friday was a day of abstinence from meat. It did not take long for the students of Uppsala, Sweden's oldest university, to invent their own version with hot punch.

For this recipe, one needs small, young nettles without flowers; once the plants have flowered they no longer have the same flavor. The vitamin content is also dependent on the cooking time. Stinging nettles should therefore be blanched for only two to three minutes. They are then chopped and added to the soup just before it is served. A quail egg looks very good as a decoration, but a small chicken egg or even a few salmon eggs will do as well.

1. Wash and blanch the nettles, rinse them under cold water, chop, and set aside.

2. Boil the chicken broth and bind with the roux while stirring with a whisk to obtain an evenly combined mixture.

Stinging Nettle Soup

3. Stir in aniseed powder and fennel powder and season to taste. Cook the quail eggs for five to six minutes.

4. Add the stinging nettles to the soup. Mix and serve in soup plates. Decorate with a quail egg and chopped chives, and serve immediately to retain the green color.

Chopped Calf's

Preparation time: 1 hour
Soaking time: 24 hours
Cooking time: 1 hour 15 minutes
Difficulty: ★★

Serves four

2 dozen large Belon oysters
2 shallots
4 slices of white bread
1 bunch of smooth-leaved parsley
coarse salt

For the calf's head:
generous 1 lb / 500 g calf's head
scant 1/8 lb / 50 g lean belly bacon
3 carrots (to yield 3 1/2 oz / 100 g cut)
1 onion (to yield 1 oz / 30 g chopped)
2 cloves of garlic
1 bouquet garni
generous 2 cups / 500 ml red wine
generous 2 cups / 500 ml veal broth
2 tbsp / 30 g butter
coarse salt, pepper to taste

At three to four years old, oysters are fully matured and suitable for consumption; in some cultures, such as the ancient Greeks, even their shells were used, ground into a powder to make a love potion. Interestingly enough, the word has some etymological coincidences, as the Latin word for oyster, *ostrea*, is not at all related to the similar-sounding Greek word that refers to a pottery tool. However, some experts point out that the pottery tool has a similar shape to an oyster shell.

Oysters are generally consumed raw, but even cooked they have an ever-increasing following, since their tender and tasty flesh can certainly withstand heating. Of all the different types of oysters offered, the so-called Belon are the ones our Dutch chef, Robert Kranenborg, prefers for this recipe. They are farmed on the banks of the Belon River in the southern part of Brittany, and are now being cultivated in the United States as

well. It is of utmost importance that the temperature never exceeds 98.6° F / 37 °C when oysters are heated, requiring the use of a good thermometer.

As Chef Kranenborg relates, in his country, calf's head is very popular. One dish, called *Kalbspolet*, is a stew made from a calf's head and brightened with lettuce leaves and peas. The recipe presented here will delight many a guest. And, though it goes without saying, we will say it anyway: only use an absolutely fresh calf's head that has been steeped in water for a full day ahead. The same applies to veal knuckles, which may, if desired, substitute the calf's head.

One last bit of advice – a heavy, sun-blessed red wine, a Côtes-du-Rhône perhaps, is excellent for the sauce.

1. Steep the calf's head in water for 24 hours, then blanch, leave to cool, and cut into big chunks. Sauté the carrots, onions, garlic and diced bacon in a pot with butter. Add the calf's head and the bouquet garni and season with a pinch of coarse salt. Add a dash of red wine and fill the pot with veal broth.

2. Cover the pot with baking paper and bake in the oven at 320° F / 160 °C for an hour and 15 minutes. Remove the chunks of calf's head and refrigerate them. Strain the stock. Cut the chilled calf's head into small cubes. Chop parsley and shallots finely. Open the oysters and filter the juice. Poach the oysters briefly over a low heat and keep warm in a cloth.

Head with Oysters

3. Reduce the juice of the oysters. Add a little stock from the calf's head, bring to a boil and whip with butter until creamy. Cut the white bread slices into small cubes and fry in melted butter to make croutons.

4. Arrange the cleaned oyster shells on a bed of coarse salt and heat up in the oven. Place the oysters in the shells, spoon the meat cubes with shallots and parsley over them, pour some sauce over, and sprinkle with bread croutons.

Poached Eggs with

Preparation time: 1 hour
Cooking time: 1 hour
Difficulty: ✷✷

Serves four

8 eggs
4¹/₂ lb / 2 kg crabs
1 lb 3¹/₂ oz / 600 g young peas
1 head of lettuce
1 bunch of chives
1 slice cooked ham
generous 2 tbsp / 40 ml crème fraîche

For the sauce:
8 tomatoes
5 carrots (to yield 2¹/₂ oz / 75 g cut)
1 onion (to yield 1 oz / 30 g chopped)
1 clove of garlic
1 shallot (to yield 1 oz / 30 g chopped)
1 bouquet garni
4 tsp / 20 ml port
4 tsp / 20 ml cognac
⁵/₈ cup / 150 ml white wine
generous 3 tbsp / 50 ml vegetable oil
4 tsp / 20 g tomato paste
1 sprig of tarragon
salt, pepper to taste

"The egg is a little universe in a thin shell" – an apt description for this inexhaustible source of vitamin A and phosphorus, for which there are a thousand ways to prepare it. Large eggs are not always the best, since the egg yolk takes up more space than the egg white. An ideally sized egg should weigh about two ounces (sixty grams).

You will need absolutely fresh eggs for poaching; they should never be older than 48 hours, and should, ideally, be from free-range chickens. With today's technology the date when the egg was laid can be printed directly onto the egg or at least onto the package seal. Some gourmet shops or health food stores may have fresher eggs.

Poaching eggs is a very delicate affair. The pot must be big enough; the water with added vinegar may only bubble slightly. Slide the eggs swiftly into the water so that the egg white around the egg yolk can coagulate immediately. You should never poach more than four eggs at a time, or they might meld together. When they are done, place them in cold water to prevent them from drying out, and trim the edges to improve the appearance.

The crabmeat filling can be prepared a day in advance. Instead of crabmeat you may prefer lobster or prawns. The suggested side dish of peas *à la française* is very popular in the Netherlands, as Chef Robert Kranenborg explains. Peas were introduced there by the French on their numerous campaigns throughout the 17th and 18th centuries.

1. Crack the eggs into individual bowls. Slide them carefully out of the bowls into simmering vinegar water and leave to steep. Drain them on paper towels, remove the egg yolk with a tablespoon, and refrigerate. Cook the claws of the crabs in salted water for three minutes. Crush the crabs' bodies and fry them in oil for five minutes.

2. Into the same pan pour on port, cognac, and white wine and add all the vegetables and the bouquet garni for the sauce. Stir in tomato paste and reduce. Add water and reduce the sauce once more. Then cover with water and cook over a low heat for 15 minutes. Remove from the heat, add a tarragon sprig to steep and then strain the sauce.

Crabmeat Filling and Peas

3. Remove the meat from the claws of the crabs. Heat a little crème fraîche in steam, whip until creamy, and mix with the crabmeat. Blanch the peas and steam together with thin ham strips.

4. Fill the empty egg white pockets with the crabmeat mixture and serve on soup plates. Add the peas and garnish with strips of lettuce leaves. Reduce the sauce a little before blending. Then spoon onto the plates, and sprinkle everything with chopped chives.

Vaudois Pie

Preparation time: 45 minutes
Cooking time: 1 hour
Difficulty: ★★

Serves eight

⁵/₈ lb / 300 g puff pastry (see basic recipes)
1 generous lb / 500 g leeks
2 large potatoes
5 slices smoked bacon
5¹/₄ oz / 150 g Raclette cheese (or Gruyère)
4 tsp / 20 g butter

1 tbsp / 15 g flour
²/₃ cup / 150 ml beef bouillon
1 egg
salt, pepper to taste

Gruyère, a pungent relation to Swiss cheese, is so famous all over the world that one easily forgets its origins in a little town situated in the canton of Fribourg in the French-speaking part of Switzerland. This town is, of course, called Gruyère. The commitment to perfection applied in the local cheese factories leaves nothing to be desired. Following old traditions passed on from generation to generation, this cheese is still produced there from raw milk and aged for up to a year. An eighty-pound (thirty-five kilo) wheel of the cheese wheel requires ninety gallons (four hundred liters) of milk. Our chef, Étienne Krebs, recommends cheese of such quality for the preparation of his pie. Other types of cheese, with a higher fat content, might melt too much when baked.

Various different types of leeks are known and enjoyed all over Europe; Wales even displays leeks in its national flag. Our chef recommends using fresh, green succulent leeks, which he likes to get from the Vaudois region. They must be washed very thoroughly before blanching to remove any soil left between the leaves. The particularly tender spring leeks have the best flavor.

One of the best kinds of potatoes for baking is the Charlotte, an early potato with very thin skin and yellow flesh; if this is unavailable, choose early potatoes, such as new potatoes, that are firm and small. The bacon should be very fatty, to best flavor and moisten the potatoes and the leeks. However, if it is too salty it will obliterate the flavors of the other ingredients.

This very filling appetizer may be decorated as desired, with puff pastry leaves, stripes, or any other design.

1. Wash the leeks and cut into 1–2 in / 4 cm pieces. Cook in salted water for 20 minutes and leave to drain. Prepare a thick roux from butter, flour, and bouillon. Season with salt and pepper and add to the leeks. Roll out the puff pastry (prepared ahead of time).

2. Line a pie dish with the rolled-out puff pastry, allowing an overlap of about an inch. Peel the potatoes, slice very thinly, pat dry and use to cover the base of the dish.

with Leeks

3. Spread the leeks with the sauce onto the potatoes and place the bacon strips and finely sliced cheese on top.

4. Brush the rim of the pie with egg yolk, cover the pie with a layer of puff pastry, fold the rim over and press down firmly with your thumb. Decorate the top with motifs or puff pastry strips as desired, brush with egg yolk and bake in the oven at 430 °F / 220 °C for an hour. As soon as the top turns brown, cover with tin foil until cooked. Serve warm.

Frogs' Legs with Mushrooms

Preparation time: 20 minutes
Cooking time: 15 minutes
Difficulty: ★

Serves four

1³/₄ lb / 800 g frogs' legs
7 oz / 200 g forest mushrooms
juice of 1 lemon
¹/₄ cup / 50 g flour
scant ²/₃ cup / 150 g butter
generous 2 cups / 500 ml cream
1 tbsp / 15 ml vegetable oil

half a bunch of tarragon
half a bunch of chervil
salt, pepper to taste

For the sesame cookies:
generous ³/₈ cup / 100 g sesame seeds
³/₄ oz / 20 g poppy seeds
3 tbsp / 40 g butter
1 tbsp / 15 g sugar
juice of 1 lemon
4 tsp / 20 ml water
1 tbsp / 15 ml honey

Sesame opens the gates to the orient, where the seeds of this oil-bearing plant are processed in various ways. In Asia the seeds are most often grilled; they also serve as an ingredient for a very nourishing Chinese drink. In the Middle East, they are ground with almonds to make a sweet delicacy known as halvah. Sesame has even entered the world of so-called fast-food production. Above all, however, sesame is the world's leading raw material for the production of high-quality odorless and colorless oil, used, for example, in dietary foods and healthy cooking.

The preparation of the sesame cookies requires concentration. Do not forget to add the crunchy poppy seeds, which will give the whole mixture a nutty aroma. The cookies are briefly baked in the oven and then placed on a cold steel or marble slab to cool and harden. They may be prepared a day in advance and then simply kept in a dry place.

For this recipe, our chef, Jacques Lameloise, recommends frogs from the area of Dombes in France (which may not be so easy to obtain in other markets). He stresses that whatever frogs you wind up using, the temperature for frying frogs' legs must not exceed 195 °F, or the butter they are being cooked in will burn.

A mixture of forest mushrooms such as chanterelles is added to this dish to intensify the tender texture of the frogs' legs. Fry the thoroughly cleaned mushrooms in butter together with the chopped shallots.

1. Coat the frogs' legs in flour; tap off any excess. Heat 1 tbsp / 15 ml oil and 7 tbsp / 100 g of butter in a frying pan, add the frogs' legs, fry over a high heat and turn. Reduce the heat as soon as they turn brown.

2. To prepare the sauce, bring 2 cups / 500 ml of cream to a boil, add the juice of a lemon, and a tablespoon of chopped tarragon. Season with salt and pepper and then leave to cook for four minutes. Add the remaining butter and whip until creamy.

and Sesame Cookies

3. To prepare the sesame cookies mix butter, sugar, the juice of a lemon, water, honey, sesame seeds, and poppy seeds in a bowl to make a paste-like dough.

4. Place small mounds of this dough onto baking paper and bake in the oven at 355 °F / 180 °C for five minutes. Arrange the frog's legs on plates and add the fried mushrooms. To serve, pour the sauce over, sprinkle with chervil leaves, and top with a sesame cookie.

Burgundy Snails with

Preparation time: 20 minutes
Cooking time: 5 minutes
Difficulty: ★

Serves four

4 eggs
4 dozen snails
3½ oz / 100 g spinach
4½ oz / 125 g button mushrooms
3½ oz / 100 g cocktail onions
4 shallots
5¼ oz / 150 g belly bacon, salted

scant ⅞ cup / 200 g butter
generous 2 cups / 500 ml water
generous ⅜ cup / 100 ml red wine
generous ⅜ cup / 100 ml vinegar
1 bunch of chervil
salt, pepper to taste

For the red wine sauce:
4 cups / 1 l red wine
generous 2 cups / 500 ml veal broth
12 red shallots
1 tbsp / 15 g butter

Imagine you are in the heart of the Bourgogne (or Burgundy), facing the ingredients for an appetizer by Chef Jacques Lameloise. In front of you are the famous snails from that region as well as other typical ingredients, like onions, bacon, and button mushrooms. The age-old recipe for eggs poached in red wine is one of the many types of *meurette*, a specialty of the Bourgogne – essentially meaning a dish cooked in red wine, and deriving from the Old French.

This method of preparation is said to be derived from an old seafarers' custom, in which eggs were cooked in hot, spiced red wine. Chef Lameloise suggests poaching them simply in a mixture of water, vinegar, and red wine; the red wine sauce should be prepared separately. Although the original recipe demands red wine for poaching, there is nothing and nobody to stop you from using white wine.

As with any poached dish, the eggs used should be absolutely fresh and of high quality. Do not add salt to the water, as it will react badly with the albumen contained in the egg white, and the egg will not be able to coagulate properly. As a matter of interest, the highest egg consumption in Europe goes to the Spaniards and the French, who hold the record of 270 eggs per inhabitant.

Regarding the snails, if you wish you can use living snails and prepare them at home, but that will require a great deal of patience. First, they must be cleaned in vinegar water and cooked twice, once in water and once in broth; the time involved in this has discouraged many an amateur. Fortunately, there are ready-to-serve snails for sale. Avoid any snail substitutions, however.

1. Finely chop the shallots and cook them with a quart / 1 l of red wine in a pot; reduce the liquid to three-quarters of its original amount. Add the veal broth and reduce again to half the volume. One should allow 1 tbsp / 15 ml of sauce per person, which will be whipped up with butter at the end.

2. Cut the belly bacon into strips and blanch. Cook the cocktail onions in water and then fry everything in butter. Cut the button mushrooms into fine slices and fry them in butter as well. Place the raw, well-washed spinach directly into the butter and steam. Proceed similarly with the snails and add more chopped shallots.

Eggs in Red Wine

3. Mix water, vinegar, and 7 tbsp / 100 ml of red wine in a pot and bring to a boil. In this mixture, which should only be allwed to simmer, bubbling lightly, poach the eggs for 3–4 minutes as usual, then take them out and drain them on kitchen paper.

4. To serve, place one egg on a bed of spinach on each plate. Surround with an assortment of snails, cocktail onions, mushrooms, and bacon, sprinkle the sauce on top, and decorate with chervil leaves.

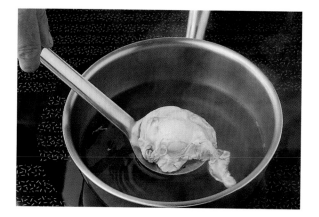

Preparation time: 40 minutes
Setting time: 2 hours
Cooking time: 1 hour, 20 minutes
Difficulty: ✼

Serves four

40 snails
1 tbsp / 15 g snail butter (see below)
scant ³/₈ lb / 170 g button mushrooms
1 small tomato
1 zucchini
juice of 1 lemon

4 cloves of garlic
2 shallots
generous ¹/₄ cup / 70 g butter
³/₄ cup / 200 ml cream
³/₄ cup / 200 ml clear broth
1 bunch of chervil
1 bunch of chives
salt, fresh-ground pepper to taste

For the ravioli dough (5¹/₄ oz / 150 g):
2 eggs
generous ³/₈ cup / 100 g semolina flour
a pinch of salt

In general, broth is used as a base for sauces. But in the recipe presented here by Chef Jacques Lemeloise, it is the main ingredient. Therefore it demands strong flavors, which are intensified during a long period of cooking. A minimum of half an hour for the vegetables and then another half hour after the wine has been added are required to produce the desired result.

Garlic haunts many a legend and has always engaged the superstitious. In the Mediterranean region it is deemed to be protection against misfortune and in the Carpathian Mountains they say it drives vampires away. Even nonbelievers concur that it has the ability to activate your circulation. If you remove the germ (or inner section, from where the garlic grows) from a clove, the garlic will be easier to digest.

The ravioli dough is prepared in the classic manner, kneaded well and then left to rest for a while at room temperature, if possible wrapped in a cloth or covered with plastic wrap. The dough is rolled out very thinly, since ravioli must not turn out too heavy, after all.

The consumption of snails can be traced back to man's early history: snail fossils have been found in prehistoric sites, and were portrayed in certain ancient frescos as well. Nowadays, the Roman snail is highly sought after, the *Helix Aspersa* from Bourgogne (also known as the Burgundy snail) being the most common type. Some varieties, such as the *petit-gris*, are now being cultivated, with much success, in the United States. To intensify the flavor of the snails, a traditional snail butter is used, which has, of course, no snails in it, but consists of that sublime, inforgettable mixture of butter, garlic, and shallots.

1. *Prepare the ravioli dough and set aside to rest for two hours. For the filling wash and chop the button mushrooms. Chop one shallot and sauté it in butter. Add the mushrooms, the juice of one lemon and 3¹/₂ tbsp / 50 ml cream and steam for three minutes. Add a little more cream, reduce for five minutes, season to taste and take off the heat.*

2. *Sauté the snails in butter, add another chopped shallot, season to taste, and set aside to cool. Roll the ravioli dough into a thin layer and cut into rectangles. Peel and halve the garlic cloves, take out the germs and steam the garlic. Dice the tomato and cut the zucchini into strips.*

Tender Garlic Sauce

3. Moisten part of the surface of the dough with a lightly watered brush, spoon on a small portion of the filling and add two snails each. Fold the dough around it, cut into shape and steam the ravioli for 4–5 minutes.

4. Finally, heat up the broth, add cream and butter, whip up with a whisk until creamy and add snail butter. Add the diced tomato and the steamed garlic and season to taste. Serve in soup plates, decorated with zucchini strips, chopped chives, and stripped chervil leaves.

Ravioli

Preparation time: 45 minutes
Setting time: 1 hour (minimum)
Cooking time: 2 hours, 5 minutes
Difficulty: ★★

Serves four

For the ravioli dough:
7 oz / 200 g semolina flour
2 eggs
scant ¼ cup / 50 ml olive oil
1 egg yolk

For the filling:
⅝ lb / 300 g pot roast (see below)

2 bunches of Swiss chard (to yield ⅞ lb / 400 g leaves)
1 clove of garlic
half an onion
1 egg
1 sprig of thyme
1 tsp / 5 g grated nutmeg
salt, pepper to taste

For the gravy:
⅝ cup / 150 ml pot roast gravy (see below)
scant ¼ cup / 50 ml olive oil
3½ oz / 100 g Parmesan

Pot roast in white wine gravy is a traditional dish of Provençal cooking (known with affection as *cousino provençalo*) and is served here as the basis for the preparation of ravioli. In Nice, such ravioli are often served as a second main course, especially over Christmas, and according to Chef Dominique Le Stanc, who brings a version here, its popularity grows each year. The pot roast, which needs to be cooked over a low heat for about two hours, is best prepared the day before. Use either beef shoulder, chuck, brisket, or rump. The following day the meat will have cooled and absorbed the flavor of the gravy. It should then be chopped as finely as possible with a sharp knife or kitchen cleaver.

As with the pot roast, the ravioli dough improves when it is prepared in advance (a minimum of one hour, a maximum of one day) and has a chance to set. The ravioli is filled, stuck together with egg yolk and cooked for only three to four minutes, which makes this dish somewhat easy to prepare, since it will require only a few minutes of your time before serving it, piping hot and covered with gravy and nestled next to shavings of Parmesan.

Presentation and first impressions play an important role in cuisine, which makes some ingredients ideal. Parmesan, with its exquisite flavor, is one such ingredient, here cut into thin shavings and arranged between the ravioli. Found on virtually every dinner table in Italy, the cheese is available in both strong and mild varieties. Whatever you choose, make sure it is fresh and imported, and never buy it already grated.

1. One day ahead of time, prepare the pot roast: rub meat with garlic and brown first over a high heat in ⅛ cup / 25 ml vegetable oil; pour off fat; add 2 cups / 500 ml stock or stock and wine mixture with an onion; slow-cook in the oven for two hours at 300 °F / 150 °C. The next day, dip the Swiss chard leaves into cold water first, then blanch, squeeze out and chop finely. Chop the cooked pot roast into fine pieces; chop the garlic clove and the onion as well.

2. Combine the meat, Swiss chard, garlic, and onion in a bowl. Add an egg, plucked thyme leaves, and grated nutmeg. Season with salt and pepper.

from Nice

3. Prepare the ravioli dough: loosely mix flour, eggs, and olive oil; set aside for an hour. Roll out the dough very thinly and cut out circles measuring 2 in / 5 cm across. Heat up the pot roast gravy and add olive oil.

4. Brush one ravioli circle each with egg yolk, spoon a little lump of the filling on top, cover with another piece of dough and press the edges together with your fingers. Cook the ravioli in salted water for two minutes. Arrange in a circle on the plates, sprinkle gravy over, and garnish with thin Parmesan shavings. Grate an additional $1/4$ cup / 50 g of Parmesan and serve separately.

Cuttlefish Risotto with

Preparation time: 30 minutes
Cooking time: 17 minutes
Difficulty: ★

Serves four

scant ¾ cup / 160 g Arborio rice
1¼ lb / 600 g dwarf cuttlefish (or small squid, or octopus)
7 oz / 200 g tomatoes
4 tsp / 20 ml olive oil
2½ cups / 600 ml clear chicken stock
1¼ cups / 300 g butter

7 oz / 200 g Parmesan
half a bunch of basil
salt, pepper to taste

There are more than fifty different ways to prepare risotto (*little rice*), which is actually a specialty of the city of Venice and its surrounding area; the dish is common throughout Northern Italy, stretching all the way to Lombardy and beyond. The rice used must, of course, be Italian, preferably coarse-grain Arborio, a starchy rice that triples in volume when it is cooked, making a tender, smooth risotto. During the entire cooking time it must be stirred gently (an Italian might say you should stir it with love), and with a wooden spoon only. If you add a little butter as you are frying it, it will be even creamier. Be careful not to let it turn brown.

Dwarf cuttlefish, which belong to the squid family, are highly popular components of Mediterraean and Asian cooking. They resemble both their relatives the octopus and the squid, but

they are only two or three inches (four or six centimeters) long. When attacked, they also hide in a cloud of ink. These small creatures are now gaining ground in European gastronomy, possibly due to the fact that they are so easy to prepare, and – given the vogue for lighter fare – are low in calories and fat.

Our chef, Dominique Le Stanc, recommends cleaning and preparing the cuttlefish the night before, since this task requires both time and concentration. Firstly they should be skinned, then the body is cut in half lengthwise and cleaned thoroughly in clear water to remove any dirt or other impurities.

Every Easter, the citizens of the town of Aigues-Mortes in the Camargue in the south of France prepare a famous specialty from such seafood.

1. Sauté the rice in heated butter in a large pot.

2. Add clear chicken stock. Simmer over a low heat and repeatedly add a little broth, which the rice must absorb.

Tomatoes and Basil

3. As soon as the rice is cooked and quite smooth, add more butter and bind with grated Parmesan cheese.

4. Prepare the cuttlefish as described above, sauté briefly in olive oil together with skinned, coarsely chopped tomatoes and basil. Serve the rice in mounds in the center of each plate, arrange the cuttlefish, tomato, and basil mixture on top, pour on the remaining juice from the pan, and sprinkle with a few drops of olive oil over all.

Crumbed Calf's Brains with

Preparation time: 1 hour, 20 minutes
Cooking time: 15 minutes
Difficulty: ★★

Serves four

4 calf's brain pieces
generous ¹/₂ lb / 250 g chanterelles
6 shiitake mushrooms
1 generous oz / 40 g fresh fava beans
1 generous oz / 40 g soybean sprouts
generous ³/₈ cup / 100 ml vinegar
1 tbsp / 30 ml soy sauce
²/₃ cup / 150 ml beef broth
²/₃ cup / 150 ml veal broth
1 head of curly lettuce

1 bunch of chervil
1 sprig of thyme
6 bay leaves
1 tsp / 5 g coriander seeds
salt, pepper to taste

For the breading:
1 egg
scant ¹/₄ cup / 50 g flour
scant ¹/₄ cup / 50 g fresh bread crumbs
2 tbsp / 30 g prepared mustard

For the vinaigrette:
⁵/₈ cup / 150 ml balsamic vinegar
generous ³/₈ cup / 100 ml grape seed oil
salt, pepper to taste

Despite numerous attempts to make brains more popular, some people are still prejudiced against this ingredient, although it is one of the most delicious types of offal. Brains are rich in vitamins, phosphorus, and proteins and should actually win over many a gourmet. If they are prepared in bread crumbs, as in this recipe, brains are a true delicacy – nice and crisp on the outside, and wonderfully tender inside.

In Europe, the soy plant has only been known for some two hundred years. We are thus lagging about five thousand years behind Asian cuisine, which has made use of this nutritious and tasty plant since the beginning of recorded time. Initially, soy was used in Europe to produce oil or margarine, and it was not until after World War I that the soy plant was fully acknowledged as a vegetable. You can use the light crunchy sprouts of this plant; wash them thoroughly and do not cook them for too long (barely more than a minute or two), otherwise they go limp and quickly lose their flavor.

Chef Michel Libotte adds a harmonious touch by serving the calf's brains in a mixture of chanterelles and shiitake, the Chinese mushrooms that grow on trees (and are rich in vitamins). Although fava beans, which as a matter of fact belong to the same plant family as the soy beans, were well known in the antique world, neither the Egyptians, nor the Greeks, nor the Romans were particularly fond of them. Only Christianity welcomed this type of pulse. In some Mediterranean countries the fava bean (or broad bean as it is also called) is the symbol of the feast of the Three Magi. It is said that Charlemagne loved these beans above all. For this recipe, according to Chef Libotte, choose very young fava beans, which are more easily digestible.

1. Steep the brains in cold salted water for an hour and a half, then remove skin, veins, and any blood stains. Poach the brains in salted vinegar water with thyme and bay leaves for 12 minutes. Scoop off the foam. Leave the brains in the stock to cool. Cut lengthwise into slices, season with salt and pepper, brush with mustard, and coat with bread crumbs.

2. Clean the chanterelles, rinse them two or three times in clear water and pat dry. Fry briefly over a high heat and remove from the pan. Add beef and veal broth to the juice remaining in the pan and cook until the liquid has boiled down. Add the whole coriander seeds, put the chanterelles back into the pan again, sauté for a few minutes and add butter.

Chanterelles and Fava beans

3. Fry the breaded brain pieces on both sides for 3–4 minutes. Prepare the vinaigrette from balsamic vinegar, grape seed oil, salt, and pepper. Add chopped chervil leaves to the chanterelles.

4. Slice the shiitake and sauté. Add the soybean sprouts, the blanched fava beans and a dash of soy sauce. Mix in the curly lettuce and season with the vinaigrette. Arrange the brain pieces on plates, place some lukewarm salad in the center, add the chanterelles, and dribble with a little sauce.

Fried Langoustines

Preparation time: 1 hour, 15 minutes
Cooking time: 15 minutes
Difficulty: ✲✲

Serves four

1 dozen langoustines
1 common crab, approximately ¹/₂–1 lb / 225–450 g
   (such as blue crab, dungeness crab, or stone
   crab)
3¹/₂ oz / 100 g shiitake mushrooms
scant ¹/₈ lb / 50 g fresh spinach
1 clove of garlic
generous ³/₈ cup / 100 g flour
generous ³/₈ cup / 100 ml vinegar
generous ³/₈ cup / 100 ml parsley oil
1 sprig of thyme

1 sprig of bay leaves
1 bunch of parsley
salt, pepper to taste

For the polenta:
generous 1 cup / 250 ml water
¹/₄ cup / 60 g cornmeal
4 tsp / 20 g grated Parmesan
1 tbsp / 15 g butter

For the sauce:
1 shallot
1 tomato
4 tsp / 20 g butter
³/₄ cup / 200 ml fish stock
³/₄ cup / 200 ml olive oil

Nobody knows for sure who really invented polenta, the much-celebrated, perennial staple of northern Italian cuisine made from cornmeal. It may have been the Venetians; it may have been the Lombards. Many generations of Italian gastronomes have argued this question without ever coming to a conclusion, but all agree that polenta has been a part of cooking there for centuries, and that originally it was cooked in large copper pots. Most chefs will tell you that, while it does not require a copper pot, it should still only be stirred with a wooden spoon.

To prepare the cornmeal correctly, you must first soak it in water and then heat it slowly until it has reached the right consistency. Then spread out the mixture and cut out any shapes you like. Corn is a very versatile cereal, used for, among other things, alcohol such as American whiskey, as well as syrup, oil, and various sauces. In this case, the polenta is embellished

with crabmeat and shiitake, or Chinese mushrooms. The latter should be medium-sized, light in color, and not too dry.

The best meat of the common crab (depending on what region you are cooking in, you may be using one of a few varieties, from stone crab to blue crab) is hidden in the claws, but, apart from the shell, any part of this crustacean is edible and delicious. It is gently stirred, along with the mushrooms, into the polenta mixture.

Our chef, Michel Libotte, insists on using langoustines from Brittany; Loctudy, situated on the southern side of the peninsula is, after all, the biggest langoustine harbor in France, if not in Europe. The meat of langoustines is very tender, and should be shelled when raw. As they toughen fast, langoustines should not be fried for too long.

1. Cook thyme and bay leaves in salted, vinegar water and poach the crab in it. Leave it to cool and then remove the shell. Heat 1 cup / 250 ml of water, stir in the cornmeal and cook over a low heat for 30 minutes. Stir in the butter and the grated Parmesan. Dice the mushrooms; fry and add, with the crabmeat, to the polenta mixture.

2. Spread the polenta about ¹/₂ in / 1¹/₄ cm thick on a flat greased surface. Sauté a chopped shallot in butter, add the fish stock and the skinned diced tomato and reduce. Then puree and pass through a sieve. Add olive oil and set aside; keep warm.

with Crabmeat Polenta

3. Sauté the garlic and spinach in butter. Shell the raw langoustines, coat in flour and fry in olive oil for five minutes. Use a pastry cutter to cut out round cakes from the polenta mixture.

4. Dust these cakes with flour and fry them in butter until golden brown. Place a tablespoon of spinach in the center of each plate, cover with a polenta cake, and top with three langoustine tails. Sprinkle a little sauce and a few drops of parsley oil around the polenta.

Preparation time: 30 minutes
Setting time: 1 hour
Cooking time: 10 minutes
Difficulty: ✲✲

Serves four

generous ¹/₂ lb / 250 g button mushrooms
generous ¹/₂ lb / 250 g shiitake mushrooms
generous 2 cups / 500 ml poultry broth

scant ¹/₄ cup / 50 ml truffle juice
¹/₃ cup / 80 g butter
2 sprigs of thyme
salt, pepper to taste

For the stef:
scant ⁷/₈ cup / 200 g durum wheat semolina flour
1 egg
1 egg yolk

The tiny nation of Luxemburg has, not surprisingly, a distinctly European flavor to its cooking, reflected here in this thoroughly European recipe from our chef, Léa Linster. Combining a pasta dough from Italy, a French manner of presentation and an assortment of mushrooms popular throughout the continent, the appetizer encompasses much that is good about European cuisine.

In keeping with the old Italian tradition, the pasta dough is made of durum wheat semolina and eggs. In the end, provided the ingredients are combined in their proper proportions, the dough should be firm enough to be rolled out very thinly: some cooks say it should be thin enough that you can see the marble pattern of the working surface through it. It is advisable to prepare the dough in advance and to keep it chilled; it should set,

after being mixed, for at least an hour before being used to prepare the rest of the dish.

The filling is meant to be a surprise; in other words, guests at your table should only discover it after their first bites, when all the flavors develop in their mouths. Cut the mushrooms for the filling as finely as possible to ensure the best impact. The quality of the sauce from truffle juice and poultry broth also plays an important role. If available, a whole truffle (*Tuber melanosporum*) can be added to the mushrooms to intensify the flavor of the sauce.

The noodles will turn nice and crisp when put in the oven. Brush them with butter to give them a golden yellow color.

1. To prepare the pasta dough, mix the durum wheat semolina with the eggs, knead well, and leave for an hour. Roll out the dough very thinly and cut into 8 in / 20 cm long strips.

2. Cut the button mushrooms and the shiitake mushrooms into sticks and sauté in oil. Season and put 2 tbsp / 30 ml aside for the sauce.

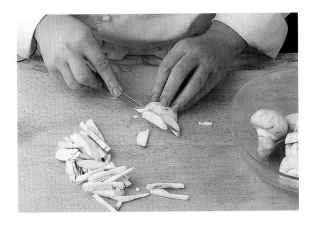

Mushroom Filling

3. To prepare the sauce, heat the poultry broth with the truffle juice, add a little butter and reduce. Whip until creamy while adding butter, add the mushrooms that were set aside, and season to taste. Spread out the dough strips on a cloth and spoon the mushroom filling on top.

4. Fold up the dough lengthwise and roll in a spiral. Grease a baking tray or a suitable platter with butter, place the noodles on top, brush with melted butter, and bake in the oven at 355 °F / 180 °C for five minutes. Cover the the plates with sauce, place a noodle spiral on top, and serve immediately.

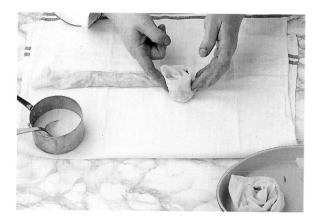

Green Bean Soup with

Preparation time: 40 minutes
Cooking time: 45 minutes
Difficulty: ✳

Serves four

generous 1 lb / 500 g fresh green beans
7 oz / 200 g belly bacon, smoked
4 smoked sausages
1 bulb celeriac
1 large leek stalk

1 onion
5¼ oz / 150 g potatoes
1 clove of garlic
generous 2 tbsp / 40 g sour cream
1 bunch of parsley
salt, pepper to taste

For the roux:
⅛ cup / 25 g butter
⅛ cup / 25 g flour
⅛ cup / 25 ml vegetable broth

With this bean soup (or *bouneschlupp*) we find ourselves right in the middle of Luxemburgian tradition. This dish, as presented here by Chef Léa Linster, is prepared all year round – in season with fresh beans, out of season with canned or frozen beans. The numerous ingredients almost make this soup a main dish; in fact, the gastronomy in the Grand Duchy generally offers very filling meals. All the tasty ingredients used for this recipe are, of course, very fresh.

Modern methods of cultivation have produced stringless beans and done away with the efforts and bother of pulling these strings out. At the same time the beans have become more tasty and tender. The other vegetables do not require any special

preparation. The celeriac (or celery root) should be firm and heavy, the leeks fresh and crisp. Charlotte potatoes are the most suitable, since they do not disintegrate while cooking; if these are not available, substitute any firm-fleshed early potato.

High-quality streaky bacon with an equal amount of fat and lean meat will not get too dry or too greasy. Use hearty boiled sausages, which should be quite fatty, as are all pork products from Luxemburg. Smoked ham is particularly popular there, and rightfully so. However, if only because of your health, you do not have to be over-generous with these ingredients: their flavors will be strong enough.

1. Wash, peel, and chop the vegetables indicated and cook them in salted water.

2. Chop a clove of garlic, add to the bacon, and cook for 30 minutes. Lastly add the potatoes and cook for another 15 minutes.

Smoked Bacon and Sausage

3. Make a roux from the butter, flour, and a little vegetable broth. Use this to bind the soup; season with salt and pepper. Cook the sausages in boiling water for 20 minutes.

4. Cut the bacon into strips and the sausages into slices. Ladle the soup into plates, add the meat, pour a teaspoon of sour cream in the middle and serve sprinkled with parsley.

Lentil Tarts with Frogs'

Preparation time: 30 minutes
Cooking time: 30 minutes
Difficulty: ★

Serves four

2.2 lb / 1 kg frogs' legs
7 oz / 200 g chanterelles
5/8 lb / 300 g spinach
4 shallots
generous 3/8 cup / 100 ml dry white wine

For the tarts:
scant 1/4 cup / 50 g lentils (see below)
5/8 cup / 150 g flour

scant 7/8 cup / 200 g rice flour
scant 7/8 cup / 200 g butter
12 large egg whites

For the decoration:
1 oz / 20 g shelled pistachios
1 oz / 20 g shelled almonds

For the parsley sauce:
3 1/2 oz / 100 g parsley
3 1/2 oz / 100 g salad burnet
1/3 cup / 80 g butter
salt, pepper to taste

As early as the Middle Ages, frogs were very sought-after, mainly consumed during the time of fasting because of their lean meat. According to an old saying, frogs turn into toads two weeks after Palm Sunday. There is, of course, no truth to that, but it does reflect the fact that frogs are preferably consumed in spring. Nowadays, frogs in France are only found in stagnant waters and along a few rivers in Alsace, Brittany, and the Auvergne, which is where our chef, Régis Marcon, obtains them from. Here, he prepares them with great style.

Chanterelles, which the French lovingly call fairy mushrooms or mountain nymphs, grow from April to September. Even when cooked for longer periods they survive undamaged, but – like frogs' legs – they should be fried only briefly.

The use of lentils dates back to antiquity, and in the past they were often scorned as poor man's food. In this recipe, lentils are processed into tarts and rounded off with the cucumber-like flavor of wild burnet, a native European herb. The lentil tarts are baked on a baking tray greased with butter and are afterwards left there to cool. The green lentils from Puy-du-Dôme in a volcanic region of central France are considered the best lentils in the world, and should be given preference in this recipe. However, if those are unavailable, substitute any high-quality, small lentils.

If you disapprove of the consumption of frogs' legs, you can use maritime ingredients for this recipe instead, substituting the frogs' legs with langoustines or crayfish.

1. Dust 12 frogs' legs with flour and set aside. Steam the rest with chopped shallots in white wine for eight minutes. Bone the frogs' legs and set the meat aside. Wash the spinach leaves thoroughly in clear water. Crush the shelled pistachios and almonds.

2. Mix the rice flour with the cooked and pureed lentils and the flour. Season with salt. Stir in the egg whites with a spatula, add 13 tbsp / 200 g of melted butter, knead gently, and set aside. Remove the stalks of the parsley and the burnet, puree them together and add 7 tbsp / 100 ml of boiling water.

Legs and Mushrooms

3. Heat the parsley and burnet puree. Just before serving, whip it with butter until creamy. Grease a baking tray with butter, spread on the lentil mixture in the shape of round tarts and sprinkle these with crushed pistachios and almonds.

4. Bake the tarts in a pre-heated oven at 355 °F / 180 °C for five minutes. Dust the frogs' legs with flour and fry in butter for three to four minutes. Proceed similarly with the mushrooms and add them to the frogs' legs. Sauté the spinach leaves in butter, and arrange all the ingredients on plates, garnished with chervil leaves.

Preparation time: 30 minutes
Marinating time: 12 hours
Cooking time: 1 hour, 15 minutes
Difficulty: ✲✲

Serves twelve

1¼ lb / 600 g Beaufort cheese (see below)
6 artichokes
40 thin slices pancetta (or 10 thin slices prociutto or other ham)
1 tbsp / 15 g flour
juice of 1 lemon

12 whole eggs
6 egg yolks
generous 1 cup / 250 ml whole milk
generous ³/₈ cup / 100 ml white wine
generous 1 cup / 250 ml cream
generous ³/₈ cup / 100 ml vinegar
1 head lamb's lettuce

For the mustard sauce:
generous 2 tbsp / 40 g prepared mustard
1¼ cups / 300 ml veal broth

The renown gastronome and writer Maurice-Edmond Sailland (1872–1956), who took the name Curnonsky as his pen name, described Beaufort as the prince among the cheeses, and the king among the Gruyère cheeses. Guy Martin, our chef, gets great pleasure out of using this cheese: particularly when it comes from Savoy. With its nutty flavor, this variety was rightfully awarded the title "alpine cheese," because it is made from the milk of the beautifully dappled cows that graze in the high mountain regions of the Alps. A round of Beaufort cheese, which can weigh up to one hundred and thirty pounds (sixty kilos), matures for six months, during which time its consistency turns dense and firm. It does not have any holes, only a few random cracks, or "threads." As an alternative to Beaufort, Guy Martin suggests Emmental cheese, which has a similar consistency, though not quite as remarkable a taste.

Chef Martin recommends preparing this terrine with pancetta, a fat-streaked bacon that has been smoked the same way for decades, according to tradition. If pancetta is unavailable, other types of European ham are also suitable, such as prosciutto from San Daniele or Parma. This area in northern Italy has special connections with Savoy in France, established in the days when spice merchants from the Orient traveled through these high mountainous regions. Savoy has thus always been a connecting link between France and Italy. High-quality Spanish hams like serrano, iberico or pata negra will also go very well with this dish.

The different flavors of this dish are well balanced and will harmonize well with a side accompaniment of poached fresh eggs, doused in mustard sauce and sprinked with parsley.

1. Cut the Beaufort cheese into ¹/₂ in / 1 cm thick cubes, add white wine and leave to marinate overnight. Clean the artichokes and strip down to the hearts, which should be cooked in a mixture of water, flour, lemon juice, and salt. Line the terrine mold with the thin slices of Pancetta.

2. Crack six egg yolks into a bowl, add cream and milk, blend with a whisk and add the drained, marinated cheese. Poach the 12 eggs in boiling water (four eggs at a time) with 7 tbsp / 100 ml of vinegar – approximately 2¹/₂ tbsp / 40 ml of vinegar per batch of four eggs.

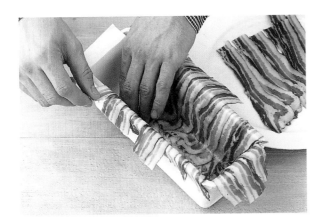

Ham and Artichokes

3. Cover the base of the terrine mold with a third of the Beaufort and a little cheese and cream mixture. In the meantime, cook 2¹/₂ tbsp / 40 g of mustard with 1¹/₄ cups / 300 ml of veal broth for the mustard sauce. Trim the artichoke hearts into squares.

4. Fill the mold with a layer each of artichoke hearts and then cheese mixture. Cover with aluminum foil. Bake in the oven at 300 °F / 155 °C for one hour and 15 minutes; leave to cool for about 15–20 minutes. To serve, place on each plate one slice of lukewarm terrine, with a poached egg resting on a bed of lamb's lettuce next to it. Sprinkle mustard sauce over the egg and around the terrine.

Master Chiquart's Filled

Preparation time: 30 minutes
Cooking time: 3 hours, 20 minutes
Difficulty: ☆

Serves four

scant $^7/_8$ lb / 400 g boneless pork shoulder
$2^2/_3$ oz / 80 g goose liver (foie gras)
generous 1 oz / 40 g figs
generous 1 oz / 40 g dried prunes
generous 1 oz / 40 g dates
2 tsp / 10 g pine nuts

$^1/_8$ lb / 60 g Raclette cheese
1 egg
1 tsp / 5 g grated white ginger root
quarter bunch of parsley (to yield 4 tsp / 20 g chopped)
1 tbsp / 5 g mixed spices: curcuma, coriander, cardamom, cloves, and cinnamon
a pinch of saffron threads
4 tsp / 20 g sugar
1 tbsp / 30 g coarse salt
generous 1 lb / 500 g puff pastry (see basic recipes)
4 gold leaves (if desired)

"Cooking is more than just composing recipes," a wise man once said, and in this case, it is in fact a historic voyage of discovery into the world of medieval dishes.

Master Chiquart was one of the most famous chefs in the Middle Ages. Hailing from Savoy, his good reputation spread to all the royal courts in Europe. While in the services of Count Amadeus VI of Savoy, he invented dishes using the new and strange spices brought by the rich merchants from Venice via the Alps to his homeland. This recipe, presented by Guy Martin, pays homage to the old master, incorporating exotic spices into a wonderful French creation.

Pork shoulder, which serves as a basis for the filling, deserves more respect than it is generally shown. Even when chopped up as in this appetizer, its taste mingles harmoniously with the flavors of the fruit, the spices, and the Raclette cheese.

Contrary to what some might believe, spices played an important part in the medieval kitchen. In this recipe they must be used sparingly, so as to not destroy the harmony of the meat and cheese flavors. If instead of Raclette you use a strong cheese like Italian Pecorino with pepper or Gouda, the blend of spices may become a bit stronger as well. The preparation of the puff pastry, as well as the filling of the pastry pockets, is best prepared the day before, which shortens the cooking time before serving considerably.

As Chef Martin notes, the medieval custom of ornamenting dishes with gold leaves has almost fallen into oblivion, and is the province of only a few confectioners, who still decorate their chocolate specialties using the material.

1. Peel and finely dice the figs, the dates, the prunes, and the cheese. Cut the pork into pieces, add the spice mixture, and mix well. Sprinkle with coarse salt and braise in the oven at 320 °F / 160 °C for two to three hours.

2. Puree the foie gras. Chop the braised pork finely, then gently fold in the pureed goose liver and all the other ingredients. Fry the pine nuts in the pan or grill in the oven until golden brown, taking care not to burn them. Finely chop the parsley.

Puff Pastry Pockets

3. Roll out the already prepared puff pastry dough into a thin layer, cut out circles of about 6 in / 15 cm in diameter and place a small mound of filling in the center of each.

4. Fold up the edges of the dough to make the shape of triangles, pockets, or a similar shape. Brush the surface with egg yolk. Bake the pockets in the oven at 390–430 °F / 200–220 °C for approximately 20 minutes. To serve, decorate with a gold leaf, if desired.

Portugese Fish

Preparation time: 15 minutes
Cooking time: 30 minutes
Difficulty: ★★

Serves four

1³/₄ lb / 800 g hardshell clams, such as littleneck,
  cherrystone, or butter clams
1 large onion
2 cloves of garlic
juice of 1 lemon
3 slices of white bread
1 tbsp / 15 g butter
generous ³/₈ cup / 100 ml olive oil

scant ¹/₄ cup / 50 ml white wine
2 tbsp / 30 g corn meal
2 egg yolks
1 bunch of fresh cilantro

For the fish stock:
 heads and bones from tuna, bluefish, grouper, or
  similar sea fish
1 leek stalk
1 celery stalk
1 bunch of parsley
4 black peppercorns
salt to taste

The clam belongs to the family of the bivalves, which has more than five hundred species. One of its nicknames is the Venus shell, a name that it owes to the Roman goddess of love who, as legend has it, emerged from the sea in such a shell. Bulhão Pato, Portugal's most famous gastronome in the 19th century, introduced this mollusc to his people, and since then, its flavor and its tender flesh have enjoyed great popularity. Witness, for example, this appetizer from Chef Maria Ligia Medeiros.

Clams can be eaten alive or cooked, cold or warm, without ever losing their flavor. In this recipe they are presented in a tasty soup with fresh herbs. Parsley, celery, and especially cilantro (fresh coriander) are widely used in Portugal. It is the taste of cilantro that dominates all the other flavors and lends this dish its typical character, which should not be over-shadowed by the other ingredients.

If necessary, this fish soup can be prepared in advance. You can then simply bind it with an egg yolk before serving, but do not bring it to a boil a second time. In this case the cilantro should also be added at the last moment, otherwise it will lose too much of its flavor. The bread croutons should be served separately, so that guests can help themselves. The croutons provide a delightful contrast to the creamy smooth soup.

1. Wash the clams carefully, rinse them at least two or three times, cook them in white wine until they open, and take out. Add fish heads and bones, leeks, celery, parsley, peppercorns, and salt to the broth. Bring to a boil again, then pass through a sieve.

2. In a fairly large saucepan, sauté the onion and the chopped garlic in olive oil over a low heat for ten minutes, then add the fish stock.

Soup with Clams

3. Make a roux of cornmeal and cold water, stir into the soup, and bring to a boil again.

4. Blend egg yolk, lemon juice, and the chopped cilantro in a bowl. Take the soup off the stove; add the cilantro mixture to bind the soup. To make the croutons, dice the bread slices and fry in butter until golden brown. Place a bit of clam flesh on the center of each plate and serve the soup immediately, with the croutons in a separate bowl.

Fricassee of Snails and

Preparation time: 1 hour
Cooking time: 2 hours,
    30 minutes
Difficulty: ✷✷✷

Serves four

40 snails
half a small calf's head
1 veal trotter
2 tomatoes, 1 carrot, 1 leek, 1 onion
quarter of a celeriac bulb
1 shallot
2 cloves of garlic
$^1/_2$ cup / 125 g fresh bread crumbs
scant $^1/_4$ cup / 50 ml olive oil
generous 2 tbsp / 30 g Parmesan, grated

1 bay leaf
4 sprigs each of thyme, rosemary, sage leaves
1 bunch of borage flowers
leaves from 1 head of celery

1 clove
half a bunch of parsley
4 sprigs each of chives, fresh marjoram
  salt, 10 black peppercorns

For the vegetables:
1 large bunch of spinach (to yield scant $^7/_8$ lb / 400 g)
2 potatoes (such as Bintje or Yukon gold)
1 shallot
scant $^1/_4$ cup / 50 g butter
$^1/_2$ cup / 125 ml olive oil

For the sauce:
scant $^7/_8$ cup / 200 ml stock made from the calf's
  head
1 cup / 250 ml Banyuls red wine
1 tbsp / 15 g butter

True gastronomes are not interested in borders. This dish, from Chef Dieter Müller, provides a good example. The calf's head is a traditional ingredient from Germany (predominantly from Baden-Württemberg), the potato cake, known as a *rösti*, is from Switzerland, the snail fricassee is done in the Burgundy (or Bourgogne) style, the Banyuls is made from the black Grenache grapes of Catalonia and, last but not least, the olive oil hails from Italy. What else does one need to build a united Europe?

Our chef suggests using Roman snails that are very similar to the ones found in Burgundy – known, naturally, as Burgundy snails, or vineyard snails, and fed a diet of grape leaves. Since the flavor of Roman snails is not very strong, Chef Müller adds

the tender meat of a calf's head, though good sweetbread would also be ideal. This tender ragout provides an interesting contrast to the crisp *rösti* cakes made from raw potatoes. Our chef recommends Bintje potatoes, as they are not floury and do not disintegrate when they are fried; otherwise, try Yukon gold potatoes.

The garnish for this complex appetizer is not exactly easy, considering that it includes fried veal trotter, borage flowers, and fresh marjoram. The herbs intensify the flavor of the fricassee and the wine from Banyuls adds a finishing touch. A product of the medieval art of winemaking, this wine only develops its aroma with time. In the past it was only available in the Banyuls region; today it is a must in every good European wine cellar.

1. Clean the calf's head and the veal trotter and cook together with the carrot, leek, and celeriac. Take the calf's head out after an hour and leave the trotter to cook for another hour. Cut the meat of the calf's head into small cubes and refrigerate. Bone the veal trotter and cut into 2 in / 5–6 cm strips.

2. Arrange the veal trotter strips on baking paper in the shape of a grid and refrigerate. Later, fry this grid in olive oil. (This task requires a lot of patience.) To prepare the sauce, mix the wine and the veal broth and thicken until it has a syrupy consistency. Take off the heat and stir in butter. Then pass through a sieve and season.

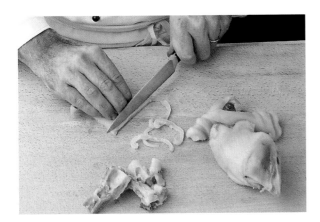

Calf's Head in Banyuls

3. Heat oil and a little butter in a non-stick frying pan rubbed with garlic. Add the snails, the diced meat from the calf's head, and the chopped shallot, and fry for 3–4 minutes. Then add the sauce, the diced tomatoes, herbs, and bread crumbs; season to taste. Cook the spinach and toss it in butter with chopped shallot.

4. Prepare the rösti from thinly cut raw potato strips and fry in a pan with olive oil. Serve the rösti on plates, spoon some spinach over, and lastly dish up the ragout. Sprinkle with grated Parmesan and briefly bake au gratin. Decorate with the borage flowers and the grid made from the veal trotter. Place a snail, in its shell, on the side.

Fisherman's Style

Preparation time: 40 minutes
Cooking time: 30 minutes
Difficulty: ★★

Serves four

8 big langoustines
1 lobster, 1 lb / 500 g
5/8 lb / 300 g baby octopus or small squid (with ink)
5/8 lb / 300 g clams and cockles
3 1/2 oz / 100 g rice
1 green pepper
2 onions
3 cloves of garlic

1 bunch of parsley
1 quart / 1 l olive oil
salt, pepper to taste

For the fish stock (to yield 2 1/2 cups / 600 ml):
1 sea robin
1 bunch of fresh savory
a pinch of saffron threads

For the lobster broth:
2 carrots
2 onions (stuck with cloves)
2 stalks of celery
1 bay leaf

This Catalan specialty was originally – and, to some extent, remains – a fisherman's dish. As rice was the only provision taken on board, all the other ingredients were caught fresh there and then. Even if this simple dish as presented by our chef, Jean-Louis Neichel, has been converted into a gastronomic delicacy, one should not forget the rough life these fishermen had to live (and still do). Victor Hugo once said: "Poor people, they have to leave at night heading into the darkness, into uncertainty. Hard work, everything is cold, everything is black, no glimmer of light."

Among a crew of eight on a small fishing cutter the task of preparing the soup always falls on one, who, for safety reasons does not bake or fry the fish, but rather crushes it and cooks it with the rice (or with thin noodles). Spanish tradition demands round-grain rice cooked in stock that is repeatedly added to. As a result, the rice is unlikely to stick together.

Octopus or squid ink is used to dye the stew a most unusual black color; either will also harmonizes with the various other flavors from the sea. If you prefer to avoid the messy task of handling the ink sacs, you can get the ink in a can instead.

Chef Neichel recommends preparing the fish stock with a small sea robin (known in Europe as a gurnard), a saltwater fish that, incidentally, makes a croaking noise as it swims near the surface. Unwashed and unscaled, this fish is cooked in water with saffron and fresh savory. After cooking, all ingredients are crushed and passed through a fine sieve.

1. Prepare the fish stock ahead of time. To begin preparing the dish, chop the onions and green pepper. Wash and rinse the octopus or squid well and reserve the ink. Fry the vegetables and the octopus or squid in a covered pan with olive oil, for 15 minutes. Cook the lobster in vegetable broth with onions, carrots, celery, and a bay leaf.

2. Sauté the garlic and chopped parsley in olive oil. Add watered-down ink and rice and mix well. Gradually stir in the fish stock.

Seafood Pot

3. Wash the clams and cockles, add to the pot with the octopus or squid, and season. Cook for 15 minutes. Midway through the cooking time season to taste, if necessary.

4. Crush some of the fried garlic with parsley and a few drops of olive oil. Add to the clams and cockles, cover and set aside. Fry the langoustine tails, shell the lobster, and cut into slices. Serve the seafood and rice mixture on soup plates, decorated with lobster slices and langoustine tails.

Glass Eel Salad

Preparation time: 30 minutes
Cooking time: 15 minutes
Difficulty: ☆

Serves four

5 oz / 150 g glass eel
generous ¹/₂ lb / 250 g small periwinkles (sea snails)
¹/₄ lb / 120 g purple potatoes
1 bunch green asparagus (to yield 8 spears)
1 red pepper
1 shallot
1 garlic clove

1 chili pepper
¹/₂ lb / 200 g seasonal assorted green lettuces
half a bunch of parsley
half a bunch of chives

For the vinaigrette:
generous ³/₈ cup / 100 ml extra virgin olive oil (from Catalonia, if possible)
scant ¹/₄ cup / 50 ml red wine vinegar
1 tbsp / 15 g prepared mustard
juice of 1 lemon
salt, pepper to taste

Because they are almost transparent, baby eels of two to three inches (five to seven centimeters) in length are also referred to as "glass eels." In France they are called *pibales* or *civelles* at this stage of growth, *angula* or *anghula* in Spain and Portugal and *cieche* in Italy. Unluckily for them, eels have hardly any eyesight at this stage and therefore get caught very easily: all it takes to lure them is a bright light at night. They are caught this way all along the Atlantic coast from Bordeaux to Bilbao, especially in winter, their price fluctuating considerably depending on the season.

Few glass eels escape the close-meshed nets now used by the fishing industry and manage to migrate upriver to grow and develop undisturbed. Most of them land, in Europe, on the Basque or Catalan plates on either side of the border. Their chances of survival would be much higher if only nets of the permitted mesh size were used.

Glass eels are normally steamed, but many gourmets fry them in olive oil. Chef Jean-Louis Neichel prefers the combination of glass eel with perwinkles, or sea snails, served with a tossed salad. Periwinkles, though difficult, at times, to find in North America, are not difficult to prepare. Our chef recommends cooking them in seawater to bring out their maritime flavor to the fullest. The purple potatoes, with their nutty, truffle-hinting taste, provide an interesting and colorful contrast to the tossed salad, and round off the flavor of the dish.

1. Prepare the vinaigrette from the ingredients indicated. Clean and wash the green lettuces. Wash the perwinkles in cold water, put them in boiling salted water, and cook them for 3–4 minutes. Remove the shells and toss the snails into the vinaigrette.

2. Fry the chopped garlic and a small chili pepper in a pan with olive oil over a high heat. Add the glass eel and fry briefly. Boil the purple potatoes for ten minutes.

with Purple Potatoes

3. Mix the glass eel, sliced red pepper, shallot, and parsley in a bowl with the vinaigrette and the periwinkles and season. Peel the green asparagus and cook in vigorously boiling water for three minutes.

4. Serve the salad on plates, add the sliced potatoes and the asparagus tips, and decorate with chives and parsley.

Blini with Crab and

Preparation time: 1 hour, 15 minutes
Cooking time: 20 minutes
Difficulty: ★★

Serves four

For the blini:
1 common crab approximately 4½ lbs / 2 kg (such as blue crab or stone crab) to yield generous ½ lb / 250 g of meat
1 Northern lobster, 2–3 lb / 1.5 kg, to 5¼ oz / 150 g of meat

2 eggs
2 tbsp / 30 g flour
1 tsp / 5 ml Worcestershire sauce
a few drops of Tabasco

For the mustard sauce:
½ tbsp / 10 g coarse Meaux mustard
1⅔ cups / 400 ml whipping cream
1 bunch of chervil
salt, pepper to taste

Blini, the small fat pancakes served with cream or melted butter that are an obligatory component of Russian appetizers, are baked lightly, and served hot, moist, and soft.

Although the common crab boasts impressive claws and a hard shell to cover its tender flesh, this aggressive-looking creature is not necessarily looking for trouble and will generally withdraw rather than risk direct confrontation. Choose a nice live specimen, weighing about four and a half pounds (two kilos). If you are an inexperienced cook, you might get an enormous fright when the crab suddenly jumps. In Europe, most of these sought-after crustaceans come from Great Britain; in the United States, they come from both coasts.

The lobster, usually from Brittany if our chef, Pierre Orsi, has his say, should weigh well over two pounds (one kilo). Northern

lobsters will also work well. Just make sure that these two crustaceans don't kill each other in your kitchen. Before cooking, the rubber band around the lobster's pincers must be removed so as not to corrupt the flavor of the lobster broth.

Dissolve the coarse mustard (*moutarde de Meaux* or *à l'ancienne*) well in the heated cream, where its grainy consistency will work wonders. It is called *moutarde de Meaux* to distinguish it from Dijon mustard. Both terms refer to the production method rather than the origin of the mustard. The mustard grains in the *moutarde de Meaux* are only coarsely crushed, and the shells remain part of the final mixture.

1. Cook the crab and the lobster in salted water. Remove the claws of the crab and set aside. Mix the flour and eggs in a bowl and whip with a whisk. Add the crab and lobster meat. Stir in Worcestershire sauce and Tabasco and refrigerate.

2. Place small molds greased with butter in a non-stick pan. Fill with blini mixture. Fry lightly for a few minutes. Then bake in the oven at 390 °F / 200 °C for ten minutes until the top is golden brown.

Lobster in Mustard Sauce

3. Mix the creamy part of the crab and the lobster (the coral) with 1²/₃ cups / 400 ml cream and cook for ten minutes. Pass through a conical strainer. Reduce to a creamy sauce. Remove from the heat and stir in ¹/₂ tbsp / 10 g of coarse mustard.

4. Remove the molds by sliding a knife along the rim. Using a suitable spatula, place the blin in the center of the pre-warmed plates. Pour the sauce around them. Sprinkle with chervil leaves and decorate with the crab claws.

Preparation time: 1 hour
Cooking time: 30 minutes
Difficulty: ✴ ✴

Serves four

For the filling:
⁵/₈ lb / 300g fresh duck liver (foie gras)
2²/₃ oz / 80 g truffles
³/₄ cup / 200 ml truffle juice
1 quart / 1 l poultry broth
1 egg yolk

scant ¹/₄ cup / 50 g melted butter
salt, pepper to taste

For the sauce:
generous 2 cups / 500 ml port
generous 1 cup / 250 ml veal stock

For the ravioli dough:
generous 1 cup / 250 g flour
1 egg
1–2 tbsp / 30 ml water
a pinch of salt

This dish, while not very complicated, consists of exquisite ingredients that deserve to be treated with great care and respect. This definitely applies to the foie gras, which should have an attractive, even pink coloring and firm consistency. Foie gras has been considered a delicacy since ancient times, as have the black truffles from the Périgord region that are carefully selected according to their freshness and weight.

Truffles should not be washed but brushed gently to remove any dirt from their surface. If fresh truffles are unavailable because they are not in season, there are various types of good canned truffles to use in the preparation of this warm appetizer.

Our chef, Pierre Orsi, concurs that the best time to prepare the ravioli dough is the night before; keep it covered in a cool place until you are ready to roll it out. Prepare it in a blender or food processor for an even consistency, which will allow you to process it easily and to roll it out thinly until it is almost transparent.

The port sauce should be light, but nevertheless elegant in flavor. You should therefore use a quality port, even a good vintage one, which can be cooked down until reduced to syrup. To round off this appetizer, the port used for the gravy may also be served as a drink to accompany the ravioli.

1. Roll out the ravioli dough into a thin layer. Cut a 7 oz / 200 g of the duck liver into eight small medallions and season. Place on a layer of dough and moisten the edge of the dough with the egg yolk. Cover with a second layer of dough and cut out with a cookie cutter (our chef prefers a round shape). Brush with melted butter.

2. In a saucepan reduce the port to syrup. Add 1 cup / 250 ml of veal stock and cook for ten minutes. Pass through a conical strainer and stir in the truffle juice.

Port and Truffle Sauce

3. Dice the remaining portion of foie gras – it should be about 3 oz / 90 g – and stir into the sauce to bind it. Leave to steep for five minutes and season to taste. Pour into a double boiler. Slice the truffles finely.

4. Bring the poultry broth to a boil. Add the ravioli and simmer for a few minutes. Take out two at a time with a skimmer and drain well. Serve on pre-warmed plates, sprinkle with truffle slices and dous with the very hot sauce.

Strips of Skate with

Preparation time: 50 minutes
Resting time: 2 days
Cooking time: 9 minutes
Difficulty: ★★

Serves four

1 large skate (such as thornback)
one dozen chicken livers
⅝ lb / 300 g mixed lettuces (for example radicchio,
  lamb's lettuce, and green lettuce)

⅓ cup / 80 g butter
¾ cup / 200 ml olive oil
⅓ cup / 80 ml balsamic vinegar
1 bunch of chervil
1 bunch of parsley (for the tips only)
1 bunch of thyme
4 bay leaves
1 tsp / 5 g peppercorns
1 tsp / 5 g coarse salt
salt, ground pepper to taste

Although skate (also known as ray) is available on the market throughout the year, in Europe it is traditionally eaten in winter. There are several species of this flat, scaleless fish. The stingray or *raie bouclée* is also known as the curly ray or thornback, and is considered the leanest and tastiest member of the family. An inhabitant of the waters off the Mediterranean coast, it is easily recognized by its "curls" – big curved spikes growing on its back and its belly. Due to its large muscle fibers it is easy to process and its fine tender flesh makes it a superb delicacy, with a flavor not unlike the scallop.

Skates are covered by a viscous substance (check for it in the market: if the skate is clear of it, it's not fresh), and must therefore be left to rest for two days before consumption. It should then be washed several times in fresh water to remove its slight ammonia smell. It is advisable to buy a large skate: allow about

one and a quarter pounds (six hundred grams) for four guests. Place the skate in a large pot of cold water and heat to a boil, then immediately remove from the stove. The ray should cool down in its own stock. Its flesh is fairly firm and can be quite easily cut with a sharp knife into narrow strips.

The preparation of the chicken livers – our chef prefers them to any other poultry livers for this recipe – requires some effort. As a precautionary measure, remove the nerves and any traces of the gall bladder that might leave a bitter taste with the liver or render it tough in places. Before the livers are diced, they should first be fried in very hot butter. Make sure that their insides remain nice and soft. This dish is served lukewarm and sprinkled with a tasty vinaigrette, accompanied by a small, fresh lettuce salad.

1. Prepare the skate ahead of time. The day of preparation, trim the parsley bunch to its tips. Place the skate into a pot and cover with cold water. Add coarse salt, peppercorns, parsley tips, thyme, and bay leaves. Bring to a boil, remove from the stove and leave to cool in the stock.

2. Clean the chicken livers carefully and cut into cubes. Drain the skate and remove the skin.

Salad of Chicken Livers

3. Cut the skate into strips. Arrange in a circle on pre-warmed plates, placing a bouquet of colorful lettuce leaves in the center.

4. Season and fry the chicken liver pieces and scatter over the skate strips. Sprinkle a warm vinaigrette of olive oil and balsamic vinegar over the arrangement, and decorate with chervil tips.

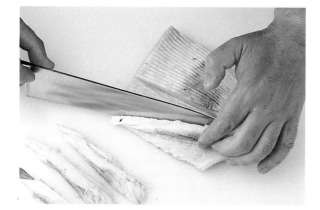

Preparation time: 35 minutes
Cooking time: 25 minutes
Difficulty: ★★★

Serves four

20 large sea scallops
1 ginger root, approximately $^1/_4$ lb / 50 g
$^5/_8$ cup / 150 g butter
salt, pepper to taste

For the stock:
scant $^7/_8$ lb / 400 g sole bones
$^3/_4$ cup / 200 ml white wine
$1^1/_2$ quarts / $1^1/_2$ l water
5 shallots
3 carrots
$^1/_4$ cup / 60 g butter
1 bunch of parsley

Sea scallops, molluscs living on the seabed, indicate their age by the number of stripes on the inside of their shell. Appearing quite placid and still, they only move when danger approaches: a starfish, for instance, can suddenly set them in motion. Scallops are most popular in the United States, Japan, and France, where the sea scallop season begins in January. In Brittany, one of the main activities in the Bay of Saint Brieuc is trawling for scallops along the sandy seabed; the scallops netted this way are the pride of the Côtes d'Armor. In contravention of health regulations, scallops are often offered with their shells open, a natural result of being removed from their natural, seawater habitat. If you touch them you can easily find out whether they are still alive – if they move it is an unmistakable indication of their freshness.

The stock for this dish must be well-spiced, but, while it is being reduced, must also be closely watched. One moment of inattentiveness and the stock could reduce too much, resulting in a far too spicy glaze that would ruin the mild flavor of the scallops. Moreover, if you use a glaze with a butter base you must be careful to spread it evenly over the mussels to obtain a uniform appearance.

The thin ginger strips will offer a spicy-flavored contrast to the sweet scallops. The strips should be cut from fresh, medium-sized ginger roots, which must be nice and smooth, and not too fibrous. Ginger originally comes from India and has been known in Europe since the Middle Ages. A vibrant ginger trade thrived until the 18th century.

1. Peel the ginger, cut it into very thin strips, and cover with water. Start with the preparation of the stock. Sauté the fish bones in butter and add the vegetables and herbs. Pour the white wine over, add 6 cups / $1^1/_2$ l of water and cook for 20 minutes.

2. Clean the scallops thoroughly in clear water and drain on a cloth, discarding the orange roe (if there is any). Cut the scallop flesh into medallions.

Scallops

3. Arrange the medallions immediately in a circle on ovenproof plates. Sprinkle lightly with salt and pepper and sprinkle on a layer of ginger strips.

4. Pass the fish stock through a sieve and reduce to a semi-firm glaze. Stir in butter, and spoon the stock evenly over the scallops. Slide the plates briefly under the grill until the glaze has browned a little, and serve immediately.

Oysters on a Bed of Leeks

Preparation time: 30 minutes
Cooking time: 10 minutes
Difficulty: ☆

Serves four

4 dozen oysters (preferably Belon)
3 leeks
juice of 1 lemon
³/₄ cup / 200g butter
1 tbsp / 15 g poppy seeds
salt, fresh-ground pepper to taste

Today we eat only the seeds of the poppy, whereas in the past the leaves of this plant were consumed like spinach. In certain regions of Asia, people use poppy seed oil or *huile d'oeilette*. The pharmaceutical application of the poppy is as well known as the fact that it is refined into opium. Poppy seeds are mainly used in bakeries but also to spice hearty dishes, like this appetizer for example, where warm oysters constitute the main ingredient. Poppy seeds become more aromatic if they are roasted in the oven for a few minutes.

For this recipe you should choose the oysters from Brittany known as Belon; they are now cultivated in the United States as well. Also known as *huitres creuses*, their shells may have a deep green color, and their succulent, firm flesh develops a distinct flavor from growing in deep water. (To test the freshness of an oyster, touch its edge with the tip of a knife. If the oyster is alive, it will immediately withdraw.)

It took a while to convince the fans of raw oysters that these delicacies may also be enjoyed when warm. However, if oysters are not cooked long enough, they lack texture, and if they are cooked for too long, they turn tough and rubbery. The same or a similar rule applies to leeks, which should neither be served half-done nor be overcooked. The success obviously depends on the right timing.

Our chef, Paul Pauvert, would be quite happy to substitute the oysters with sole fillets, which also harmonize very well with the poppy seeds.

1. Open the oysters, remove their shells, and strain and reserve their juice. Poach them for a few minutes in their own juice and drain. Roast the poppy seeds lightly in the oven.

2. Slice the leeks diagonally across the stalk, into diamonds. Sauté in 3¹/₂ tbsp / 50 g of butter. Add 1 tbsp / 15 ml of oyster stock and slowly reduce the heat. Season with pepper and simmer over a low heat for five minutes.

with Poppy Seed Butter

3. Set the leeks aside. Make a butter sauce from the remaining portion of butter, the reduced oyster stock, and the juice of a lemon.

4. Finally, add the poppy seeds and a pinch of fresh-ground pepper. Serve the leeks on plates and arrange the oysters in rosettes on top. Cover with butter sauce and serve hot.

Snail Muscadette with

Preparation time:	1 hour, 30 minutes
Rinsing time:	2 hours
Cooking time:	1 hour
Difficulty:	✶✶

Serves four

4 dozen snails
4 button mushrooms
5/8 lb / 300g green beans
5/8 lb / 300g young peas
1 fennel root

2 carrots
3 celery stalks
1 onion
3 shallots
3 egg yolks
scant 1/4 cup / 50 ml brandy
1²/₃ cups / 400ml Muscadet (dry white wine)
generous 2 cups / 500 ml cream
generous 3/8 cup / 100g butter
juice of half a lemon
1 bunch of chives
salt, pepper to taste

The origins of wine are lost in the darkness of the distant past, always the subject of much speculation. One persistent hypotheses purports that the Egyptians spread the cultivation of wine all around the Mediterranean. As early as the Middle Ages, wine production was already becomng an art: the medieval monasteries, almost all of which owned several acres of vineyards and produced their own wine, contributed greatly to refining wine production.

Our chef, Paul Pauvert, takes us to the fertile region of the Muscadet to find a dry white wine from the environs of Nantes. The controlled designation of origin "muscadet" (*appelation d'origine controlée*) is shared by three cultivation areas: the muscadet from Sèvre-et-Maine, the Muscadet, and the muscadet from the Loire valley. Each designation refers to a particular cultivation area, and only regulates the wine produced in that area. This wine, which is generally enjoyed very young, goes well with seafood and is an excellent accompaniment to the button mushrooms and snails in our recipe.

The small gray snail (*petit gris*), less fleshy than its relative from Burgundy, is also called *cagouifle* in the Charente. These molluscs with their fruity flavor (they feast on grape leaves) are mostly collected in winter. Their preparation requires a lot of time and patience. But, as our chef likes to ask, would a self-respecting cook really make do with canned snails, prepared by a merchant, shelled or even deep-frozen, when he or she can experience every detail and nuance involved in preparing an ingredient from scratch? The button mushrooms sharing the plate with the snails are far less complicated: they can be prepared in advance and kept in lemon water, which will retain their white color.

Cook the vegetables, carrots, celery, and fennel, until *al dente*. Cut them into small cubes to intensify their flavor, and serve the dish in a small copper pan for an attractive, appropriate presentation.

1. Peel the button mushrooms and remove their stalks. Carve in a pattern of spiral grooves. Mix 2 cups / 500 ml of water, the juice of half a lemon, a knob of butter, and a pinch of salt and bring to a boil. Add the button mushrooms. Cook over a high heat in rapidly boiling water for two minutes. Cook the vegetables and reserve the stock.

2. Put the snails in water for two hours to rinse out. Then wash them twice, using lots of water. Blanch them in plenty of water for 5–6 minutes, drain and leave to cool. Remove their shells. Sauté the chopped onion and the shallots in butter. Add the snails and flambé in brandy.

Choice Vegetables

3. *Cover and simmer. Add muscadet and bring to a boil again, uncovered. Add the mushroom water and the vegetable stock. Let the snails settle.*

4. *Cook the snail stock for a few minutes, then bind with three egg yolks and add the cream. Carefully stir some chopped chives into the sauce with the vegetables and the snails and season. Serve on plates with each topped by a spiral-patterned button mushroom.*

Artichokes Filled with

Preparation time: 1 hour
Cooking time: 30 minutes
Difficulty: ★

Serves four

4 artichokes
3½ oz / 100 g chévre
4 tomatoes
juice of 1 lemon
generous 1 lb / 500 g baking potatoes (such as Idaho)
2 anchovy fillets (preserved in brine)
scant ⅛ lb / 50 g black olives
1 tsp / 5 g coriander
1 tsp / 5 g peppercorns
1 bunch of basil
1 bunch of thyme

1 bay leaf
1 clove of garlic
2 egg yolks
scant ¼ cup / 50 ml whole milk
scant ¼ cup / 50 ml cream
generous ⅜ cup / 100 ml olive oil
4 tsp / 20 g fresh butter
salt, pepper to taste

For the parsley juice:
¾ cup / 200 ml vegetable or poultry broth
1 bunch of smooth-leaved parsley
1 bunch of young spinach (to yield scant ⅛ lb / 50 g leaves)
half a bunch of chervil
3 cloves of garlic (to yield 1 tbsp / 15 g chopped)
2 tbsp / 30 g cold butter
salt, fresh-ground pepper to taste

The artichoke, a remote relative of the thistle, was only introduced to the kitchen fairly recently, after a most honorable career as a diuretic in the medical field. Only during the Renaissance period, after a remarkable introduction to the court, did it become popular on royal dinner tables. Here, in a dish presented by our chef, Horst Petermann, it assumes a starring role.

There are two major artichoke families: the southern type, a small purple artichoke or *poivrade* grown in Italy and in Provence and often consumed raw, and one from Brittany or from the north, which is cooked in boiling water. The large green artichoke from Laon and in particular the blunt-nosed one from Brittany recommended for this recipe belong to the second category. Before you prepare the artichoke, it is important to twist off the stem with a quick movement, pulling out,

at the same time, a number of tough, fibrous strings reaching right into the heart of the artichoke (otherwise known as the choke).

France boasts a great variety of chèvres, or goat's milk cheeses, partly matured in ashes, and available in various degrees of maturity. Only six of these have a controlled designation of origin. With great zeal, manufacturers monitor their refined quality, and the improvements become evident in the texture and flavor. For this appetizer, choose a small cheese that has only ripened for two weeks and still has a soft consistency.

The anchovies preserved in brine must be thoroughly rinsed in water or milk to weaken their salty taste. Use the more aromatic smooth-leaved parsley instead of the curly parsley to give the sauce a stronger flavor.

1. Remove the artichoke leaves. Twist off the stem. Cut out the artichoke hearts, trim them to pleasing, round shapes and sprinkle with lemon.

2. To cook the artichoke hearts, cover peppercorns, bay leaf, crushed coriander, thyme, and finely sliced garlic with water. Add 3½ tbsp / 50 ml of olive oil. Add the hearts and cook over a low heat for about 20 minutes. Remove the strings (chokes) of the artichokes.

Olives and Chévre

3. Blanch, skin, and chop the tomatoes. Seed the olives and chop. Dice the goat's milk cheese. Desalinate the anchovy fillets in cold water for ten minutes. Chop the basil. Mix these ingredients with 3¹/₂ tbsp / 50 ml olive oil and spread onto the artichoke hearts. Prepare the mashed potatoes with the milk and season to taste.

4. Cover the filled hearts with a tablespoon of mashed potato until they look like small hemispheres. Blend the egg yolk with the cream, use to brush the mashed potato and brown under the grill. Heat the vegetable broth, add chopped herbs and spinach and bring to a boil. Puree and pass through a sieve. Whip up with butter. Arrange on plates, served with parsley juice.

Goose Liver Papillotes

Preparation time: *30 minutes*
Cooking time: *15 minutes*
Difficulty: ★★

Serves four

1 pre-cooked goose liver (foie gras), approximately
   ¹/₂ lb / 250 g
4 rice paper parchment sheets (8 x 8 in / 20 x 20 cm)
half a red pepper
4 shallots

4 cornichons
1 tbsp / 15 g capers
1 egg white
1 tbsp / 15 g poppy seeds
1 tbsp / 15 ml walnut oil
¹/₂ cup / 125 ml red wine vinegar
¹/₂ cup / 125 g all purpose flour
1 bunch of chives
1 bunch of chervil
salt, fresh-ground pepper to taste

The objective of this recipe from Chef Roland Pierroz is to bring out the full flavor of the foie gras. For this reason, one should select a firm, pre-cooked goose liver, because it can be fried over a high heat that can sometimes sap the flavor of a weaker ingredient. This dish is doubtlessly very high in calories, but even if it upsets any diet schedule, its rich and superb flavor and outstanding texture and color will delight any guest and more than make up for a momentary violation of any principle. Moreover, how could anyone resist such a work of art, particularly when its creator is generous enough to reveal its secrets?

The innovation in this recipe is the use of the egg white to ensure that the rice paper envelopes are perfectly sealed – with this method, the problem of water permeability is solved for good. This is crucial, for if the rice paper sheets are not hermetically sealed, they will not become puffed up by the steam released from the wrapped-up hot goose liver – which in turn will cook the contents inside. If you also baste the papillotes with hot oil while they deep-fry, you will further improve the effect of this chemical procedure.

Your guests will certainly enjoy the contrast between the mild flavor of the liver and the tart vinaigrette of the vegetables. The instructions for the preparation of the vinaigrette should be followed closely.

1. Remove the nerves of the goose liver, cut into slices of about 2 oz / 50 g each, then season and coat lightly with flour. Brown in a non-stick pan over a high heat for about 20 seconds per side and leave to cool.

2. Brush the edges of the rice paper sheets with egg white. Place a slice of fried goose liver on each sheet on the diagonal. Fold the sheets into triangles. Press the edges firmly to seal well, and brush the bundles with egg white as well as sprinkling them with a few poppy seeds.

with Marinated Vegetables

3. Brown the bundles in a pan with oil heated to 355 °F / 180 °C, basting them often with oil to make them puff up. Drain on paper towels. Chop a sufficient amount of chives and chervil to fill a small soup spoon of each.

4. Dice the cornichons finely and chop the capers. Chop the shallots finely, place in a saucepan, cover with red wine vinegar and simmer until the liquid has boiled away. Add oil, capers, red pepper, cornichons, a dash of vinegar, herbs, salt, and pepper. Serve the papillotes with vegetables on the plates, with the vinaigrette trickled over them; garnish, if you desire, with a generous sprig of chervil.

Tortelloni

Preparation time: 45 minutes
Cooking time: 20 minutes
Difficulty: ★★

Serves four

For the lasagna sheets
scant ³/₈ lb / 200 g fresh spinach
2³/₈ cups / 700 g durum wheat flour
2 eggs

For the filling:
3¹/₂ oz / 100 g Séré cheese (Ricotta or Sérac)
2 red peppers (to yield 4 tsp / 20 g chopped)

2 yellow peppers (to yield 4 tsp / 20 g chopped)
2 green peppers (to yield 4 tsp / 20 g chopped)
1 eggplant
1 egg
¹/₂ cup / 125 ml olive oil
salt, fresh-ground pepper to taste

For the decoration:
¹/₈ cup / 25 ml extra-virgin olive oil
4 olives
2 cloves of garlic
2 basil leaves
¹/₄ lb / 50 g Parmesan cheese

This Mediterranean recipe, with its fragrances of olive oil and basil, is certainly attributable to Roland Pierroz' Italian ancestors and, though he is based in Switzerland, it has little to do with Swiss cooking. "Niçoise" refers to the tortelloni filling based on eggplants, peppers, and olives: the combination has been a part of the cuisine of the old county of Nice since long before it became part of France, in 1860.

Start with the preparation of a very smooth dough, dyed with spinach, and roll it out very thinly with a rolling pin. It should be made of gluten-rich Italian or Canadian durum wheat, which produces the tastiest noodles you could wish for. After rolling out the dough you should wind up with twelve, five-inch (twelve centimeter) squares.

These tortelloni go particularly well with vegetables from the Mediterraean region, like eggplants. Choose a medium-sized

eggplant with a smooth and very shiny skin. The peppers are an essential component; they give the filling color and a soft consistency, as does the olive oil, which also evokes the magical scent of Mediterranean cuisine. Our chef, bringing in some of his Swiss influences as well, includes Séré in his recipe, a white Swiss cheese of Latin origin (the name is derived from the word *serum*, i.e. "whey"), which has the right consistency to bind the filling.

A few changes are allowed so long as they fit the recipe's Mediterranean flair – tomatoes and zucchini, for example, are also suitable for the filling. Filled Italian pasta dishes, of which there are innumerable variations, offer constant opportunities for imagination and innovation.

1. To prepare the dough, wash, cook, and chop the spinach; mix with the flour and eggs. Cut the Parmesan cheese thinly using a slicer. Chop the basil. Peel, slice, and fry the garlic. Drain on paper towels.

2. Dice the eggplant and green, red, and yellow peppers. Boil briefly in salted water, making sure that they remain firm. Drain and sauté briefly in olive oil. Drain on paper towels. Roll out the dough to make 12 sheets, about 5 in / 12 cm on each side.

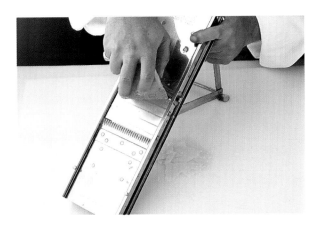

Niçoise

3. Whip up the egg. Bring a pot of water to a boil. Pass the egg through a sieve to set in the water. Strain the contents of the pot once more. Combine the egg in the sieve with the vegetables and the cheese and season. Place a tablespoon of this mixture onto the lasagna squares.

4. Fold the squares into triangles. Stick the rims together and adjust. Steam the tortelloni until done. Slowly heat 5 tbsp / 75 ml olive oil with the basil in a saucepan. Arrange the tortelloni in the center of the plate. Sprinkle with basil oil and Parmesan; decorate with olives and fried garlic.

Zucchini Flowers

Preparation time: 14 minutes
Cooking time: 15 minutes
Difficulty: ★★

Serves four

1¹/₃ lbs / 650 g clams
one dozen baby zucchini with flowers intact
2 tomatoes
1 large zucchini
generous 1 oz / 40 g truffles
1 egg yolk

1–2 tbsp / 30 ml wine
³/₄ cup / 200 ml cream
³/₄ cup / 200 ml olive oil
¹/₄ cup / 60g * butter
1 bunch of basil
salt, fresh-ground pepper to taste

This symbol of abundance and fertilly in the Orient is ubiquitous in home gardens, where it sometimes grows to enormous proportions. But the tastiest zucchini are smaller ones, and the most well-known variety among all of them, in France, is the *Diamant*. According to our French chefs, Jacques and Larent Pourcel, this type outshines all the others, with its lack of seeds and refined flavor. And, the chefs point out, there are many ways of preparing this vegetable, using any number of different sauces or cooking methods.

Judging by the impression one gets in the south of France, zucchini flowers are a common and popular dish. The baby zucchini itself, while very small, becomes all the tastier when the wide-open and well-developed flower is filled. Of course, these small zucchini have to be harvested at the right moment and processed as soon as possible. To open up the flower, blow into it gently. Remove the pistil, blanch the flowers quickly, and immediately dip them in ice water to keep them from going limp. Filling the flowers of this young vegetable is not all that easy and will probably require an extra set of hands, as well as a lot of practice.

To accompany the zucchini, our chef recommends seafood, which requires hardly any preparation apart from serving. If the clams, or *clovisses*, are nice and fresh, they will meet any expectations, particularly if they come from Sète, the Mediterranean harbor where these bivalves are mainly caught. *Clovissère*, derived from *clovisse*, is the name of a fishing device used to comb the bed of the lagoons of Languedoc-Roussillon. Especially in summer, this dish is an ideal combination of fruit from the sea and from the garden. If these clams are not available in American fish markets, subsitute them with any variety of high-quality, hardshell clams.

1. Carefully remove the pistils of the zucchini flowers. Cut off the zucchini stems. Blanch in boiling water for 15 seconds. Leave to cool and cut in half lengthwise. Set the cut-off halves aside.

2. Cook the cut-off zucchini halves and the chopped zucchini for the filling, reduce the cream and set aside. Cook the clams in wine until they open, then take them off the stove. Shell and rinse them and add them to the wine again. When the zucchini have cooked for a few minutes, take them off the heat and combine them with the egg yolk and the reduced cream.

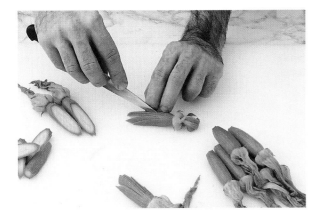

with Clam Filling

3. Skin and dice the tomatoes. Clean and peel the truffles and cut them into fine strips. Add half the clams and season. Fill this stuffing into the zucchini flowers; a pastry bag could be used.

4. Place the zucchini in an ovenproof dish. Pour a little water and the olive oil over the bottom and season. Cover with aluminum foil and bake at 355 °F / 180 °C for 25 minutes. Add the remaining clams and season. Mix butter and truffle peels into the zucchini stock. Serve the zucchini sprinkled with the sauce, and decorated with truffle strips, tomatoes and fresh herbs.

Potato and Boletus

Preparation time: 30 minutes
Cooking time: 10 minutes
Difficulty: ☆

Serves four

5/8 lb / 300 g boletus mushrooms
scant 7/8 lb / 400 g potatoes
3½ oz / 100 g raw ham (finely sliced)
6 shallots (to yield 3/8 lb / 180 g) chopped)
2 egg yolks
1/3 cup / 80 g butter

scant 7/8 cup / 200 ml cream
3½ tbsp / 50 ml olive oil
2 sprigs of smooth-leaved parsley
1 bunch of chives
salt, white pepper to taste

Perhaps we do not pay mushrooms sufficient respect. After all, these small crumbly fungi are capable of breaking through the surface of a road. Not all of them are edible, some are even poisonous, but how can one resist the delicious chanterelles or boletus that melt on one's tongue? Our chefs, Jacques and Laurent Pourcel, have a preference for mushrooms, and therefore invite us to sample this delectable boletus and potato cake.

Boletus grow all over Europe. You can hardly go wrong with the robust fleshy variety from Bordeaux, which is one of the most delicious. The Pourcel brothers, however, prefer the small boletus found near the Cevennes, which, unfortunately, is so delicate that it will hardly survive long distances undamaged.

Use young firm mushrooms with immaculate white flesh for this recipe. And take note as well that the boletus available in summer are less spicy than those collected in fall.

Boletus are first fried to expel their moisture content, a process that will render them more tender in the pancake. This way, they also avoid the risk of becoming discolored due to having an excess of liquid. Another tip: the more finely you grate the potato, the smoother your potato and boletus cakes will be.

The ham should be cut very finely, *à l'italienne*, into almost transparent slices, to intensify the meat's aroma.

1. Peel the potatoes and cut them into fine strips with the grater. Chop the shallots and the parsley and dice the ham finely. Cut the boletus into thin slices.

2. Brown all these ingredients apart from the potatoes in olive oil and set aside.

Pancakes with Ham

3. Wash the potato strips well under running water. Place them in a non-stick frying pan 8 in / 20 cm in diameter, so that the base of the pan is covered. Fry them in clarified butter and brown nicely. Blend ³/₄ cup / 200 ml cream with two egg yolks, season, and set aside.

4. Place a mixture of fried boletus, parsley, and chives onto the potato cake. Add the egg and cream mixture and bake in the oven at 390 °F / 200 °C for 7–8 minutes. Serve the cake on a plate with a mixture of olive oil and meat juices, if desired.

Warm Duck Liver

Preparation time: 1 hour
Cooking time: 10 minutes
Difficulty: ★★

Serves four

$^1/_2$ lb / 225 g duck liver
1–2 bunches of Swiss chard
generous 2 tbsp / 40 ml sherry vinegar
generous $^3/_8$ cup / 100 ml brown veal stock

1 bunch of smooth-leaved parsley
$^1/_2$ tsp / 5 g fresh-ground pepper
$^1/_2$ tsp / 5g coarse sea salt
fine salt

The chefs along the Côte d'Azur use Swiss chard regularly in a variety of dishes. It also has a number of other names there, like *poirée* and *bléas* in Nice, and *joutte* in Poitou. Swiss chard is a vegetable from the beet family (or, in German, the family of the mangel-wurzel); it has large dark-green leaves with a big white rib in the middle, though it also comes in a stronger-flavored, red variety. Both leaves and ribs are edible and rich in vitamins, iron, and calcium. Swiss chard is predominantly available in winter and spring. Choose fresh leaves with a strong green color, large enough to wrap in layers around each piece of duck liver.

You should preferably use a whole duck liver for this recipe, and then cut it into eight equal pieces. As our chef, Stéphane Raimbault will attest, duck liver is smaller and tastier than the goose liver and its fat melts in hot steam, which is a great advantage here. According to this recipe, this melted (yet not burnt) fat is used to soak the three layers of Swiss chard leaves enveloping the duck liver. The result is a rare and exquisite blend of flavors and a superb Swiss chard ragout in veal stock. Make sure that no liquid escapes through the three layers of leaves; the duck liver should not lose any fat when it is cooking.

It is quite unusual to cook duck liver in steam, but this seemingly unorthodox technique makes for a most refined and easily digestible dish.

1. Remove the fat of the duck liver. Cut the liver into eight equal slices. Remove and set aside the ribs of the Swiss chard leaves, blanch well, let cool, and drain. Season each slice of liver, wrap each slice with three leaves, and refrigerate.

2. Peel and wash the Swiss chard ribs and cut them into diamonds. Cook in salted water. Set aside.

in Swiss Chard

3. Boil 2 quarts / 2 liters water with salt in a couscous pot (or pressure cooker). Place the plate with the wrapped liver slices onto the couscous grid (or pressure cooker grid) and steam them for 6–8 minutes.

4. Sauté the Swiss chard rib pieces in a pan with butter and sprinkle with a dash of vinegar. Add the veal stock, the fat of the duck liver and parsley. Serve the Swiss chard diamonds on pre-warmed plates and place two Swiss chard parcels in the middle of each plate. Pour veal stock over and sprinkle with parsley. Season with fresh-ground pepper and coarse sea salt.

Grilled Chèvre with

Preparation time:	1 hour
Marinating time:	2–4 hours
Cooking time:	1 hour
Difficulty:	★

Serves four

scant ³/₄ lb / 350 g chèvre (in a cylindrical form)
5¹/₄ / 150 g fava beans
6 ripe tomatoes
1 shallot

1 clove of garlic
2 tbsp / 30 ml balsamic vinegar
1 sprig of tarragon
1 stalk of fennel
1 sprig of chervil
scant ¹/₄ cup / 50 g butter
generous ³/₈ cup / 100 ml olive oil
2 tbsp / 30 ml light olive oil
1 tbsp / 15 g sugar
1 tbsp / 15 g salt
pinch coarse black pepper

It was a sojourn in California that inspired our Irish chef, Paul Rankin, to create this recipe, which builds on his well-known preference for Provençal cooking.

The flavor of chèvre, or goat's milk cheese, depends on the condition of the milk it was made from. It is very mild if raw or pasteurized goat's milk is used, and it develops more character if pure goat's milk is added. All goat's milk cheeses are prepared the same way, so it is up to you to choose the cheese you like best – though for this dish, it is crucial that you use a chèvre in a cylindrical, instead of squat and round, shape. It is important not to cook the cheese for too long, or else it will disintegrate and destroy the intended effect. One should also take note that, after about two weeks, the cheese will lose its flavor, so once again the chef's cardinal rule of only using fresh ingredients should be in effect.

The fava beans should be fresh, young, and medium-sized. The skin is often indigestible, but if it is tender enough, it can be left on. Cooked *al dente*, they harmonize perfectly with the fresh and aromatic herbs complementing this dish. Apart from the herbs suggested here, you can also use savory, which goes very well with goat's milk cheese.

Tomatoes lend this beautifully presented and impressive appetizer a touch of color. They must be ripe, tasty, and preferably very fleshy so that they maintain their shape despite the loss of water.

Other spring vegetables like peas, for example, may also be used for this recipe. The only ingredient that may not be substituted is the goat's milk cheese, since it constitutes the center of this dish.

1. Four hours prior to the preparation of the dish, combine the shallot, garlic, vinegar, light olive oil, sugar, salt, pepper, and a tablespoon of mixed herbs (chopped tarragon, chervil, and fennel). Halve the tomatoes and add to the mixture. Leave to marinate for 2–4 hours. Blanch and drain the fava beans.

2. Take out the tomatoes and place them round side down onto a grill. Bake in the oven at a low heat (265 °F / 130 °C) for an hour.

Beans and Tomatoes

3. Slice the goat's milk cheese, brush the slices with liquid butter. Bake them under the hot grill for about two minutes until they are lightly browned and soft.

4. Arrange three tomato halves and three little heaps of the previously blanched and drained fava beans in a ring on each pre-warmed plate. Place one slice of cheese in the center. Cover with olive oil, and sprinkle with the remaining herbs.

Warm Salad with

Preparation time: 1 hour
Soaking time: 24 hours
Cooking time: 15 minutes
Difficulty: ★

Serves four

1¼ lbs / 600 g monkfish tail
1 large potato
½ lb / 250 g mixed lettuce leaves, such as Bibb
   lettuce, raddichio, or mesclun
1 egg

generous ³/₈ cup / 100 g flour
3 cups / 750 ml oil or lard for deep-frying
2 tbsp / 30 ml vinaigrette (see basic recipes)
salt, freshly ground white pepper to taste

For the mustard sauce:
¾ cup / 175 ml heavy cream
2 tbsp / 30 g coarse prepared mustard

This way of preparing fish is very common in Great Britain. It proves how easy it is to combine very economical ingredients to make a tasty and cleverly designed dish. The contrast between the creamy salad and the crisp French fries and deep-fried fish is particularly delicious.

By the choice of monkfish you can tell where our chef, the Irish Paul Rankin, comes from. The two main types of monkfish caught in Irish waters are the common monkfish (*lophius piscatorius*) and the red monkfish (*lophius budegassa*). Their strong flavor and fleshy consistency have made them both popular. If you steam the monkfish pieces before you deep-fry them, they will retain their succulent texture.

The Irishman's much-loved (and at times, much depended upon) potato is a component of innumerable recipes in Ireland. Maris Piper potatoes are ideal for crisp French fries, but Stella or Apollo are very suitable too. To make them lighter, Paul Rankin leaves the cut potatoes in cold water for twenty-four hours where they lose a considerable amount of their starch. They turn wonderfully crisp if you deep-fry them slowly.

Representing a British tradition, this appetizer can be enjoyed anywhere and at any time, possibly with a hot cup of tea.

1. Set aside 2 tbsp / 30 ml of heavy cream, bring the rest to a boil. Simmer for a minute until it has thickened slightly. Take off the stove and add mustard. Peel the potato and cut it into matchstick-thick strips. Place them in cold water for an hour to lose their starch.

2. Cut the tail of the monkfish into ½ in / 1 cm thick pieces. Blend the egg and the remaining heavy cream and use to coat the fish pieces. Then cover them thoroughly with flour until all the egg and cream mixture has been absorbed.

"Fish and Chips"

3. Deep-fry the monkfish pieces at 375 °F / 90 °C for three minutes. Take out and drain on paper towels. Season with salt and pepper. Then prepare the French fries in the same manner.

4. Just before serving, dip the lettuce leaves into the vinaigrette and distribute them on four plates. Arrange the French fries and the monkfish pieces on top of the salad. Finally, add a touch of mustard sauce.

Pike Sausages in

Preparation time: 15 minutes
Cooking time: 10 minutes
Difficulty: ★★

Serves four

scant ⁷/₈ lb / 400 g pike fillet
¹/₂ cup / 125 g coarse prepared mustard
generous 1 lb / 500 g spinach
5¹/₄ oz / 150 g button mushrooms
1 shallot
scant ⁷/₈ cup / 200 g butter

1¹/₄ cups / 300 ml cream
¹/₂ cup / 125 ml white wine
salt, pepper to taste

Though it may not be common to prepare fish in a similar manner to meat, this is exactly what our chef, Joël Roy, does- and he does it very skillfully, to the delight of any gourmet. The sausages consist of a white, very thin sausage "skin" that forms around the outside of a delicious mixture, sometimes coated with bread crumbs, jelly or lard. Since the foundation of the A.A.A.A.A. (*Association amicale des amateurs d'authentiques andouillettes*) with its strict quality controls, the quality of the sausages is rated even higher. This association has not yet given its approval to our chef's pike sausages, which – admittedly – are slightly outside the norm, but they would hardly be detrimental to the A.A.A.A.A.'s collection.

As usual, use only very fresh ingredients for this recipe. This applies in particular to the pike, which should preferably be a river pike, which is tastier than its counterpart from stagnant waters. The flesh of this predatory fish is delicious and often consumed cold. Next to the trout, it takes first place amongst the freshwater fish in flavor.

It is advisable to process the fish fillets under cool conditions and as rapidly as possible. Season them just before you finish cooking; the salt improves their consistency.

For the filling you could consider button mushrooms, oyster mushrooms or boletus, depending on your preference. Their flavor will be brought out even more by the coarse-grained mustard. Select an old-fashioned coarse mustard (such as Pommery) since, unlike most of the basic mustard types, it does not contain any added seasonings.

1. Process the fish fillet with 3¹/₂ tbsp / 50 g butter in a food processor. Add 1¹/₄ cups / 300 ml of cream, blend again, season with salt and pepper and set aside.

2. For the mushroom filling chop the mushrooms finely. Add a pinch of chopped shallot as well as salt and pepper. Sauté with a pat of butter and leave to cool. Clean the spinach leaves, sauté in butter and leave to cool. Season and keep warm.

Coarse Mustard Sauce

3. Add the mushroom filling to the fish mixture. Form small sausages using a pastry bag. For the white butter sauce, reduce the shallot with $^{1}/_{2}$ cup / 125 ml wine until the liquid has almost evaporated. Stir in 7 tbsp / 100 g of butter. Add a teaspoon of coarse mustard and season to taste.

4. Clarify the remaining butter. Fry the pike sausages in the clarified butter in a non-stick pan for 7–8 minutes, turning them frequently. Arrange them on pre-warmed plates, surround them in sauce, and decorate with spinach leaves.

Fricassee of Snails and

Preparation time: 40 minutes
Cooking time: 10 minutes
Difficulty: ★★

Serves four

2 dozen small squid
32 snails
1 dozen sea cucumbers
1 blood sausage
7 oz / 200 g small onions

For the sofrito:
generous 1 lb / 500 g ripe tomatoes
2.2 lbs / 1 kg onions
sugar, salt

For the sauce:
tentacles from the squid
generous 2 cups / 500 ml vegetable broth
    composed of leeks, parsley, leafy lettuce, and
    1 shallot
a pinch of saffron
1/2 cup / 125 ml olive oil from the first pressing

For the decoration:
1 bunch of chervil
1 bunch of chives
1 bunch of parsley
1 bunch of basil
1 tbsp / 15 g gray salt
2 tbsp/ 30 g almonds (if desired)

The restuarant *El Racó de Can Fabes*, where Chef Santi Santamaria presides, is situated in a favorable spot at the foot of the mountains only a few miles from the Mediterranean. It is thus predestined for this combination of snails and squid, which represent, on a plate, the classic union of land and sea. The ingredients combined here are presented on a base of simple *sofrito*, a traditional Catalan side dish made with tomatoes and onions.

The ingredients are not hard to come by. The small gray snails you find in masses on a rainy Sunday morning are just right. These *bouer*, as their fans call them, are plentiful on both side of the Pyrenees (though, in the United States, you may have to improvise).

The squid, on the other hand, have to be selected carefully, preferably towards the end of summer, when they're in season. If

you want to fish them yourself, try to avoid the use of a trawl net and rather catch them a *la potera* (fishing rod with a special hook), like Santi Santamaria does to avoid damaging them. If you obtain them in the more ordinary way, buying them from a fish market, you may also buy *chipirones*, the small squid that the Spaniards love and eat as *tapas* at all hours of the day and night. As an alternative, look for dwarf squid, which are similar.

You might also discover the sea cucumber while you're there, a marine animal also known as a sea slug whose iodine flavor complements this crunchy appetizer. Contrary to its appearance, this creature has a tough skin covered with mobile tentacles.

1. Clean the squid. Sever the tentacles. Cut the tentacles into pieces and fry in a pan until golden brown and set aside for the sauce.

2. Remove the cooked snails from their shells. In a non-stick pan, fry the small onions and the squid separately. When they are nearly done, add the snails. For the sofrito, slice the onions finely, brown in oil and add chopped tomatoes. Steam, then reduce the liquid in the oven. Season to taste with salt and sugar.

Squid with Sofrito

3. For the sauce, add the chopped shallot, the other vegetables and the saffron to the browned tentacles. Add vegetable stock and reduce by 20%. Leave to steep for five minutes for everything to take on color. Mix with olive oil from the first pressing and season to taste.

4. Fry the blood sausage slices in a pan. Halve the sea cucumber (after having cleaned the extremities), sauté in a pan and add to the squid mixture. Serve the squid and the sea cucumber in the center of the plate. Arrange the snails and a small heap of sofrito around them. Decorate with herbs.

Grandfather's Wild

Preparation time: 30 minutes
Cooking time: 12 minutes
Difficulty: ☆

Serves four

1 lb / 450 g various wild mushrooms
5¼ oz / 150 g farmer ham
1 black truffle
1 clove of garlic
2 shallots
½ cup / 120 ml red wine
1–2 tbsp / 15–30 ml vegetable oil

1 bunch of smooth-leaved parsley
1 bunch of thyme
salt, pepper to taste

If you've ever lived in the country, you may have experienced the marvelous challenges and joys of collecting mushrooms. Our chef, Santi Santamaria, is no exception. This nearly ceremonial ritual starts with mushroom-lovers dispersing widely, some searching the well-known spots, others exploring supposedly virgin territory. Finally, after a successful day of mushrooming, all sit around a campfire to sample their haul. This warm and friendly ambience is favorable for culinary inventions. Santi Santamaria's father, for instance, once wrapped sausages in an improvised bag made from newspaper soaked in wine – the sausages, heated in the ashes, were delicious.

Our chef revels in such childhood memories of the Montseny, the mountains of Catalonia that form the "green lung" of Barcelona, when he prepares mushrooms in a sulphurized paper bag (ask in your gourmet market or high-end cooking shop).

A variety of other ingredients round off the flavor of the mushrooms – ham, garlic, shallots, red wine, and a touch of thyme.

Feel free to select any mushrooms you like (so long as you are sure they're edible!) – chanterelles and ringed boletus are particularly good in this recipe. A collection of noble mushrooms should always be crowned by the truffle, the queen of fungi, which gastronimic man of letters Brillat-Savarin calls "the black diamond." It harmonizes very well with the rustic components of this dish, such as the ham or, in Spanish, *jabugo*. Spain prides itself of being Europe's main producer and consumer of this fat gold, *el oro grasso*. Clean the mushrooms carefully, bearing in mind that quite a few types do not react well to water: these mushrooms, especially the boletus, should therefore be cleaned dry, on a sheet of paper towels.

1. Clean all the mushrooms. Do not wash the boletus, but wipe them with a damp cloth or paper towel. Peel the mushroom stalks.

2. Cut the mushrooms into ¼ in / 5 mm thick slices, leaving caps and stalks of the boletus together.

Mushrooms from Montseny

3. Fry the mushrooms in oil until they are dehydrated, but they take them off the heat before they have a chance to brown. Season with salt and pepper. Add red wine.

4. Add the finely diced ham, the thinly sliced truffle, the garlic, and the chopped shallots. Season to taste again. Fold four bags of sulphurized paper and fill them with the mushrooms and the other ingredients. Cook in the oven for seven minutes. Place the paper bags on plates and serve immediately.

Fresh Pistachio

Preparation time: 15 minutes
Cooking time: 4 hours
Difficulty: ★

Serves four

For the light stock:
1 chicken approximately 4¹/₂ lbs / 2 kg
¹/₄ of a veal trotter
generous 1 lb / 500 g beef knuckle
2 turnips
1 rutabaga
2 leeks
3 carrots
2 onions

1 celery stalk
2 cloves of garlic
1 bunch of parsley
1 bunch of herbs
salt, pepper to taste

For the cream:
7 oz / 200 g fresh shelled but not skinned pistachios
1 bunch of parsley
1 quart / 1 l chicken broth
5 tsp / 25 ml olive oil from first pressing

To garnish
1 oz / 25 g pistachios

The fully laden pistachio trees planted in Spain's Catalonia have been an irresistible temptation for our chef Santi Santamaria. His recipe brings out the full flavor of these fresh pistachios, which are far less well-known than the roasted version people nibble and enjoy (despite their high calorie content).

In flavor, texture, and versatility, pistachios can certainly compete with almonds and hazelnuts. Originating from the Near East, they were brought to Europe via Sicily, Turkey, Syria (which was the source of the biggest pistachios) and Tunisia (where the pistachios are small but very aromatic). In all of these countries people either love them or avoid them – which is the usual scope of criticism in the field of gastronomy. With its high fat content, the pistachio nut is used for the pressing of

a special oil. In some dishes, like calf sweetbreads for instance, it is very tasty in combination with olive oil. But unless refrigerated (no warmer than 37–39 °F / 3–4 °C), it may go rancid within a few days.

Chef Santamaria gives us two options: this cream can either be served cold, as in an almond cream for example, or else lukewarm, enriched with poultry stock. What is really important is the consistency of the cream, which you can perfect by using a blender.

The green color of the pistachios can be intensified by means of parsley leaves that are blanched just before being used. Add vegetable stock to lend the dish a particularly aromatic flavor.

1. Place 1 oz / 30 g of pistachios into a saucepan with boiling water. Cook for two minutes and drain. Skin them by pressing them between your thumb and forefinger. Set aside. Pick off the parsley leaves and blanch to intensify the cream's color.

2. For the light stock, place all the ingredients indicated into a large pot with 7 quarts / 7 l of water. Simmer over a low heat for four hours. Pass through a sieve. Reserve the chicken and the beef knuckle for other meals.

Cream

3. For the cream, add the 7 oz / 200 g of unskinned pistachios to 4 cups of the light stock, the olive oil, and the parsley. Puree in a blender.

4. As soon as the pistachio cream is blended well, strain and season to taste. Pour into stef small tureens, or cups, and decorate with the skinned pistachios.

Lasagnettes with

Preparation time: 30 minutes
Cooking time: 20 minutes
Difficulty: ✶

Serves four

10 tomatoes
half a red pepper
half a yellow pepper
2 zucchini
1 eggplant
1 red onion
1 clove of garlic

3 cups / 750 ml vegetable broth
1 bunch of basil
$^1/_2$ cup / 125 ml extra-virgin olive oil
salt, pepper to taste

For the lasagnette dough:
$1^1/_4$ cups / 300 g durum wheat flour
9 egg yolks
1 tbsp / 15 ml olive oil
2 tbsp / 30 ml water
pinch of salt

This is, in fact, a lasagnette – a small puff pastry lasagna filled with vegetables. It is baked immediately before being served, unlike the ordinary lasagna, which is prepared in advance and then served piece by piece according to demand. Garnished with a light and colorful ratatouille, this lasagnette is a very popular summer dish for pasta-lovers who are concerned with eating a less fat-laden version of their favorite food.

The various ingredients, prepared in different ways, are combined just before being served; in this step lies the art of preparing this dish. The lasagnettes are cooked twice. After first being cooked in boiling water they are drained very well. Then, before they are cooked again, each vegetable is processed separately, depending on its consistency and on how long it must cook. The flavor of the Italian eggplant from Calabria or Sicily goes particularly well with this recipe. Lastly, add the longish very sweet tomatoes, if possible, the San Marzano type.

The overall flavor of the dish is influenced by the typically Italian ingredients, such as *beneventano*, a large-leaved basil, which the Italians also use in pesto, their popular pasta sauce, as well as the red onions from Tropea in southern Italy. Of course these particular varieties may not be available, as Chef Ezio Santin would concur, in U.S. markets. Instead, look for similar large-leaved basil (in season particularly in late summer), as well as the imported, similarly small red onions.

Since the diced vegetables are prepared *al dente*, some of the pieces may slip off the dough layers onto the plate. Take that in your stride and do not try to remedy it, as the accident will give the dish an invitingly informal look.

1. Dice zucchini, eggplant, five skinned tomatoes, and the skinned peppers. Chop half an onion finely. Heat oil with half a clove of garlic and the rest of the onion. Sauté briefly, add the diced eggplant and zucchini and braise. Lastly mash the remaining five skinned tomatoes and add to the other vegetables.

2. Add two ladlefuls of broth and finish cooking over a low heat. Puree the vegetables in the food processor. Prepare a dough from the ingredients indicated and shape into a ball. Leave to rest for an hour. Roll out the dough thinly and cut out twelve rectangles of about 2$^1/_2$ x 4 in / 6 x 10 cm. Cook in simmering saltwater for 2–3 minutes and leave to cool.

Ratatouille

3. In a non-stick frying pan fry the diced vegetables (tomatoes, peppers) in olive oil until al dente. Add a tablespoon of chopped basil.

4. Reheat the lasagette squares over steam. Serve them on hot plates. Make a three-deckered sandwich of ratatouille and three dough sheets. Stir two tablespoons of olive oil into the pureed hot vegetable sauce, and pour it liberally around the lasagnettes.

Lasagnettes with Leeks,

Preparation time: 45 minutes
Cooking time: 10 minutes
Difficulty: ✷✷✷

Serves four

4 leek stalks
4 fresh onions
7 oz / 200 g black truffles
generous 1 oz / 40 g smoked bacon or Pancetta
5/8 cup / 150 ml crème fraîche
1/4 cup / 60 g butter
2/3 cup / 150 ml extra virgin olive oil

2 tbsp / 30 ml black truffle juice
1 tbsp / 15 ml balsamic vinegar
salt, pepper to taste

For the dough:
1 1/4 cups / 300 g flour
9 egg yolks
1 tbsp / 15 g olive oil
2 tbsp / 30 ml water
1 pinch salt

When our chef, Ezio Santin, invented this recipe prepared with the white part of leeks mixed with onions, his friends, great admirers of this delicious vegetable, were delighted. The combination of onions and leeks has long been valued by both gardeners and gourmets. Spring leeks are well-known for their tenderness and their sweetness, which is due to the sweet-tasting sucrose contained in the white part of their leaves.

Small young onions are the ones to use for this lasagnette: if they have green and succulent shoots, this is an indication that they're fresh. The combination and proportion of leeks and onions are ideal and completely harmonious. They constitute the essential basis of the filling.

The chopped black truffles add another distinctive quality to this refined appetizer. While cooking, they develop the full flavor and aroma they were endowed with by nature. If at all possible, choose winter truffles from Italy, near Norcia in Umbria, or else truffles from Périgord. But a warning on possible substitutions: Chef Santin says he would sooner leave out the truffles altogether than use the brown truffle with the white veins from Saint-Jean, for instance.

The vegetables and truffles are cooked in crème fraîche at a high temperature and need to be stirred constantly to avoid the formation of lumps. Lastly, one should not forget that it is easier to win a gourmet over with a spoonful of genuine balsamic vinegar than with a whole barrel of ordinary vinegar.

1. Cut onions and leeks into rings. Sauté in butter and 4 tbsp / 60 ml olive oil. Fry for 15 minutes over a high heat while stirring continually. Season with salt and pepper. Add the smoked bacon strips that were blanched and browned in advance.

2. For the dough, make a well in the flour and add all the ingredients indicated. Knead the dough fast and roll into a ball. Leave to rest for an hour. Then roll it out thinly and cut out 12 rectangles of about 2 1/2 x 4 in / 6 x 10 cm. Cook in simmering salted water for 2–3 minutes and leave to cool.

Onions and Truffles

3. Chop the truffles finely and add to the leek and onion mixture. Add crème fraîche and cook for about six minutes while stirring continually. Prepare the lasagnettes by placing three dough sheets and filling in alternate layers on top of each other. Reheat over steam.

4. Heat 6 tbsp / 90 ml of olive oil, the truffle juice, and the balsamic vinegar over a low heat. Serve the lasagnettes on pre-warmed plates. Garnish with a few truffle slices. Add salt and pepper and a little olive oil sauce.

Poached Eggs with Goose

Preparation time: 5 minutes
Cooking time: 20 minutes
Difficulty: ★★

Serves four

4 eggs
3 1/2 oz / 100 g goose liver (foie gras)
1 white truffle
1 shallot
scant 1/4 cup / 50 g butter
1/2 cup / 125 ml port
1/2 cup / 125 ml chicken broth

generous 3/8 cup / 100 ml crème fraîche
vinegar
salt, pepper to taste

In season from late September to January, white truffles are most delicious. They are found in Piemont, Italy in the area of Alba, the name meaning *the white one*. The wines from that region, Dolcetto and Barolo (the latter is "the king of wines," according to our chef, Ezio Santin), are famous all over Europe. Unlike the black truffle, the white truffle exudes its aroma even before it is cooked. Get to know it through this superb, traditional recipe presented by Chef Santin who has prepared it for years, and this can guarantee its success.

Select very fresh grade A eggs with a uniform weight of about two ounces (sixty grams) each. Larger eggs, Santin reminds us, are of course not necessarily fresher or better. Poach them in unsalted water with a little added vinegar, making sure that the water merely simmers to prevent the egg white from spreading too much.

The sauce is prepared from a goose liver and butter mixture, and must not be spiced excessively, since very strongly flavored ingredients may conceal and thus inevitably destroy the truffle aroma. Before the foie gras is added, the port wine serving as a base for the gravy needs to be reduced and the shallots must be totally cooked away. It goes without saying that a high-quality port should be used, despite the fact that it plays only a secondary role here.

The presentation of this appetizer requires a little care. For an even appearance, the eggs should be turned over and covered with sauce in all sides.

1. Place a knob of butter in a frying pan and add the chopped shallot. Pour on the port and reduce by three-quarters. Then add the chicken broth and crème fraîche.

2. Bring to a boil again and reduce by half Take off the stove and blend the chopped liver and the butter in a food processor. Season to taste and keep warm in a double boiler.

Liver and White Truffle

3. Poach the eggs in boiling unsalted water with a little added vinegar. Drain on a cloth and trim into shape.

4. Serve the poached eggs on plates, pour the goose liver sauce over and sprinkle with thinly sliced white truffle flakes.

Small Potato Gnocchi

Preparation time: 10 minutes
Cooking time: 25 minutes
Difficulty: ★★

Serves four

1¼ lbs / 600 g Bintje potatoes
1½ lbs / 750 g small boletus
2 cloves of garlic
half a bunch of parsley (to yield 1 tbsp / 15 g chopped)
5 sprigs of thyme
scant ½ cup / 110 g flour

⅛ lb / 25 g Parmesan
2 tbsp / 30 g butter
4 tbsp / 60 ml extra-virgin olive oil
2 tbsp / 30 ml chicken or vegetable broth
salt, pepper to taste

Gnocchi (Italian for "dumplings") are prepared in very different ways. Their first reference in literature was made by the writer Vincenzo Corrado in his *Cuisinier galant* in the early 19th century. That was the time when the potato, that had previously been fairly unknown as a food item in Italy, began to be consumed. The fact that gnocchi are made of durum wheat semolina in Rome and of cornmeal around Venice proves that cooks have a large degree of freedom when preparing this world-renowned dish. Gnocchi, it seems, can take a hundred delicious forms.

Our chef suggests cooking the unpeeled potatoes in salted water to retain their consistency. He recommends certain types that stay firm when cooked, like the potato from Bologna or the prolific Bintje potato from the Netherlands, which is available at markets all year round. If these are unavailable, just choose potatoes that are firm and fresh, such as Yukon Gold

and round whites. When cooking, make sure the potatoes do not fall apart, otherwise you will not be able to process them.

The combination of these ingredients with fresh boletus will allow hardly any alternatives. If worse comes to worse, the boletus could be substituted with morels, provided they are fresh (and prepare yourself for a lengthy cleaning process). This recipe demands softer and more aromatic ingredients than the dried morels normally used for sauces.

The ingredients for the gnocchi should be very simple. Do not use eggs, which could make the dough tough and chewy. Indenting the gnocchi by means of a fork follows the traditional presentation. Our chef, Ezio Santin, has admitted that at least twice a week he and his staff enjoy gnocchi with tomato sauce – their way of relaxing away from the busy schedule of the kitchen.

1. Cook the potatoes in salted water. Clean a boletus, dice it finely and sauté it in a non-stick pan in 2 tbsp / 30 ml oil with a clove of garlic and a sprig of thyme. Put the potatoes through the grinder. Mix the diced hot mushrooms, flour, and grated Parmesan with the warm potato paste. Combine well and add salt.

2. Make long rolls the thickness of a finger and cut into about 1 in / 2 cm pieces. Use the back of a fork to make indentations.

with Mushrooms

3. Cut the remaining well-cleaned mushrooms into large chunks and place them on a damp cloth. Then fry them in a pan with 2 tbsp / 30 ml of oil and a clove of garlic. Add parsley and salt and gradually pour the stock over. Set the mushrooms aside.

4. Cook the gnocchi uncovered in a big pot of salted water for 3–5 minutes. Drain in a strainer and then reheat in the pan with the mushroom sauce finished off with a knob of butter. Serve on very hot plates and decorate with a sprig of thyme.

Tagliolini with

Preparation time:	25 minutes
Sitting time:	1 hour
Cooking time:	2 minutes
Difficulty:	✳

Serves four

4 large artichokes
12 shrimps
2 cloves of garlic
juice of 1 lemon
1 oz / 20 g smoked bacon (or raw ham)
6 tbsp / 100 ml extra-virgin, native olive oil
salt, pepper to taste

For the tagliolini:
1¼ cups / 300 g flour
9 egg yolks
1 tbsp / 15 ml olive oil
2 tbsp / 30 ml water
pinch of salt

Although this recipe was designed for the small tender artichokes of Sardinia or the Ligurian coast, there is no reason why you could not use the purple Provençal artichokes, which are normally consumed raw *en poivrade* (with a pepper sauce), or the short Breton artichokes. Or, considering the different markets, globe artichokes from California.

The same flexibility applies to the small crustaceans, though Chef Ezio Santin would certainly advocate using the popular Italian *gambero rosso*, the red shrimp caught in the same region. Instead, look for comparable red shrimp of the same size, about two ounces (six grams) a piece. They should be shelled carefully and cooked immediately. Observe them closely: when cooking, they must not turn rubbery. If these *bouguets* as they are also known are unavailable, prawns, also

called *gambas*, are a good alternative. The use of olive oil is a delicious and inevitable must: try, for regionality's sake, to use native Italian, extra-virgin olive oil.

As with many issues concerning the rules of preparation, experts disagree on when the tagliolini dough should be prepared. Chef Santin prepares it an hour before cooking, thus shortening the cooking time as well. Other cooks leave the dough to rest for a longer period, for example overnight. Traditionally, this dough is prepared the way grandmother used to make it; in other words the only tools permitted are arms and a rolling pin to get it paper-thin. The color and smooth texture of the dough are mostly determined by the number of egg yolks it contains. Do not hesitate to add more if necessary. Of course, the tagliolini are only cooked until *al dente*.

1. To make the noodle dough, make a well in the flour and add egg yolks, a tablespoon of oil, and salt. Knead well, adding two tablespoons of water. Let sit for an hour. Roll out the dough into a long sheet, cut it up (with the noodle machine) to make tagliolini. Leave to dry for ten minutes.

2. Prepare the artichokes and quarter the hearts. Remove the strings. Place the quarters into cold water with the juice of a lemon. Cut smoked bacon into strips; blanch these in boiling water for one minute and take them out.

Artichokes and Shrimps

3. In the meantime, fry the sliced artichoke hearts with two cloves of garlic, 3 tbsp of oil and the bacon strips. Sprinkle with a few drops of lemon. Season with salt and pepper and add 2 tbsp / 30 ml water.

4. Fry the shelled shrimps tails in the remaining oil. Add salt and pepper and the fried artichoke hearts. Cook the tagliolini in saltwater. Serve on plates. Spoon on the shrimp and artichoke sauce after having removed the garlic cloves.

Saffron Risotto

Preparation time: 10 minutes
Soaking time: 4–5 hours
                     (for the saffron)
Cooking time: 15 minutes
Difficulty: ✶

Serves four

generous 1 cup / 250 g Arborio rice (see below)
$^1/_4$ lb / 125 g goose liver (foie gras)
1 pinch saffron threads
1 small onion

$^3/_4$ cup / 200 ml beef broth
scant $^1/_4$ cup / 50 g butter
$^1/_2$ tsp / 5 ml balsamic vinegar
half a bunch of rosemary
salt, pepper to taste

Saffron originally served as a pigment, was used extensively for the different greens of the frescos and stained glass windows when the *duomo* was built, a great Milanese cathedral that is still one of the most impressive buildings of Christianity. Legend has it that this risotto had its origin in a comment made by a master glazier to his apprentice working with saffron on the site of the cathedral: "You could even manage to use this for cooking!"

If one is to believe a story passed on for generations, and related here by our chef, Nadia Santini, this dish was served at the wedding of the daughter of Master Valery of Flanders. From then on the golden yellow risotto became popular in the whole of northern Italy and was particularly enjoyed in Milan by the artists of the Scala and high society. One must not forget that the climate of sun and rain had a positive influence on rice cultivation and that, as a result, there is a multitude of rice dishes from northern Italy.

To prepare this dish, you should try to choose a type of rice that is characteristic of this region, such as *vialone nano*, which is cooked *mantecato* or until *al dente*, to make it more easily digestible. If this is unavailable, choose a robust-grained Arborio. Coloring with saffron is easier if you soak the saffron threads for about four or five hours in advance. As an alternative to the goose liver slices our chef suggests artichoke hearts, or finely sliced mushrooms.

1. Fry the small, finely chopped onion in butter until golden.

2. Add the rice and stir it with the onion for 2–3 minutes so that the butter nicely moistens the rice. Pour on very hot beef stock, ladle by ladle, as it is absorbed by the rice.

with Goose Liver

3. Add saffron (previously soaked in cold water for four to five hours until almost red) to the par-cooked rice. If necessary, add a little more beef stock until the rice is cooked al dente.

4. Cut the goose liver into pieces and fry in a non-stick pan. Remove and set aside. Add balsamic vinegar and chopped rosemary to the contents of the pan. Heap a tablespoon of risotto onto each plate and arrange the liver on top, garnished, if you wish, with saffron threads.

Preparation time: 1 hour
Cooking time: 25 minutes
Difficulty: ✶

Serves four

generous 1 lb / 500 g pumpkin
1/8 lb / 60 g macaroons (see below)
3 1/2 oz / 100 g mustard fruits (see below)
3 1/2 oz / 100 g Parmesan (to yield generous 3/8 cup /
    100 g grated)
generous 3/8 cup / 100 g butter

1 tsp / 5 g grated nutmeg
1 tsp / 5 g cinnamon
1 tsp / 5 g additional spices, per your preference
salt, pepper to taste

For the dough:
2 eggs
2 egg yolks
generous 1 cup / 250 g semolina
salt

In and around Mantua, pasta is served in a large variety of shapes and combinations. Tortelli is the traditional Christmas midnight meal. It seems as if the dish was originally invented by Bartoloméo Stéfani, the chef of the famous Gonzagua family, whose gastronomic culture was influenced by Italian, German, and even Chinese cooking, when Marco Polo and his successors brought spices from the Far East.

The shapes of tortelli differ from village to village. Sometimes they look like a priest's hat, other times they are rectangular or square. In this version, from our chef, Nadia Santini, they are served three at a time in little, succulent bundles, stuffed with pumpkin filling and dribbled with butter and grated Parmesan.

To prepare the filling, use an American pumpkin with its characteristic, orange-yellow skin, or a similar squash with a yellow and green skin; either way it should be one whose width exceeds its height, and should be firm and heavy. Make sure that it is neither too dry nor too watery.

Mustard fruits are not from the mustard plant, but made from firm green fruit, such as Api apples (*apianum malum*), or pears or watermelons. The fruit is diced finely and caramelized in butter with a little sugar, and a few drops of mustard oil are added to this mixture after cooking. Mustard fruits used to be a common sight on the dinner tables of both noblemen and commoners, where they were offered as a digestive after particularly opulent and sumptuous meals. At that time it was not fashionable yet to eat raw fruit, so the mustard fruits helped to restore the digestion and provide a relatively balanced diet.

Regarding the macaroons, these should be the sandwich style ones, available in many specialty shops or Italian bakeries: look for the imported Italian version of this delectable almond, sugar, and egg white cookie.

1. Heap the flour onto the working surface. Make a well in the middle and add two eggs, two egg yolks, and salt. Mix with a kitchen knife until the eggs are completely combined with the flour. Knead well and refrigerate. Cook the pumpkin in water for about 20 minutes. Leave to cool.

2. Pass the pumpkin through a fine sieve. Add the chopped mustard fruits, the crushed macaroons, 1 3/4 oz / 50 g of Parmesan and all the spices. Combine well into a semi-firm mixture.

Pumpkin Filling

3. Roll out the dough on the working surface. Cut out squares of 3–4 in / 8–10 cm. Spoon pumpkin mixture the size of a walnut onto each square, fold them up and press the edges firmly with your fingers to seal the tortelli tightly.

4. Cook the tortelli in boiling salted water for 3–4 minutes. Take them out with a skimmer and drain on paper towels. Arrange on plates, cover with grated Parmesan and melted butter, and serve piping hot.

Tomato Soup

Preparation time: 15 minutes
Cooking time: 1 hour, 30 minutes
Difficulty: ✶

Serves four

5 vine-ripened tomatoes in season
1 green chili pepper
1 onion
2 cloves of garlic
1 bunch of parsley
4 eggs

4 slices country bread (or white bread)
2 tbsp / 30 ml light grape vinegar
2 tbsp / 30 ml oil
1 tbsp / 15 g butter
salt, pepper to taste

The Portuguese seafarers not only played a central role in the discovery of unexplored sea routes, but also brought from distant countries fruit, vegetables, and spices that were integrated into European cooking. Vasco da Gama from the province of Alentejo, for example, discovered the Cape of Good Hope in 1497 and thus promoted the trade in spices and fruit with all the authority of a viceroy of Portuguese India.

The tomato came to Europe from the New World. The numerous different names it was given (golden apple, love apple, paradise apple) prove that it enjoyed extraordinary popularity and, like many foods, was thought to have powers that went beyond just nutrition. It has remained an ingredient of innumerable sauces and meals. In the province of Alentejo in southern Portugal, farmers live predominantly on tomatoes and country bread as well as goat's or sheep's milk cheese. Apart from country bread, cornmeal bread is also very popular in Portugal.

Only ripe, fleshy, and tasty tomatoes ripened under the afternoon sun are suitable for this soup. So, as our chef Maria Santos Gomes advises, it is far better to save making this soup until it can be made in season. In other words, ignore the tomatoes offered all year round no matter how red they are, for nothing can replace a tomato's natural ripening in full sun. Cook these fully ripened tomatoes of the season very slowly with a green pepper or, better still, a pinch of sugar if you want to conceal their slightly acid flavor.

1. Skin and seed the tomatoes. Slice the onion and green chili. Chop garlic and parsley. Place everything into a saucepan.

2. Add oil, butter, pepper, and salt to the vegetables. Braise over a low heat.

Alentejo

3. Pour 2 tbsp / 30 ml unsalted grape vinegar into a pot three-quarters full of water. Bring to a boil. Add the eggs and poach for 3–4 minutes. Then dip them into cold water straight away, drain and trim the edges.

4. To serve, place a slice of bread in each soup plate. Top with a poached egg and ladle the boiling tomato soup around it.

Preparation time: 30 minutes
Cooking time: 15 minutes
Difficulty: ✶

Serves four

1 ocean perch, generous 2 lbs / 1 kg
generous 2 lbs / 1 kg eggplants
7 oz / 200 g tomatoes
3 cloves of garlic
3 onions
$^5/_8$ cup / 50 ml red wine
1 tbsp / 15 ml olive oil

1 tbsp / 15 g butter
7 oz / 200 g Kefaloti cheese (or Parmesan)
1 bunch of basil
salt, pepper to taste

For the Mornay sauce
scant $^1/_4$ cup / 50 g butter
3 tbsp / 50 g flour
$2^1/_2$ cups / 600 ml milk
2 eggs
1 oz / 30 g Parmesan (to yield 2 tbsp / 30 g grated)
salt, pepper to taste

This moussaka, especially designed by Chef Nikolaos Sarantos for Eurodélices, was inspired by the layered combination of minced or ground meat and eggplants that is traditional in Greece. Although it is of Turkish origin, moussaka is served in Greece in a large number of varieties; with potatoes, zucchini or even cheese.

The Jewish inhabitants of Thessalonika have, in fact, developed a number of methods of preparing this meal without contravening their religious principle that prohibits the mixing of milk and meat.

In this recipe, fish takes the place of the meat in a most original composition. Sea perch (or ocean perch, which is actually a member of the rockfish family) is quite common in the Medi-

terranean and a very popular ingredient there. The fillets require a minimum of preparation and are processed without the usual marinade containing cinnamon, bay leaves, and cloves.

Chef Sarantos recommends selecting ripe and tasty eggplants of high quality. Peel them and use only firm and tender flesh of an even color. You can, if you prefer, prepare the ingredients and combine the moussaka in advance. Covered with foil, it will keep in the refrigerator for up to three days. The moussaka is served lukewarm in a big dish, and sprinkled at the last minute with Kefaloti cheese, the spicy goat's or sheep's milk cheese that is ideal for au gratin dishes. As an alternative, try Parmesan instead.

1. Fillet the perch, remove the bones and cut the flesh into fine strips. Use these to line the molds.

2. Wash, peel, and slice the vegetables. Sauté in a pan with olive oil and add red wine.

Mediterranean Sea Perch

3. Cover the base of the greased molds with the vegetables. Then place perch strips and vegetables in alternate layers on top of each other until all the ingredients are used up. Mash the tomatoes and make a puree; season with basil.

4. Prepare a classic Mornay sauce with the ingredients indicated, adding the egg yolks last. Pour into the molds and bake in the oven at 355–375 °F / 180 °–190 °C for ten minutes. Take out and sprinkle with grated cheese. Serve with tomato puree and decorate with basil leaves.

Preparation time: 30 minutes
Cooking time: 15 minutes
Difficulty: ☆

Serves four

4 sheets phyllo dough (or puff pastry – see basic
  recipes)
30 mussels
4 langoustines
scant ⁷/₈ lb / 400 g sea bass
4 asparagus tips
⁵/₈ lb / 300 g carrots
scant ⁷/₁₆ lb / 200 g onions
¹/₈ lb / 60 g leeks
scant ⁷/₁₆ lb / 200 g zucchini
generous ³/₈ cup / 100 ml white wine

scant ¹/₄ cup cognac (or brandy) / 50 ml
generous ³/₈ cup / 100 ml vegetable oil
2 cloves of garlic
8 tsp / 40 g butter
salt, pepper to taste

For the sauce:
2 tomatoes
1 clove of garlic
1 bouquet garni
scant ¹/₄ cup / 50 g butter
scant ³/₄ cup / 200 ml crème fraîche
scant ¹/₄ cup / 50 ml olive oil
generous ³/₈ cup / 100 ml white wine
1 tbsp / 15 g tomato paste
salt, pepper to taste

The Aegean Sea, center of Greek mythology, could well be described as a maze of remote islands and bays, were it not for fear of insulting the peoples of the antique world. Aeacus in his desperation, waiting for his son to return, drowned himself in its waters, and Icarus, flying too close to the sun, also fell to his death into the Aegean. Today, with its variety of scarce fish and crustaceans, the Aegean Sea is worthy of being protected. It is a true treasure chest, with products that therefore deserve being being presented in a "purse," at least in Nikolaos Sarantos' opinion. He adjusted the traditional recipe to use seafood instead of lamb. Phyllo dough, prepared exclusively from flour, water, and salt, has been part of Greek cuisine for centuries, and no culinary fashion has ever been able to diminish its success. In Greek shops you may be able to buy it ready-made;

if unavailable, replace it with puff pastry. If you brush the phyllo layers with butter and oil, they will turn golden brown in the oven.

The contents of this "purse" should include sea bass or a similar fish, such as ocean perch, but stay away from fatty fish. The fish must be fried in a pan, separately from the langoustines, before it is flambéed with alcohol. The other ingredient that our chef recommends is the white, extraordinarily sweet onion from the island of Cephalonie (the largest of the Ionian Islands) which gives the brunoise of finely cut vegetables a perfect consistency. Fortunately, the United States has its own version of a sweet onion in the Vidalia variety, primarily grown in the southern states.

1. Shell the langoustines and dice them as well as the fish. Sauté with the chopped garlic and half an onion, add white wine and then steam. Set aside sixteen mussels in their shells, and open the rest. Cut the vegetables into fine strips and blanch. Sauté half an onion with salt and pepper in butter and add cognac. Combine the ingredients to make the filling.

2. For the "purses," butter the phyllo sheets and place some filling in the middle. Close the sheets to make pouches and tie them up with blanched and cooled leeks. Brown in the oven at 340 °F / 170 °C for about ten minutes. Blanch the asparagus tips and leave them to steep in butter until done.

Aegean Sea

3. For the sauce, sauté the carcasses of the langoustines with some finely chopped onion, garlic and carrot. Add the tomatoes and pour wine and the mussel water over the mixture. Add a tablespoon of tomato paste and the bouquet garni. Reduce and pass through a sieve. Add crème fraîche and reduce again. Add butter.

4. To serve, place a "purse" in the center of each plate, sprinkle with sauce, and decorate with mussels, asparagus tips, and carrots.

Cannelloni with Brandade

Preparation time: 2 hours
Cooking time: 45 minutes
Difficulty: ★★

Serves four

generous 1 lb / 500 g cod, salted
1 potato
4 cloves of garlic
1¼ cups / 300 ml cream
scant ¼ cup / 50 ml olive oil
1 bay leaf
1 sprig of thyme
juice of 1 lemon
salt, black pepper to taste

For the pasta dough:
generous 1 cup / 250 g flour

5 egg yolks
2 tsp / 10 ml olive oil
1 pinch of salt

For the pike-perch filling:
generous 1 oz / 40 g pike-perch fillet
half an egg white
1 tbsp / 15 g capers
2 anchovies
juice of 1 lemon
4 tsp / 20 ml heavy cream
⅛ cup / 20 ml Noilly Prat (vermouth)
salt, pepper to taste

For the tomatoes *à la vierge*:
4 ripe tomatoes
scant ¼ cup / 50 ml olive oil
8 basil leaves
½ tbsp / 10 g poutargue (dried roe)
1 clove of garlic
salt, to taste
pepper, to taste

The terms *boutargue* or *poutargue*, derived from the Provençal *boutargo*, refer to a preparation from dried, salted, and pressed fish eggs often consumed in the Mediterranean region. This exquisite recipe by Franz Schilling was inspired by his Italian friends, who come from a country where cod is prepared in innumerable ways.

The *poutargue* (dried roe) is made from the roe of tuna, swordfish or – on the Côte d'Azur – goatfish, also known as red barbel or red mullet. This is a matter for specialists who have to take into account the maturity of the eggs and the fishing season, both of which influence the duration of the drying period and the dosage of the salt. Buy it ready-made and make sure that it is not too dark, otherwise its salty flavor will be too strong. It must not conceal the delicious flavor of the pike-perch filling, which contrasts nicely with the different salty and sour ingredients, such as anchovies or capers. In Germany the pike-perch, known as a zander, is considered one of the finest of the freshwater fish.

Cod is the basis of every *brandade* (dish made from pureed fish); according to our chef, it should have white rather than yellow flesh, which bears too strong a taste. The *brandade* is presented in small dough tubes as tasty cannelloni made of a delicious pasta dough. Do not poach them too much – the *brandade* will run out if its coat is too soft. Place the rolled cannelloni in the freezer briefly, so that the pasta dough will harden and that the open ends can be sealed perfectly with the pike-perch filling. The second filling should stick even better than the *brandade* filling and therefore needs to be of a firmer consistency.

1. To make the brandade, boil an unpeeled potato. Steep the cod in water. Bring the cream with the garlic cloves to a boil, leave to steep for five minutes, add thyme and a bay leaf and poach the cleaned cod in this liquid for 5–6 minutes. Remove skin and bones, and puree the cooked fish fillet with the garlic cloves, the boiled potato, olive oil, and lemon juice.

2. Using a pastry bag with a medium-sized plain nozzle, pipe the cod puree onto plastic wrap. Roll up into an even sausage and freeze. Remove the plastic wrap and cut into 2½ in / 6 cm long pieces. Roll out the pasta dough thinly, roll it around the brandade center with the pasta dough extending just over an 1 in / 2 cm on either side.

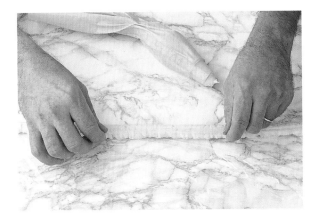

Filling and Poutargue

3. For the pike-perch filling, chop capers and anchovy fillets. Prepare a classic fish filling from pike-perch flesh, egg white, and heavy cream. Lastly add a tablespoon of Noilly Prat (vermouth), the juice of half a lemon and the chopped capers and anchovies and season.

4. Seal the ends of the cannelloni with this filling and cook in boiling water for four minutes. Skin and seed the tomatoes. Dice two-thirds of the tomatoes, combine with four chopped basil leaves and add the olive oil. Pass the remaining potatoes through a sieve and add to the above. Serve the cannelloni with the tomatoes. Sprinkle with poutargue and garnish with baked basil leaves.

Noodles with Boletus Filling

Preparation time: 30 minutes
Setting time: 1 hour
Cooking time: 40 minutes
Difficulty: ★★★

Serves four

For the noodle dough:
8 egg yolks
generous 2 cups / 500 g flour
4 tsp / 20 ml olive oil, salt

For the mushroom filling:
generous 1lb / 500 g boletus
2 shallots each, 1 clove of garlic
1 sprig of parsley
2 tbsp / 30 ml poultry stock, veal stock
salt, pepper to taste

For the frothy Gruyère sauce:
scant $1/8$ lb / 50 g Gruyère
2 tsp / 10 g Parmesan
3 egg yolks
1 bay leaf, 2 sprigs of thyme, 1 clove of garlic

$2/3$ cup / 150 ml cream, 4 tsp / 20 ml whipping cream
$1/2$ tsp / 5 g nutmeg
salt, pepper to taste

For the boletus juice:
$5^1/4$ oz / 150 g boletus, 2 dried morels
$5^1/4$ oz / 150 g button mushrooms
$3^1/2$ oz / 100 g vegetables for roasting
2 tbsp / 30 g butter
scant $1/4$ cup / 50 ml olive oil
generous $3/8$ cup / 100 ml white wine or champagne
1 clove of garlic, a pinch of coriander, 1 bay leaf,
  2 sprigs each of thyme, parsley
salt, pepper to taste

To garnish:
8 boletus caps
4 tsp / 20 g Parmesan, parsley

Our chef, Fritz Schilling, once had to improvise an original composition with a noodle base for the editors of another cookbook. Inspired by the idea of a snail shell, he cut long noodles and rolled them around a suitable filling in the shape of a spiral. The concept allowed him to focus attention on the boletus, which he is most partial to. The recipe developed into a great classic, and he is now presenting it to us.

Irrespective of whether you use boletus from Bordeaux or any other region, wild mushrooms should not be washed in water but cleaned carefully with a brush. This also applies to other types of mushrooms, like the funnel-shaped chanterelles with their irregular edges, the meadow mushrooms, and many others. If you dry the noodles on a kitchen towel as soon as they are cooked and leave them to cool, they will stick better to

the cold filling, provided the filling is not too fluid. The success of this recipe depends to a large extent on the right temperature and the right consistency of both the noodles and the filling.

The frothy Gruyère sauce is a most interesting and tasty creation that definitely leaves scope for further variations, such as adding Emmental cheese or Comté. Even Normandy and Brittany produce excellent Gruyère which can definitely bear comparison with the products of where the cheese originated-the region of Gruyère in the Swiss canton of Fribourg. For the whipped cream use liquid cream with a 32 percent fat content (basic whipping cream) and whip it at a temperature of over 41 °F until thick but not firm.

1. Knead all the ingredients indicated into a noodle dough and leave to rest for an hour. Roll out thinly with a rolling pin and cut into 1 x 20 in / 2 x 50 cm long strips. Cook in salted water, leave to cool and dry on a cloth.

2. For the mushroom filling, chop the boletus, brown them and add the chopped shallots, the veal stock, garlic, and herbs. Reduce the liquid for a few minutes. When cool, spread onto the noodles and roll up the dough into a spiral. Place in an ovenproof dish lined with buttered baking paper and add 2 tbsp / 30 ml poultry stock. Scatter Parmesan over and bake au gratin.

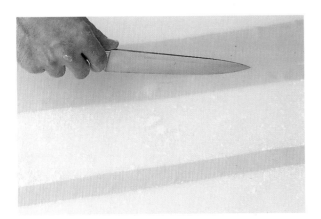

in Frothy Gruyère Sauce

3. To make the frothy Gruyère sauce, bring ²/₃ cup / 150 ml of cream to a boil and add garlic, bay leaf, thyme, and grated nutmeg; leave to steep for 5–6 minutes. Add the egg yolks and whip to a froth in a double boiler. Add grated Gruyère and Parmesan and melt in the hot froth. Pass through a sieve and complete with whipped cream.

4. For the boletus juice, sauté mushrooms and vegetables in olive oil, add herbs and white wine and season with salt and pepper. Pass through a fine sieve after two minutes. Reduce the juice a little and blend with butter. Serve decorated with the two contrasting sauces, small fried boletus caps, Parmesan, and parsley.

Baked Goose Liver

Preparation time: 10 minutes
Cooking time: 25 minutes
Difficulty: ★

Serves four

generous 1 lb / 500 g goose liver (foie gras)
generous 1 oz / 40 g truffles
1¹/₈ cups / 270 g flour
1 egg yolk
2⁷/₈ cups / 700 ml clear beef broth
scant 5 tbsp / 70 ml truffle juice

1 bunch of chives
¹/₄ cup / 50 g sea salt

Geese do not exactly have the reputation for being intelligent. This might be unjustified; it was, after all, the geese of the capital that warned the Romans of an attack by the Gauls. In those days, the first force-feeding methods were developed that would lead to the preparation of foie gras; the methods have hardly changed since then.

Frenchmen often claim that their Gallic predecessors were the true inventors of foie gras. Whatever the true source is, its production varies from region to region. The southwest (Toulouse and Gers) is famous for having achieved real mastery in this respect, and Alsace is known for its pâté de foie gras with truffles, prepared according to old traditions. For years our chefs,

Jean and Jean-Yves Schillinger from Colmar, prepared foie gras in broth, and the reputation of this dish has reached far beyond the boundaries of the area.

It is not true that the biggest goose liver is always the best. On the contrary, its fat content may be very high and its texture might be coarse. Depending on the quality of the corn used for force-feeding, the liver will be white, yellow or pink. Its ideal weight varies between one and one-and-three-quarter pounds (six hundred to nine hundred grams). Our chefs recommend cooking it in an ovenproof glass dish, which allows you to observe it during this critical phase.

1. Wait as long as possible before you halve the liver with a long and very sharp knife; it will then be easier to cut into even slices. Serve this exquisite appetizer in soup plates because the juice is an integral part of the dish.

2. Salt the whole goose liver and brown in a pan without oil, but do not fry. Lay it into an ovenproof glass dish and place the truffles on top. Blend the beef broth with the truffle juice and pour around the liver. Add chives. Cover with a lid.

in its own Juice

3. Seal the dish hermetically with a dough of flour and water as depicted. Brush the dough with egg yolk, and cook in the oven at 480 °F / 250 °C for 25 minutes.

4. Cut the liver into fine slices on a board. Serve two slices on each plate with some broth. Decorate with finely sliced truffles and sprinkle with chopped chives and sea salt.

Preparation time: 10 minutes
Cooking time: 5 minutes
Difficulty: ★★

Serves four

scant ⁷/₈ lb / 400 g cockles
scant ⁷/₈ lb / 400 g periwinkles
scant ⁷/₈ lb / 400 g clams
scant ⁷/₈ lb / 400 g mussels
8 oysters (such as Belon)
3 leeks

1 shallot
1 cup / 250 ml dry white wine
³/₄ cup / 200 ml sherry vinegar
2 tbsp / 30 ml olive oil
1 bunch of chives
1 bunch of dill
salt, pepper to taste

For this appetizer, the bivalves have to be of a certain size, and they should be alive, that is closed, when you buy them. Ideally you should collect them yourself by means of large fishing nets – but who has the chance to do this?

First the shellfish need to be washed in plenty of water, sometimes they must be soaked in salted water to wash out any sand they might still contain (this is a necessary precaution for cockles and clams, which dig themselves into the sand at low tide). Then our chefs, Jean and Jean-Yves Schillinger, stew them to

open up their shells, retaining the condensed water. If you prepare the shellfish ahead of time you can leave them in that same liquid.

Handle the bivalves with great care at all stages, especially when you open them to collect their juice, which serves as a basis for a tasty vinaigrette that is served hot. However, be very careful not to boil the vinaigrette and thus ruin its consistency. Combine it with the seafood and herbs just before serving.

1. Cut the leeks at an angle and cook in rapidly boiling water. Wash the periwinkles in plenty of water and cook them in unsalted water for three minutes. Leave to cool. Use a pin to pull them out of their shells.

2. Wash the cockles and clams in plenty of water. Cook them in a pot with olive oil until they have opened. Remove their shells, clean, and retain the juice.

Marinated Shellfish

3. Open and clean the oysters. Wash the mussels in plenty of water. Finely dice the shallot and then sauté. Add the mussels and equal amounts of white wine and water and cook, covered, for three minutes. Discard the shells, clean the mussels and retain the stock.

4. For the vinaigrette (see basic recipes), blend all the stock with a little olive oil and sherry vinegar. Reheat the seafood in the vinaigrette and use to fill the leek pieces. Serve six or so on a plate, garnished with periwinkles, mussels, and fresh herbs, and dribbled with olive oil.

Crabmeat Crapiau in

Preparation time: 30 minutes
Cooking time: 8–10 minutes
Difficulty: ★

Serves four

scant ⁷/₈ lb / 400 g crabmeat (from a large crab such
   as a blue or stone crab)
4 large potatoes
1 red pepper
1 green pepper
juice of 1 lemon
2 tbsp / 30 g mayonnaise (see basic recipes)
a pinch of cayenne pepper
a little olive oil
salt, to taste
pepper, to taste

For the sauce:
³/₄ cup / 200 ml heavy cream (38% fat)
1 tbsp / 15 g fresh grated horseradish
3 shallots
1 egg yolk
¹/₃ cup / 80 g butter
scant ⁷/₈ cup / 200 ml dry white wine
1 cup / 250 ml poultry stock
1 tbsp / 15 g Dijon mustard
1 bay leaf
1 sprig of thyme
salt, pepper to taste

For the garnish:
2 Italian tomatoes
1 onion
1 bunch of chervil

The term *crapiau* (or *grapiau*) developed from *crapeau*, the French word for toad, through the influence of dialect. In this dish, the crabmeat is pressed flat and thus assumes the shape of a toad. It is comparable to an English fish cake made of fried salmon and finely cut potatoes. In this recipe, this typically British method of preparation is applied to the French *crapiau*, with a crab of American origin in the lead role – a gastronomic combination of three countries.

If possible, use a living crab and cook it in a court bouillon (spiced broth) yourself. Otherwise a deep-frozen crab will do. Season with a basic mixture of salt, pepper, and mustard,

according to the rule. The horseradish must be absolutely fresh; add it at the very last minute because of its strong and prominent flavor. The *crapiau* must be baked immediately before serving; all the other preparations involving the crab may, however, be done in advance.

This combination had a remarkable effect on the promenade decks of the *Queen Elizabeth II*. They were all deserted, because the passengers rushed to the restaurant where our chefs work to sample the delicious crabmeat and the indispensable piquant sauce. If desired, *crapiau* may also be prepared from cod or salmon.

1. Poach the crab in a pot of boiling water. Remove the shell. Dice the peppers finely and blanch. In a metal bowl, combine the crabmeat, the mayonnaise, and the diced peppers. Season with cayenne pepper, lemon juice, salt, and pepper.

2. Peel the potatoes and grate finely. Make a crab crapiau in a round mold. Start with a layer of grated potatoes, continue with a layer of crabmeat and finish with potatoes. Press down lightly.

Horseradish Cream

3. Heat the olive oil in a non-stick pan and fry the crapiau for 3–5 minutes on each side until golden brown. Bake in the oven until done and serve immediately.

4. For the sauce, sauté the shallots and the herbs in a knob of butter. Add white wine and reduce. Add the poultry stock and reduce. Then add the cream, egg yolk, mustard, herbs, and the grated horseradish. Bring to a boil and season to taste. As soon as the sauce has thickened pass it through a sieve and round off with butter. Serve hot, garnished with chopped tomatoes and chervil.

Preparation time: 20 minutes
Cooking time: 20 minutes
Difficulty: ✷✷

Serves four

1/8 lb / 60 g Cheddar cheese
1/8 lb / 60 g blue cheese
1 bunch of asparagus (to yield 12 tips)
2 tomatoes
1 shallot
4 eggs
1/4 cup / 50 g grated Parmesan cheese

scant 7/8 cup / 200 ml cream
generous 1 cup / 250 g butter
1 cup / 250 ml dry white wine
generous 2 cups / 500 ml poultry stock
1 bunch of chives
1 bunch of chervil
salt, pepper to taste

For the Béchamel sauce:
scant 1/4 cup / 50 g butter
scant 1/4 cup / 50 g flour
generous 3 cups / 750 ml whole milk

An "accident" often results in the most creative recipes – in the case of our chefs, Rudolf Sodamim and Jonathan Wicks, that is what happened one day in the *Queen Elizabeth II* kitchens. The chefs forgot their soufflés were baking in the oven, and the only way to rescue them was with a hastily prepared Béchamel sauce. However, the guests were not quite as punctual as they should have been, so the chefs had to put the soufflés back into the oven. That was when they noticed that they could, in fact, be baked twice. In front of all the guests, they were then lifted out of their molds and served covered with butter and asparagus. This creation subsequently became a classic.

As a basis for the soufflés, our chefs recommend Cheddar, a typically English cheese that originated some time in the 16th century, during the reign of Queen Elizabeth I. The little village in Somerset from which it came, situated at the mouth of the picturesque Cheddar Gorge, is certainly less well-known than the yellowish cylindrical or rectangular cheese. Although it is firmly pressed, the cheese is still soft to the touch. Legend has it that Queen Victoria was presented with an impressive thousand pound (five hundred kilo) Cheddar on her wedding in 1840. But you will certainly not need that much to appreciate this slightly fatty cheese, with its pronounced, distinctive flavor.

For harmony, add some soft blue cheese, which the English are particularly partial to without producing it themselves. The Bleu d'Auvergne, Bleu de Bresse or Bleu de Causses would be suitable. The cook will finally decide, of course, but according to our chefs even a Boursin with garlic will guarantee an exciting moment.

1. In a saucepan make a roux from butter and flour. Carefully add the boiling milk.

2. Grate the Cheddar and chop the blue cheese. Add the egg yolks (retaining the egg whites), the Cheddar and the blue cheese to the Béchamel sauce. Whip the egg whites until stiff and fold in gently.

Cheese Soufflé

3. Grease four small soufflé molds and sprinkle with Parmesan. Spoon the mixture into the molds and cook in a double boiler in a hot oven for 8–12 minutes. In a stockpot cook the chopped shallot and the white wine and reduce. Add the poultry stock and the cream and reduce by two-thirds. Stir small pats of butter into the cream over a low heat.

4. Season the sauce to taste and pass through a fine sieve. Slide the soufflés back into the oven until they have puffed up nicely. Dip the tomatoes into boiling water, skin and seed them. Add chives, asparagus, and the diced tomatoes to the sauce. Lift the soufflés out of their molds, serve on plates and sprinkle with the sauce. Decorate with chervil leaves.

Fried Belgian Endive

Preparation time: 30 minutes
Cooking time: 15 minutes
Difficulty: ☆

Serves four

3 Belgian endives
½ lb / 250 g raw goose liver (foie gras)
2 tsp / 10 g butter
1 tbsp / 15 g black truffle
1 tsp / 5 g sugar
1 tsp / 5 g grated nutmeg

1 tsp / 5 ml sherry vinegar
1 tbsp / 15 ml olive oil
salt, fresh-ground pepper to taste

"I am a great friend of chicory," admits our chef, Roger Souvereyns, who has had this recipe on his menu since his 40th birthday. For Roger Souvereyns chicory is a vegetable that lends itself continually to new gastronomic variations, and it has accompanied him throughout his career as a chef. In this case, he is using a close relative of chicory – the Brussels, or Belgian endive (called *chicon* or *witloof* in Belgium), which is popular for its bitter substances and its digestive qualities.

Interestingly, the antique Greeks referred to Belgian endive as "friend of the liver," which might have inspired this combination with foie gras. Very low in calories and with a water content of ninety-five percent, it is a frequent component in health-conscious diets. In our recipe, the fine endive leaves are cooked over a high heat so that the water evaporates. They

should never be kept in the water they were cooked in, or they will acquire a bitter taste. Caramelize them by cautiously adding sugar and keep them warm at an adequate temperature until they are served.

In principle, a raw goose liver has no fat. Cut it carefully into very thin slices to allow these to warm by conduction from merely touching the warm chicory leaves. The also finely cut truffles serve to intensify the flavor of the foie gras.

This recipe is exclusively designed for the endive, and Roger Souvereyns refuses to substitute his beloved vegetable with anything else.

1. Cut the endives into fine strips of 1¼ in / 3 cm. Wash well and dry.

2. Fry the endive strips in oil and butter over a high heat for two minutes. Season with nutmeg, salt, pepper, and sugar. Leave to caramelize and add sherry vinegar.

with Foie Gras

3. Add the finely cut truffles and braise for ten seconds.

4. Spoon the chicory onto the center of the pre-warmed plates. Place the paper-thin liver slices on top to be warmed by the chicory. Season with a little fresh-ground pepper.

Crunchy Vegetable Cake

Preparation time: 1 hour, 30 minutes
Cooking time: 45 minutes
Difficulty: *

Serves four

For the crunchy vegetable cake:
1 large potato (to be cut into 12 thin, lengthwise slices)
4 carrots with greens
scant $1/8$ lb / 50 g green peas
scant $1/8$ lb / 50 g thin green beans
4 large oyster mushrooms
$3^1/2$ oz / 100 g spinach
1 small-medium eggplant (to be cut into 4 slices)

2 tbsp / 30 ml veal stock
1 tsp / 5 ml balsamic vinegar
generous $1/2$ cup / 125 g butter
beef drippings
salt, pepper to taste

For the pea cream:
$2^2/3$ oz / 80 g peas
$1/3$ cup / 80 ml whole milk

For the shallot fondant:
7 oz / 200 g shallots
scant $1/8$ lb / 50 g potatoes (to be finely sliced)
$1/4$ cup / 60 ml cream
light stock

A passionate friend of vegetables, Chef Roger Souvereyns enjoys what he calls "making a meal of them." He only prepares this simple, yet tasty appetizer – where he uses nothing but vegetables – for a dinner with friends, such as a welcome-home party, for example. Any garden vegetable may go into this low-fat and easily digestible delicacy.

The foundation consists of potato sheets that can be cut from any well-sized potato, for instance the yellow-skinned Bintje, which the Belgians claim to have grown since the end of the 17th century, or the popular American Yukon Gold. Slice the potato lengthwise to give the cake structure. Deep-fry the slices in oil that is not too hot; they must remain light brown and slightly juicy.

The garnish of this crunchy cake may be left up to your imagination or preference, and to the vegetables of the season. The pea cream reminds us of the excitement this strange little green ball caused when it was first introduced to the French Court towards the end of the 17th century. Some ladies-in-waiting, so the story goes, could not even resist sampling this new vegetable for breakfast.

If you cook all the ingredients for this appetizer until just *al dente*, you can prepare this dish in advance and heat it up in a warm oven just before serving.

Finally, this recipe is dedicated to Clément, the gardener who faithfully (and skillfully) looks after our chef's vegetable garden.

1. Cook the peas in salted water and leave to cool. For the pea cream, bring the milk to a boil and mix it with the peas in a blender. Pass through a fine sieve, season and keep warm.

2. For the shallot fondant, cook the shallots with the finely cut potatoes, add the light stock and boil down to half the amount within 30 minutes. Add cream.

"Gardener Clément"

3. Deep-fry the potato slices in beef dripping, drain on paper towels and salt. Cook the vegetables in rapidly boiling saltwater and set aside. Sauté the eggplant in a knob of butter, season, and add a dash of balsamic vinegar. Add the veal stock, cook for about three minutes and then keep warm.

4. Reheat all the vegetables separately in butter, sauté the spinach lightly and season. Spoon some onion fondant onto the center of each plate. Then create a crunchy cake with alternate layers of potato, eggplant, potato again, then oyster mushrooms, peas, and green beans. Lastly spoon some pea sauce around the cake and garnish with a carrot, as well as any other herbs or vegetables you might prefer.

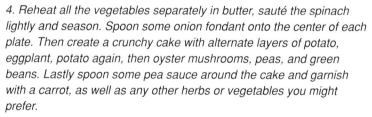

Preparation time: 15 minutes
Soaking time: 12–24 hours
Cooking time: 1 hour, 30 minutes
Difficulty: ★

Serves four

20 prawns
⅝ lb / 300 g dried chickpeas
4 nasturtium flowers
1 onion
1 bunch of chives
scant ¼ cup / 50 ml white wine

½ cup / 125 ml olive oil
½ cup / 125 ml sherry vinegar
½ cup / 125 g flour
salt, pepper to taste

For the green pepper sauce:
2 green peppers
half an onion
scant ¼ cup / 50 ml white wine
scant ¼ cup / 50 ml fish stock
¼ cup / 50 ml extra-virgin olive oil from first pressing
salt, pepper to taste

In Spain the chickpea is an indispensable component of a very popular stew called *cocido*. The best type, according to Chef Pedro Subijana, is grown in the little village of Fuente Saucedo close to Zamora. In the old days people used to retain the left-over chickpeas from lunch and fry them for supper. Our chef applies a similar method.

Chickpeas need to be soaked for a whole night and then cooked for a long time until their indigestible skins are shed. Only then are they fried in sufficient olive oil to cover them. The prawns are only lightly grilled. The best Mediterranean prawns are caught in Andalusia – unfortunately they are also wasted, used as bait for salmon fishing in England.

The nasturtium flower serves two purposes in this recipe. The decorative flower lends the dish a Japanese flair, and its piquant and peppery taste emphasizes the flavor of the chickpea puree. Its taste reminds one a bit of red radish, cress, and capers, and it is most often marinated in vinegar to increase this effect. The Germans call this plant "capuchin cress," a name it owes to its calyx, which resembles the shape of a Capuchin monk's hood. With this flower, Chef Subijana wants to honor his father who, a chef himself, was very fond of this plant.

1. Soak the chickpeas overnight. Heat the chopped onion in a pan, dust with flour and sauté. Add some wine and chickpeas. Cover with water, add salt and cook for 90 minutes. Take out some of the stock for the vinaigrette and add vinegar, salt and pepper. Pass through a sieve.

2. Prepare a chickpea puree in a food processor with part of the peas and the stock. Drain the remaining chickpeas and fry them in hot oil.

Fried Chickpeas

3. Shell the prawns just before cooking them, leaving the last ring of the shell (including the tail) on. Remove the guts and season with salt, pepper, and olive oil. Place in the pan under the grill and cook gently.

4. Seed the peppers, cut into large strips and fry in oil. Add the finely cut onion midway during the cooking process. Pour the oil off and combine the mixture with wine and fish stock. Pass through a sieve, season to taste and add a dash of olive oil. Spoon some chickpea puree onto the plates, garnish each with a nasturtium flower and arrange the prawns decoratively.

Spanish

Preparation time: 1 hour, 30 minutes
Cooking time: 20 minutes
Difficulty: ★★★

Serves four

For the white dough (see basic recipes)
3¹/₂ oz / 100 g flour, 1 pinch of salt
2 egg yolks,
1 egg
2 tsp / 10 ml olive oil

For the black dough (see basic recipes)
7 oz / 200 g flour
1 egg yolk
1 egg
2 tsp / 10 ml olive oil
ink of 3 squid

For the spider crab filling:
generous ¹/₂ lb / 250 g spider crab flesh
3¹/₂ oz / 100 g lobster roe
1 onion, 1 green pepper, 1 red pepper
2 tsp / 10 ml cognac, 4 tsp / 20 ml white wine

For the zucchini cream:
7 oz / 200 g zucchini, 3 shallots
2 tsp / 10 g butter, ³/₈ cup / 100 ml cream
cognac, flour, salt, pepper

For the langoustine sauce:
generous 1 lb / 500 g langoustine carcasses
7 oz / 200 g periwinkles with their shells
1 carrot, 1 leek, 1 onion
3¹/₂ oz / 100 g tomato paste
4 peppercorns, bay leafs, bunches of thyme
4 tsp / 20 ml cognac, 2¹/₂ tbsp / 40 ml white wine
1 quart / 1 l fish stock
¹/₈ cup / 30 ml vegetable oil
scant ¹/₄ cup / 50 g butter
scant ¹/₄ cup / 50 ml cream
2 sprigs of tarragon
salt, pepper to taste

Txanguro is the Spanish name for the spider crab, a crab that Pedro Subijana chose for this recipe after numerous experiments. Thanks to the dyed lasagna dough this dish is a most colorful recipe. In our chef's opinion, it is also the best way of preparing this awkward crustacean. To dye the dough black and to achieve this remarkable color mixture, Subijana uses the ink of *chipirones*, those small squid the Spaniards enjoy from mid-July to mid-September. If *chipirones* are unavailable, any other squid ink or octopus ink is an alternative. All these creatures use the same camouflage system to confuse their enemies – a sudden squirt of black ink.

The spider crab should be bought alive. It should feel heavy and be fairly young, because adult spider crabs move more easily and are often damaged in vicious fights. The female spider crabs carry their eggs in a large fold in the abdomen; these eggs are very sought-after for certain sauces. The crab will be cooked in boiling water for a very short time.

As an accompaniment, our chef recommends a zucchini cream; its mild flavor and creamy consistency complements the maritime essence of this lasagna. Be careful not to season it too heavily and not to combine it with a different vegetable that has an overly pronounced taste.

1. Prepare a white and a black dough (see basic recipes); the results should be of even consistency, and not too sticky. Before you finish processing the white dough, add a few black strips to it. Use a noodle machine to make a thin dough sheet and cut into 3 in / 8 cm squares. Set aside to dry.

2. Clean, cook and shell the spider crab. Sauté the diced peppers in oil and add the chopped onion. Add the crab meat, fry, and flambé with cognac. Pour the wine on, reduce and add the lobster roe. Simmer over a low heat for 20 minutes, adding liquid occasionally.

Txanguro Lasagna

3. For the zucchini cream, sauté the chopped shallots in butter. Add the finely diced zucchini. Keep frying, dust with flour, brown lightly and flambé with cognac. Add the cream and reduce. Season to taste and set aside. Cook the lasagna until al dente in boiling salted water with a dash of oil.

4. To make the langons fine sauce, fry the vegetables and spices (except the tarragon) in oil. Sauté the langoustine carcasses with the tomato paste in oil, flambé with cognac, and add the wine. Pour on the fish stock and reduce by half. Pass through a sieve, add the cream and blend with butter. Add tarragon. Shell the periwinkles. Alternate layers of lasagna and fillings, and serve in a light ring of sauce, garnished with parsley and periwinkle.

Lentil Cream with Frogs'

Preparation time: 20 minutes
Cooking time: 45 minutes
Difficulty: ★★

Serves four

7 oz / 200 g green lentils
1 carrot
1 onion, studded with cloves
1 bouquet garni
$1/3$ cup / 80 ml cream
$2/3$ cup / 150 g butter
scant $1/4$ cup / 50 ml fish stock

salt, pepper to taste
one dozen frogs' legs
4 thin dough sheets (phyllo or Tunisian brek pastry)
$51/4$ oz / 150 g chanterelles
1 bunch of smooth-leaved parsley
1 shallot
1 oz / 30 g black truffles
2 tsp / 10 ml port
$1/4$ cup / 50 g flour

It is high time that we did away with unnecessary prejudices about the quality and the cooking time of lentils. To this end, our chef Émile Tabourdiau has created an appetizer that is ideally suited to altering preconceptions about this starchy food. In France, lentils are grown on a large scale, particularly in the area of Puy-en-Velay where the small, green variety are so esteemed they have earned the *Appelation d'Origine Contrôlée*, which regulates their production. Although they last very well, it is advisable to choose lentils, preferably green ones, of the current year.

Frogs' legs have always been easily available in France. There are excellent frogs from Alsace, and comparable pinkish-skinned ones from central France. If you are unable to obtain frogs' legs or would prefer using another ingredient, you can replace them with fried lobster or finely diced salmon fried in butter. The lentils themselves may be exchanged for an asparagus cream or crushed peas. Remember that dried lentils, unlike other dried vegetables, do not need to be soaked beforehand.

The combination of truffles and lentils adds another subtle touch to this recipe, providing a harmonious accompaniment to the soft frogs' meat. The chanterelle, with its gentle apricot aroma, moreover contributes a rural accent to this dish that suits the frogs' legs – "Aurora's thighs," as Escoffier, the famous chef, once called them.

1. Cook the lentils with a carrot, an onion studded with cloves and a bouquet garni for 30 minutes. Set aside 2 tbsp / 30 g for garnishing and puree the rest in a blender. Add the fish stock and the boiling cream and strain. Add butter and season to taste.

2. Separate the frogs' legs, coat with flour, and fry briefly in a little butter. Add the chanterelles.

Legs and Parsley

3. Chop the shallot and the smooth-leaved parsley and combine with the frogs' legs. Dice the truffles finely, sauté in butter and add port. Add the remaining 2 tbsp / 30 g of lentils.

4. Cut the paper-thin phyllo or brek dough sheets into triangles, place two each with the tips pointing upwards into a brioche mold, and bake at 300 °F / 150 °C for three to four minutes until these "bowls" are crisp. Serve the dough bowls filled with frogs' leg ragout on soup plates, spoon the truffle and lentil cream around the arrangement, and offer the lentil cream separately.

Oyster Fricassee

Preparation time: 15 minutes
Cooking time: 5 minutes
Difficulty: ★★

Serves four

28 medium-sized oysters
8 young carrots
8 turnips
8 young leeks
3½ oz / 100 g fava beans
8 cherry tomatoes

8 radishes
1 dozen snowpeas
generous ³/₈ cup / 100 ml muscatel
⁵/₈ cup / 150 g butter
3 chive sprigs
a pinch of sugar
salt, pepper to taste

At the beginning of spring, the small young vegetables that have not fully matured in flavor are beautifully accompanied by the Beaumes-de-Venise muscatel. This appetizer, from Chef Émile Tabourdiau, is inspired by the traditional spring lamb ragout, though the variation of preparing oysters in a fricassee is probably foreign to most of us.

Some oysters unfortunately "shrink" when they are cooked, like the clear oysters, for example. Our chef therefore prefers using special oysters from the famous oyster beds of Marennes-Oléron. Very fleshy with a slight fat content, these perfect oysters offer all the desired qualities. They must not be cooked too long, however. If these are not available, look for bluepoint or Belon oysters.

Combined with young vegetables, fava beans provide an interesting and refined color effect, and lend the dish the right consistency. Another interesting feature of this appetizer is the balanced interaction between the muscatel and the juice of the oysters: the outstanding wine harmonizes extremely well with the flavor of the algae that the oysters feed on. Rich in mineral substances, they are responsible for the oysters' dark coloring. Nicely chilled, muscatel is also a good wine to drink with this appetizer. When oysters are out of season, our chef recommends substituting them with frogs' legs, which go very well with the muscatel and the garnish.

1. Clean the vegetables and cook individually in water with salt, butter, and sugar. Then combine all the vegetables in a saucepan and keep warm.

2. Open the oysters, drain, and reserve the oyster juice. Shell the oysters and fry in 3½ tbsp / 50 g of very hot butter.

in Muscatel

3. Add the muscatel. Remove oysters from the pot and add to the vegetables.

4. Blend the oyster juice with the oyster stock and reduce slightly. Stir in a few small pats of butter and strain. Arrange the vegetables and oysters harmoniously on the plates, pour some sauce over, and sprinkle with chives.

Flan of Frogs' Legs

Preparation time: 30 minutes
Cooking time: 40 minutes
Difficulty: ★★

Serves four

2.2lb / 1 kg frogs' legs (fresh or deep-frozen)
4 red beets
2 zucchini
1 celery stalk
1 onion
1 carrot

scant ¼ cup / 50 ml white wine
generous 2 cups / 500 ml milk
scant ¼ cup / 50 g butter
scant ¼ cup / 50 g flour
4 eggs
½ cup / 125 ml vegetable oil
salt, pepper to taste

Lombardy, an area of lakes, rivers, and ponds in northern Italy, is home to thousands of amphibians, the best varieties living in the rice fields of the Po plains. For this dish, our chef, Romano Tamani, recommends the small frogs for their tender meat. They can be serve in a sauce, an omelet or in a flan. In principle, the larger frogs should be avoided, since they do not have the same tender quality.

Italian frogs, which are mainly the green frogs, have a similar exquisite taste. In some countries, only deep-frozen, imported frogs are available: these should be thawed in a mixture of water and milk to regain their succulent consistency.

Since the Italian Renaissance, all the knowledge and skills of the chefs employed in the ducal palaces of Ferrara, Bologna, Parma, and Mantua have been focused on the exclusive use – and promotion – of local and regional products. Chef Tamani follows this tradition by suggesting red beets as an accompaniment, which are grown in Lombardy on a large scale. Their color and slightly sweet mild flavor will harmonize well with the frog meat. Season the sauce lightly if you find it too sweet.

Choose firm and shiny zucchini – fairly small ones, if possible – with few seeds. These will brown faster, and they do not lose their consistency.

1. Melt a little butter in a saucepan, add the flour, and make a roux. Bring the milk to a boil in a different pot and gradually add to the roux, until it has an even consistency. Season with salt and pepper and leave to cool.

2. Cook the frogs' legs for ten minutes in a bouillon made of carrot, celery, onion, white wine, and salt. Drain, cut up the frogs' legs and stir them into the Béchamel sauce. Wash and grate the zucchini. Fry them in a knob of butter until golden brown and add to the sauce.

on a Red Beet Sauce

3. For the beet sauce, peel and grate the beets. Cook in plenty of salted water and drain. Heat in a pan with a little oil. Season with salt and pepper.

4. Separate egg yolks from egg whites. Whip the egg whites until stiff. Butter four individual soufflé molds. Blend the egg yolks carefully with the Béchamel sauce, then fold in the whipped egg whites. Pour into the individual molds and bake in the oven in a double boiler at 340 °F / 170° C for 30 minutes. Leave to cool for ten minutes, turn them out of their molds and arrange them on a bed of red beets, garnished with a contrasting green leaf of fresh lettuce or chervil.

Gramigna with Mild Bacon

Preparation time: 30 minutes
Cooking time: 40 minutes
Difficulty: ★

Serves four

For 7 oz / 200 g green "gramigna":
2 eggs
1²/₃ cups / 400 g flour
3¹/₂ oz / 100 g spinach
7 oz / 400 g mild bacon
generous ³/₈ cup / 100 g Parmesan
generous 1 cup / 250 ml balsamic vinegar

¹/₂ cup / 125 ml olive oil
salt, pepper to taste

For 7 oz / 200 g yellow "gramigna":
2 eggs
1²/₃ cups / 400 g flour

Originally this meal was prepared with couch grass, a wild-growing herb that gave the bacon a tangy flavor further emphasized by the balsamic vinegar. Following the century-old culinary traditions, the grass is still used for the fresh pasta that Italians are particularly partial to. As our chef, Romano Tamani attests, *gramigna*, in whatever color, is a fine alternative to tagliatelli, especially in appetizers.

It would certainly be ideal if you could prepare the two-tone *gramigna* yourself, possibly with the help of a special noodle machine that pushes the dough through a grid and produces spaghetti-like threads. If you do not own such a machine you may use ready-made spaghetti (though make sure it is imported, or at least from durum wheat), and break them carefully into small pieces.

Aceto balsamico, the indispensable balsamic vinegar used everywhere in Italy and far beyond Italy's borders, lends this dish its typical character. The Italian town of Modena, where it originated, looks back onto a long tradition. Since the Italian Renaissance, unfermented Trebbiano grapes have been processed into a particularly valuable vinegar that has to mature for up to ten years in specially constructed small vats in order to develop its incomparable aroma. A bottle labeled *aceto balsamico tradizionale di Modena* guarantees its origin and its traditional method of production. The particularly high price is also indicative of the exclusivity of this product used in cold and warm dishes. Here, its prominent flavor seasons the fried bacon, which is one of the other main components of this dish.

1. Dice the mild bacon finely. Prepare the dough to make the gramigna. For the yellow gramigna, blend eggs and flour. For the green gramigna, add the cooked, drained, and chopped spinach to the eggs and the flour. Put both doughs through the noodle machine and cut into small pieces.

2. Fry the finely diced bacon in a pan with very hot olive oil for a few seconds.

and Balsamic Vinegar

3. Season with salt, add the balsamic vinegar and braise until the liquid has boiled down completely.

4. Cook the noodles in a big pot of water, drain and combine with the bacon. Sprinkle with grated Parmesan cheese.

Preparation time: 30 minutes
Cooking time: 1 hour, 40 minutes
Difficulty: ★

Serves four

7 oz / 200 g rabbit meat
generous ⅛ lb / 70 g bacon
2 oz / 50 g tomato
½ lb / 250 g assorted vegetables for roasting
   (celery, carrots, shallots)
1 cup / 250 ml white wine
generous ⅜ cup / 100 ml beef bouillon

5¼ oz / 150 g Parmesan
2 bay leaves
2 sprigs of rosemary
¼ cup / 50 ml oil
1 tbsp / 15 g butter
salt to taste

For the macaroni (generous 1 cup / 250 g):
1⅔ cups / 400 g flour
3 eggs

What would Italian cooking be without pasta? This dish, normally served as an appetizer, is closely linked to the traditions of the neighboring regions of Lombardy and Emilia-Romagna. It is, moreover, a very balanced appetizer incorporating equal amounts of pasta, vegetables, meat, and cheese.

Italians are particularly fond of rabbit meat. They consume more than eight pounds per inhabitant per year and thus take first place worldwide. Try to find firm meat without an excessive amount of fat, dice it finely and cook until light pink. There is, in fact, a more economical version of this recipe, without meat but with plenty of vegetables to obtain the required amount of liquid.

Traditionally, noodles are prepared by hand. It is common to make use of very specific instruments to refine presentation.

For instance, macaroni are shaped into little pipes by means of a small wooden rod, a "pettine," and a grooved board is used for the even pattern of finely crossed grooves on the outside of the noodles. Other instruments applied are, for example, the "chitarra," a wooden frame with metal strings, or the ravioli board.

To round this dish off, our chef, Romano Tamani, recommends a cheese from the Po region, the Grano Padano Parmesan, which he prefers to its classic competitor, the Parmigiano Reggiano from the south. However, if chef Tamani's favorite is unavailable, you may substitute it with the latter.

1. Chop carrots, celery, and shallots very finely. For the macaroni, knead flour and eggs into a dough, roll it out and cut into rectangles. Roll these over the pettine, (a little wooden rod), shape into macaroni and decorate by rolling them over a grooved board.

2. In a pan with olive oil, sauté the diced bacon and the vegetable mixture consisting of carrots, celery, and shallots.

Rabbit Sauce

3. Cut the rabbit meat into small pieces. Add the tomato and the small rabbit pieces, then bay leaves, rosemary, wine and bouillon. Braise for 90 minutes until the liquid is slightly reduced and thickened.

4. Cook the macaroni until al dente. Rinse under cold water, drain and season with the sauce and the grated Parmesan cheese. Serve on pre-heated plates, garnished with fresh herbs.

Filled Tortelli with

Preparation time: 1 hour
Soaking time: 24 hours
Cooking time: 10 minutes
Difficulty: ★★

Serves four

4 langoustines
4 cloves of garlic
1 bunch of parsley
1 tomato
$^1/_4$ cup / 50 ml olive oil

For the dough:
$3^1/_2$ oz / 100 g spinach
$1^1/_4$ cups / 300 g flour
2 eggs

For the filling:
$5^1/_4$ oz / 150 g dried red beans (or dried pinto beans)
$5^1/_4$ oz / 150 g chestnuts
1 onion
$3^1/_2$ oz / 100 g tomatoes
1 cup / 250 ml white wine
scant $^1/_4$ cup / 50 g butter
$^5/_8$ lb / 300 g Parmesan
1 bay leaf
1 cup / 250 ml red wine
1 tbsp sugar
salt, pepper to taste

This recipe unites the agricultural products of the Italian Po plains with the gifts from the sea, symbolized here by the langoustines. Tortelli, tortellone, and tortellini, a few among the numerous varieties of pasta, are all members of the same family and only differ from each other in the way they are cut. The smallest of them, the tortelli, are also affectionately called "navel of Venus" in Bologna.

As is usual for green pasta (but by no means the rule), dye the pasta dough by adding chopped spinach to the eggs and the flour. Even in cooked pasta the spinach flavor will still be recognized. Doctors sometimes refer to spinach as "the stomach's broom" on account of its digestive qualities. If you substitute spinach with the green part of Swiss chard leaves, the color will be the same, but the taste might be more neutral.

According to some sources it was Catherine de Medici who imported beans and chestnuts into France. It is more likely, though, that the bevy of Italian cooks in her company brought a multitude of recipes to France, and that their knowledge then spread among their French colleagues.

Although our chef Romano Tamani recommends Saluggia beans, they are certainly hard to come by anywhere but Italy, so any other red or pink bean that is rich in mineral substances may be used. Green peas are another alternative, even though their taste is somewhat sweeter. The chestnuts have to be soaked for twenty-hours before cooking, as do the dried beans. In the case of fresh chestnuts, the time needed to peel and skin them must also be taken into account.

1. The day before, soak the chestnuts and the beans for 24 hours. Begin the next day's preparations by cooking the chestnuts for 30 minutes with tbsp sugar, and the beans for one hour with the white wine. Melt the butter in a pan, add the finely diced onion as well as the beans and the chestnuts, and fry. Add the tomatoes and the bay leaf and simmer over a low heat. Add red wine and season to taste.

2. Leave this mixture to cool for a few minutes and pass through a sieve. Blend everything with the grated Parmesan into an even mixture.

Langoustines

3. Clean the langoustines well and fry for a few minutes in a roasting pan with olive oil, the chopped garlic, and the small tomato pieces. Then shell the langoustines.

4. For the dough, mix stet eggs, flour and the finely chopped spinach. Roll out the dough, cut out squares of about 4 in / 10 cm for the tortelli and fill with the bean and chestnut mixture. Cook in simmering water for a few minutes. Drain on a cloth and toss them in a little butter. Serve together with the langoustines, dribbled with the remaining tomato, garlic, and olive oil mixture.

Sardine Fritters with

Preparation time: 1 hour
Cooking time: 30 minutes
Difficulty: ★

Serves four

12 sardines
4 zucchini flowers
4 celery leaves
2 red peppers
1 onion
scant ¼ cup / 50 ml olive oil
5 quarts / 5 l peanut oil

4 sprigs of basil
4 sprigs of sage
4 sprigs of cilantro
4 sprigs of smooth parsley
salt, pepper to taste

For the batter:
generous ⅓ cup / 85 g flour
generous ⅓ cup / 85 g cornstarch
3 tsp / 15 g baking powder
generous 1 cup / 250 ml warm water
scant ¼ cup / 50 ml olive oil
fine salt to taste

Fritters are served in various ways, savory or sweet, as appetizers or desserts. They are available in all kinds of shapes and are loved for their lightness as well as for the contrast between the crisp dough and the juicy, succulent contents.

The basic principle of fritter-making is simple. You dip a small piece of vegetable, meat or fish into the batter, and then deep-fry it. Apart from batter you may also use choux pastry or even a yeast dough, though this will need time to rise.

Our chef, Laurent Tarridec, chose a light batter in which to dip the sardines and herbs. As he notes, when you coat frozen food with a batter and then deep-fry it, it experiences a strong thermal shock, and the fritters puff up in weird and wonderful shapes.

Chef Tarridec has his origins in Brittany, but his heart belongs to the Mediterranean. In his opinion, sardines from the Atlantic coast, from Douarnenez or Saint-Gilles-Croix-de-Vie, are just as good as those from Marseilles, Sète or any other harbor of the Midi where they are caught with the aid of lantern lights at night. Most inappropriately, this classic fish with its shiny skin and its moderately fat flesh is squeezed into cans, a complete contradiction of its incomparable quality when fresh.

Serve this dish hot and garnished with parsley. Instead of sardines, fritters may also hide other secrets, like langoustine or cod fillet pieces.

1. Make a well in a mixture of flour, cornstarch, baking powder, and salt and gradually pour in water and olive oil. Blend all these ingredients well. Leave this batter to rest for half an hour.

2. Gut and de-head the sardines. Remove the backbone above the stomach with a filleting knife. Wash and dry the sardines as well as the herbs.

Aromatic Herbs

3. Peel and chop the onion and sauté in olive oil. Add the washed, seeded, and diced peppers. Simmer, covered, for half an hour. Puree in a food processor and keep warm.

4. Dip the sardines celery leaves, zucchini flowers, and the herbs into the fritter batter. Drain and deep-fry separately in hot peanut oil at 320 °F / 160 °C. Drain on paper towels and add salt. Serve three fritters on each plate with a few herbs, garnished with a generous tablespoon of pepper puree and parsley.

Spider Crab Ragout

Preparation time: *1 hour, 30 minutes*
Cooking time: *30 minutes*
Difficulty: ★★

Serves four

2 spider crabs (approximately 1 lb / 12 oz each /
    800 g)
2 zucchini
generous 1 lb / 500 g button mushrooms
4 tomatoes
2 shallots

2–3 cloves of garlic
5/8 cup / 150 g butter, salted
1 quart / 1 l white wine
1¼ cups / 300 ml heavy cream
1 bunch of chervil
1 bunch of basil
1 bunch of parsley
2 bunch of thyme
4 bay leaves
salt, pepper to taste

The appearance of the spider crab and the name it was given (in some languages it translates into "sea spider" are not very flattering. Nevertheless it is a crab *par excellence*, with flesh that is particularly flavorful in spring and in fall. The spider crab has nothing in common with the agile land spider. Rather, it moves quite awkwardly, and its claws are not very effective.

Whenever possible, buy the spider crab alive; its legs should still be moving and its eyes should be shiny. In a good fish market you may also find spider crabs with closed eyes (watch their claws nevertheless). The male ones with slightly larger claws and longer feelers are less meaty than the female ones, but have a more delicious flavor. Their ideal weight generally varies between twenty and thirty ounces (six hundred and eight

hundred grams). Make sure not to cook them for too long, as the stock could neutralize their flavor.

The button mushrooms help to clarify the soup and provide the necessary liquid. Unless you use fresh garlic cloves, add them unpeeled so that the skin filters out any excessive garlic flavor. Zucchini and button mushrooms round off the dish, and the tomato completes it with a touch of sharpness.

Bearing in mind the old Breton traditions according to which "there is no kitchen without butter," our chef, Laurent Tarridec, adds salted butter to the spider crab stock to intensify the flavor of the other ingredients without dominating it.

1. Poach the first spider crab in broth and cook over a low heat for 10–15 minutes. Take the spider crab out, shell it and set it aside. Wash the second spider crab and break it into pieces. Cut the button mushrooms and retain the caps.

2. Cut the stalks into chunks, halve the tomatoes, and mix with parsley, shallots, the remaining herbs and two to three unpeeled garlic cloves. Fry in olive oil. Add the white wine and simmer for 30 minutes. Pass through a sieve and add all the juice squeezed out of the spider crab carcass.

with Salted Butter

3. Swirl butter and heavy cream into the spider crab stock and pour through a sieve. Keep warm.

4. For the ragout, finely dice the mushroom caps as well as the peeled and seeded tomatoes and zucchini. Sauté gently in butter for a few minutes, then season and add the spider crab flesh. Spoon the ragout into the center of the plates and pour the hot soup around it.

Mushroom Cream with

Preparation time: 1 hour, 15 minutes
Cooking time: 30 minutes
Difficulty: ★★

Serves four

generous ¹/₂ lb / 250 g button mushrooms
2.2 lbs / 1 kg river crayfish
2 thin slices Bayonne ham
3¹/₂ oz / 100 g shallots
1 bouquet garni
1 quart / 1 l light poultry stock

scant ¹/₄ cup / 50 g butter
scant ¹/₄ cup / 50 ml cream
1 bunch of chervil leaves
salt, pepper to taste

The art of cooking is subjected to a continual metamorphosis, in which the skills of a great master chef adapts to various quality products, and products are developed to meet the demands, or satisfy the whims, of master chefs.

Hence this creamy soup, which is as delicious in summer as it is in winter. The firm white button mushrooms are a popular ingredient on account of their strong flavor. And, as our chef, Dominique Toulousy cautions, do not use mushrooms with black lamella (the fringe underside of the caps), since that would affect the color of the soup. Rub the mushrooms lightly with lemon juice when you clean them to keep their color, which will help to ensure that the cream will be nice and white. A pinch of curry or saffron will add the final touch to the cream.

Despite all the measures applied to protect the river crayfish, it is threatened with extinction and the fans of this small fresh-water crustacean have good reason to worry. If you have the opportunity, choose crayfish from the rivers of the Languedoc, in Lozère, Gard or Hérault; according to our chef these are the best quality crayfish. Those living in Louisiana in the United States, however, would certainly beg to differ. Do not forget to remove the alimentary canal, that is the black thread below the tail.

It is the incomparable Bayonne ham that finally rounds off this dish. The ham comes from Basque pigs, which, up to the age of nine months, are fed with corn, grain, and barley in accordance with the traditions of this region. The ham has to mature for at least four months. Chef Toulousy recommends in particular the Ibaïona type, an oustanding ham that is a superb treat for any gourmet.

1. Scald the crayfish. Peel the tails and do not forget to remove the alimentary canal. Sauté 3¹/₂ tbsp / 50 g of chopped shallots. Add chopped mushrooms, crayfish shells, and the bouquet garni. Steam covered for five minutes. Pour on the light stock. Cook over a low heat for another 30 minutes.

2. In the meantime, cut one slice of ham into very fine strips and dice the other. Sauté the finely chopped shallots and the finely diced ham in butter. Add the flesh of the crayfish claws, then line four small ovenproof molds with the crayfish tails.

Crayfish and Ham

3. Spoon the ham mixture into the molds lined with crayfish tails, cover with aluminum foil, and place in a double boiler to keep them warm. Remove the crayfish shells and the bouquet garni from the stock.

4. Puree the soup, adding the cream and butter, in a blender. Arrange the contents of the molds in the center of the soup plates. Sprinkle with ham strips and garnish with some chervil leaves. Serve the soup separately in a tureen.

Skate Salad with Lentils

Preparation time: 50 minutes
Cooking time: 35 minutes
Difficulty: ☆

Serves four

4 skate fillets, approximately $^5/_8$ lb / 300 g)
7 oz / 200 g lentils

For the bouillon:
1 bouquet garni
1 carrot,
1 onion
$^1/_4$ cup / 60 ml white wine
1 tbsp / 15 g coarse salt

For the garnish:
1 carrot
1 zucchini
1 onion
1 celery stalk

For the vinaigrette:
$^1/_3$ cup / 80 ml olive oil
scant $^1/_4$ cup / 50 ml sherry vinegar
$^3/_4$ cup / 200 ml poultry stock
1 bunch of chives
1 pinch of curry powder
1 bunch of chervil
1 tbsp / 15 g mustard

It is time to discard those awful memories of a tepid mush of tasteless lentils stuck together in a gooey lump. We are not in a canteen, and the exquisite Ponote lentils that our chef recommends are a totally different story. (Ponote is also the name given to the inhabitants of Puy-en-Velay, a select area for growing green lentils.) The dreaded sessions around the kitchen table sorting out lentils are also a thing of the past, since the little stones have long disappeared. In other words, there is no valid reason to look down on the main ingredient in this delectable warm appetizer, with juicy vegetables that contrast well with the tender flesh of the ray.

"The lentil represents both tradition and modernity. It enchants us with its authenticity and simplicity yet sets no limits to imagination," proclaimed Michel Troisgros, the master chef

from Roanne, in celebration of the lentil from Puy. This variety of lentil boasts a controlled designation of origin and therefore presents itself as a lentil *de luxe*.

To cook the lentils, put them on the stove in cold water and make sure they remain *al dente*. Unlike dried beans, they do not have to be soaked ahead of time. The best accompaniment for them is the skate, also known as a stingray, with its sweet-tasting, somewhat scallop-like flavor. Put the skate on the stove in cold water and take it off when the water has reached boiling point. The salad dressing for the dish, with the pure aroma of sherry vinegar, lends a special character. If you like strong seasoning, you could add horseradish or galangal root for an added bite.

1. Make a bouillon from the ingredients indicated, add the skate fillets, and cook for 12 minutes. Leave to cool in the stock, drain, and set aside to dry on a cloth. Remove the skin and the fat (the black part on the flesh) of the skate.

2. Cook the lentils the classic way for 30 minutes. Mix the ingredients for the vinaigrette.

in Sherry Vinaigrette

3. Dice the carrot, zucchini, onion, and celery stalk finely.

4. Sauté the diced vegetables in butter, add the cooked and rinsed lentils, the poultry stock, and the vinaigrette. Arrange the ray fillets on the plates and scatter the vinaigrette with the lentils evenly around them. Decorate with chervil leaves or sprigs of chives.

Preparation time:	1 hour
Cooking time:	3 hours
Difficulty:	★

Serves four

2.2 lbs / 1 kg veal knuckle
1¹/₂ quarts / 1¹/₂ l light stock
1 carrot
1 onion
1 clove
1 leek
1 bouquet garni of parsley, thyme, and bay leaves
salt, pepper to taste

For the garnish:
scant ¹/₄ cup / 50 g almonds (finely ground)
scant 2 tbsp / 25 g sliced almonds (to be roasted)

For the roux:
scant 2 tbsp / 35 g flour
scant 2 tbsp / 35 g butter

As a binder:
generous ³/₈ cup / 100 ml crème fraîche
1 egg yolk

In this recipe, the only purpose of the veal knuckle is to make a tasty bouillon. The meat itself can be reserved for a different dish, such as a cold salad.

This recipe was designed by a great almond-lover, our chef José Tourneur, who would not hesitate to use ground almonds as a base for any appetizer and sliced almonds as a garnish. Ground almonds are particularly delicious in the cream bouillon, a most subtle blend of different flavors.

The seeds of the almond tree have been known since antique times. From Greece they were passed on to the Romans, who called them "Greek nuts." There are two main types of almonds, the sweet almond that tastes particularly good when fresh and the bitter almond that contains a minimal amount of hydrocyanic acid. Did not Hercule Poirot, the meticulous Belgian inspector of Agatha Christie's detective novels, immediately identify a poisoning by the bitter almond smell?

That said, choose sweet almonds from Morocco, if possible. Ideally, they should be crushed with a pestle and mortar to extend their fresh flavor, but who finds the time for that in this day and age? So do not hesitate to use your grinder.

Preparing this dish is relatively time-consuming because the veal knuckle takes a long time to cook. It is, however, very easy and rewarding, especially if you prepare the light stock a day in advance and use a thick cream. Place the veal knuckle into cold water so that all the meat juices can develop their flavor, and only then add the bouquet garni.

1. Place the veal knuckle into a saucepan with 6 cups / 1¹/₂ l of light stock. Add carrot, onion, clove, leeks and the bouquet garni. Cook it for about two hours until the knuckle is done. Strain the liquid.

2. Prepare a roux from flour and melted butter. Gradually add the bouillon to make a light white sauce and season to taste.

Almond Soup

3. Remove from the stove and bind with egg yolk and crème fraîche before it cools. Blend well until creamy.

4. Grind the almonds into a powder; roast or lightly toast the slivered almonds to be used for the garnish. Place one tablespoon of almond powder onto each plate and add the hot smooth cream. Lastly, sprinkle the cream with roasted slivered almonds.

Preparation time: 1 hour
Cooking time: 5 minutes
Difficulty: ★★

Serves four

4 dozen snails
3 lbs / 1¹/₂ kg spinach
2¹/₂ oz / 75 g cheese (see below)
generous ¹/₂ cup / 125 g butter
4 anchovy fillets packed in oil
scant ¹/₄ cup / 50 g dried bread crumbs

¹/₂ tsp nutmeg
salt, pepper to taste

Namur is justifiably proud of its little spotted snails (*petits gris*), which are famous all over Europe for their fine flesh and flavor. Our chef, José Tourneur, created this recipe especially for Eurodélices; it is also an allusion to a poem by Jacques Prévert ("Funeral of a spinach leaf left behind by two snails").

The preparation of these small molluscs requires a certain amount of care. Since snails are eaten whole, they must be taken out of their shells very gently. Soak them in vinegar water first to rid them of sand. It is quite easy to cook them in butter, but they can also be prepared in a brunoise with tender chopped vegetables and a fragrant bouquet garni.

The snails are served on plates with blanched and steamed spinach leaves. Season the spinach just before you spoon it over the snails. The flavor of the snails mingles with the juicy consistency of the spinach and the sautéed shallots seasoned with pepper and nutmeg. The anchovy fillets in oil should be used sparingly so as to not spoil this precious balance by an excessive amount of olive oil. As for the cheese to be grated into the spinach and then sprinkled on top, the choice is up to you, but try Emmental or Gruyére if you need some inspiration.

There is much competition amongst restaurant owners around Namur, who are constantly vying for new ways to prepare their famous snails for their menus. This extremely original appetizer will gradually draw you closer to this famous town, with its impressive castle and remarkable snails.

1. Sauté the shelled snails in a pan with butter, making sure they remain moist and do not dry out.

2. Blanch the spinach for a few minutes and then sauté in butter. Stir over a high heat to make a thick puree.

Au Gratin

3. Season the spinach with salt, pepper, and nutmeg. Grate the cheese. Add two-thirds of the grated cheese and a teaspoon of finely diced anchovy fillets.

4. Spoon a third of the spinach into a buttered dish suitable for au gratin baking. Place the snails on top and cover with the rest of the spinach. Combine the bread crumbs and the remaining grated cheese, and sprinkle over the spinach. Trickle melted butter on top before browning under the grill for five minutes. Serve immediately.

Green and Yellow Farfalle

Preparation time: | 1 hour
Setting time: | up to 12 hours
Pickling time: | 2 hours
Cooking time: | 15 minutes
Difficulty: | ✶✶

Serves four

For the yellow dough:
generous 1 cup / 250 g durum wheat semolina flour
1 egg
4 egg yolks
1 tbsp / 15 ml olive oil
a pinch of salt

For the green dough:
generous 1 cup / 250 g durum wheat semolina flour
1 egg

4 egg yolks
3 spinach leaves
1 tbsp / 15 ml olive oil
salt, pepper to taste

For the sauce:
1 eggplant
4 boletus or button mushrooms
1 ripe tomato
1 shallot
2 sprigs of parsley
2 sprigs of thyme
2 sprigs of basil
1 tbsp / 15 g butter
salt, pepper to taste

You have to have some background in Italian cuisine to be able to distinguish the traditional pasta shapes from the new specialties invented daily. Italian gourmets put aesthetics above everything, incessantly varying shapes and colors to please the eye and palate in new ways. Green noodles (with spinach, basil or parsley) are the great classics. The butterfly shape (farfalle or farfallini) has long been popular in Italy and abroad.

Here our chef, Luisa Valazza, demonstrates how green pasta is prepared. Start with lightly blanched spinach, which you squeeze in a cloth to remove any excess water and to retain the consistency of the dough later. Refrigerate the dough for a while before you roll it out. Ideally, you should prepare the dough a day ahead and leave it, covered, in the fridge overnight. Then roll out the dough very thinly, join the different color rectangles together and pinch them with your fingertips to give them the desired bowtie shape.

Dried boletus stalks, and the eggplants that are so bountiful in Campania, Sicily and Calabria, are also a traditional accompaniment. Before you prepare the eggplant, pickle it in salt for two hours; it thus will be drained of water and much easier to cook. Thyme, a wonderful herb that is valued in every kitchen, lends the warm pasta a delicate aroma. It also has important medicinal qualities. Thyme has an antispasmodic effect and its essential oil provides a very strong antiseptic.

1. To prepare the green dough, blanch the spinach and squeeze it out well. Combine the egg, egg yolks, and spinach leaves and add flour, oil, and salt to make a dough. Prepare the yellow dough similarly, but without spinach. Leave to rest for at least an hour.

2. Roll out the two dough balls into thin strips. Join the green strips with the yellow ones by simply moistening the edges and sticking them together. Cut into 2-in / 5 cm squares. Pinch them in the middle with your thumb and index finger into the shape of butterflies (or bow ties).

with Button Mushrooms

3. Dice and blanch the eggplant. Chop the mushrooms. Sauté the shallot, tomato, eggplant cubes, and mushrooms in a pan with a little oil and season to taste.

4. Cook the noodles for five minutes until al dente. Drain and add to the sauce. Also add chopped parsley, thyme, basil leaves, and a pat of butter. Leave to braise for a few minutes, then and serve very hot, garnished to your taste.

Pennette with

Preparation time: 20 minutes
Cooking time: 8 minutes
Difficulty: ★

Serves four

scant $^7/_8$ lb / 400 g fresh or dried pennette
tomato sauce from fresh tomatoes (if desired)
1 garlic clove
4 tomatoes
1 shallot

1 anchovy fillet
1 tsp / 5 g capers, chopped
1 tsp / 5g black olives,
1 tsp / 5g chili pepper
1 bunch of basil
$^1/_4$ cup / 50 ml olive oil
$^1/_4$ lb / 50 g Parmesan cheese
salt, pepper to taste

Preparing pasta without turning it into an unappetizing mush requires a fair amount of skill. To avoid a temperature shock that could have disastrous effects (for one, it could ruin the consistency), do not submerge the cooked and drained noodles in cold water to stop the cooking process. And, if you serve the noodles in a sauce, thin it with a few tablespoons of the noodle water before you stir them in. These are helpful tricks for this very subtle recipe with its rich flavors that will, if prepared right, undoubtedly delight your guests.

The noodles chosen here are pennette, or small penne rigate. Their shape is inspired by the larger macaroni cut at an angle. There are medium-sized penne as well (mezze penne), which are relatively common.

The success of this recipe depends to a large extent on the quality of the tomatoes, a fruit of American origin that was introduced to Europe in the 16th century via Naples and Genoa. In our recipe, this "golden apple" accompanies typical Mediterranean ingredients, the amount and combination of which is left up to your personal preference. This kind of option is what causes debates in the Valazza family: Mr. Valazza enjoys this dish with red peppers, whereas Mrs. Valazza insists on Parmesan. In this case, domestic peace is restored by accepting variety as the rule. Our chef, Luisa Valazza, recommends the tasty black olives from Liguria, but green olives may be used as an alternative. The fine aroma of basil, however, is indispensable.

1. Chop the black olives, chili pepper, garlic, and shallot; slice the anchovy. Heat the olive oil in a pan and sauté the chopped garlic, shallot, anchovies, capers, the black olives, and chili pepper.

2. Then add the sauce made of fresh tomatoes (essentially pureeing garlic and fresh tomatoes before adding them to the mélange). Cook for a few minutes, while stirring.

Mediterranean Flavors

3. Cook the pennette in boiling salted water until al dente, drain, and set aside. Dip the tomatoes briefly into boiling water, leave to cool, cut the tops off and hollow them out.

4. Fry the pennette in the sauce. Add a 1 tbsp / 15 g of Parmesan and 1 tbsp / 15 g of chopped basil. Fill the tomatoes with pennette and sauce, arrange on plates, and sprinkle with the tomato sauce.

Spaghetti with

Preparation time: 20 minutes
Cooking time: 15 minutes
Difficulty: ★

Serves four

14 oz / 400 g spaghetti
3 small artichokes
3 dried boletus mushrooms
1 onion (approximately 1 oz / 30 g)
1 garlic clove
juice of half a lemon

1 tbsp / 15 ml fresh tomato sauce (see below)
2 tbsp / 30 g butter
1 tbsp / 15 ml olive oil
2–3 tbsp / 40 ml dry white wine
1 bunch of parsley
salt to taste

You may feel lucky if you have genuine durum wheat flour to prepare pasta with a high gluten content. In this respect only, Canada (especially the area around Manitoba) and parts of the United States can keep up with southern Italy, where this type of flour has always been used for spaghetti. These noodles, with their remarkable structure, have nothing in common with the pale industrial products you find on any supermarket shelf. If you do wind up shopping for pasta, in the U.S. and Canada you should certainly be able to find Italian imported pasta, which will be made with the right kind of flour.

Chef Luisa Valazza prepares a typically Mediterranean recipe here, including products from several Italian regions – artichokes from Liguria and tomatoes from Sicily. The Italians are the main producers of artichokes and export them predominantly to France. The small Ligurian artichoke is still very similar to the thistle. With lots of prickles but without a choke (or

beard) it is mainly consumed raw in salads. These artichokes' hearts do not need to be blanched; it suffices to cut them into fine slices and to cook them until *al dente* like noodles. Prepared like this, they retain their exquisite flavor. Prepare the artichoke as soon as you have cut it to prevent it from oxidizing and thus developing a sharp taste. If Ligurian artichokes are not available, search for small globe artichokes, which will have a similar flavor. The tomato sauce can be made simply, by pureeing tomato with garlic, salt, and pepper, or these ingredients can be sautéed ahead of time so there is sauce on hand. In any case, the sauce should be fresh.

This *primo piatto* must not be burdened with cheese, as that would weigh too heavily on the diner. Rather add a modest amount of dried boletus that have been briefly soaked in water to regain their volume and consistency. Keep the artichoke leaves to decorate the plates.

1. Prepare the artichokes, cut the hearts into fine slices, and place them in cold water with a dash of lemon juice. Leave the boletus to soak in a little lukewarm water.

2. Sauté the clove of garlic, the onion, and the soaked boletus in a pan with a little olive oil.

Artichokes

3. Add the artichoke heart slices and cook. When a third of the cooking time has lapsed, add a tablespoon of tomato sauce. Increase heat after ten minutes and add 2–3 tbsp / 40 ml tablespoons of white wine.

4. At the same time, cook the spaghetti in saltwater until al dente and drain. Add butter and chopped parsley to the artichokes and combine with the spaghetti. Serve on plates, decorated with artichoke leaves.

Eggplant Cakes

Preparation time: 10 minutes
Cooking time: 10 minutes
Difficulty: ★★

Serves four

3$\frac{1}{2}$ oz / 100 g bonito tuna (or yellowback, skipjack, or bluefin tuna)
3$\frac{1}{2}$ oz / 100 g salmon trout
1 eggplant
3$\frac{1}{2}$ oz / 100 g carrots
3$\frac{1}{2}$ oz / 100 g spinach

3$\frac{1}{2}$ oz / 100 g green beans
$\frac{7}{8}$ cup / 200 g flour
1 bunch of smooth-leaved parsley
1 tbsp / 15 g oil
4 tsp / 20 ml cream
$\frac{1}{8}$ cup / 30 ml whole milk
1 tsp / 5 g nutmeg
salt, pepper to taste

The bonito, a large type of tuna, lives mostly in warm waters, and is found in the Mediterranean, the Atlantic, and the North Sea. Its flesh, with characteristic white stripes, is perhaps slightly fatty, but very tender. Bonito and bluefin tuna have much in common, and are also prepared similarly. The salmon trout, which accompanies the bonito in this inventive appetizer from Chef Freddy Van Decasserie, is at its best from April to June; the fish is actually a trout that has matured on a seafood diet, which colors its flesh. This light pink flesh is a delicacy and must always be prepared when very fresh. A firm round belly and a very stiff body with shiny scales are indications of its freshness.

Although eggplants are available all year round, their flavor is best in summer. Choose medium-sized unblemished specimens with a very shiny dark skin, as large eggplants often have too many seeds. If you dip the slices into milk, then coat them with flour and gently tap off any excess, they will turn out tender and succulent.

The vegetables should provide some color variety to intensify the visual impression of this appetizer. Choose anything you like, except early green peas with their soft green hue. Add a little water and cream to the spinach and carrot purees to give them a creamier texture.

You can build the pyramid form of this without any difficulty if you first cut the fish into very thin slices. Baked on the grill, bonito and salmon trout retain their succulent consistency and freshness.

1. Cut the eggplant into $\frac{1}{4}$ in / $\frac{1}{2}$ cm rounds. Season with salt and pepper. Dip the slices into milk and coat them with flour. Fry in oil over a high heat for two minutes on each side.

2. Steam and dice the carrots finely. Proceed similarly with the beans. Blanch the spinach, chop finely and heat with 4 tsp / 20 ml cream and a pinch each of salt and nutmeg. Use part of the spinach and the carrots to make a puree.

Fisherman's Style

3. Clean the salmon trout and the bonito carefully. Fillet them and remove the bones. Cut both fish into thin, even slices.

4. Slide the fish slices briefly onto the grill. Then, build a pyramid of eggplant slices covered with salmon trout and bonito. Place them in alternate layers on top of each other with vegetables in-between. Spoon a green and orange ring of spinach and carrot puree around the pyramid, and garnish with parsley leaves.

Asparagus, Morels, and Young

Preparation time: 30 minutes
Cooking time: 30 minutes
Difficulty: ✳

Serves four

20 small potatoes
20 green asparagus shoots
3¹/₂ oz / 100 g fresh morels
scant ¹/₄ cup / 50 g butter
³/₄ cup / 200 ml chicken stock
scant ¹/₄ cup / 50 ml chicken juice
1 bunch of smooth-leaved parsley

For the sauce:
scant ¹/₄ cup / 50 ml cream
scant ¹/₄ cup / 50 ml olive oil
1 pinch of nutmeg

Several centuries ago, people believed that mushrooms had diabolic powers. The poisonous ones do present a real danger, whereas the edible ones offer great culinary pleasures: if there is anything diabolical about a morel, perhaps it would be how delectable this mushroom is. The morel, highly esteemed for its refined taste, is best between March and May. The conical honeycomb-patterned cap protruding over its white stalk is often full of sand or small stones and has to be brushed very thoroughly. Since fresh morels are very scarce, you may use dry morels, which you have to soak in water for a few moments until they regain their original shape and tenderness.

The green asparagus should be fresh, medium-sized and firm. If you rinse the spears under cold water right after they are cooked, they will retain their fresh color. In spring they are outstanding, just like the small potatoes, preferably the Grenaille, which turn both creamy and crisp when prepared. Early potatoes, such as new potatoes, can substitute for the Grenaille if the latter are not available.

Nutmeg has many useful qualities: it is applied in the pharmaceutical field for a variety of cardiotonic and digestive drugs. It is the kernel of the fruit of the nutmeg tree, common in the Antilles, on Réunion Island, and in southeastern Asia. It contains a substance called nutmeg butter with a high fat content. You should always buy a whole nutmeg and grate off as much as you need at the time; this way it will retain its aroma for years.

1. Trim the stalks of the morels and clean the mushrooms thoroughly in clear water. Halve or quarter them depending on their size.

2. Melt 5 tsp / 25 g of butter in a hot pan. Salt and pepper the morels and sauté them with the chicken (or poultry) juice for a few minutes. Set aside.

Potatoes in Nutmeg Cream

3. Fry the potatoes in clarified butter. Add the asparagus and the chicken stock after five minutes. Cover with baking paper and cook in the oven for 20 minutes.

4. Add the morels and cook for another five minutes. Add the whipped cream and the grated nutmeg. Arrange the drained asparagus on plates, and place the morels and potatoes on top. Reduce the sauce and whisk in the olive oil. Cover the dish with sauce, and decorate with smooth-leaved parsley. Serve immediately, while still hot.

Cream of Bean Soup

Preparation time: 2 hours, 30 minutes
Soaking time: 12 hours
Cooking time: 2 hours
Difficulty: ✶

Serves four

7 oz / 200 g dried navy beans
16 preserved duck stomachs
1 scant 2 oz / 50 g black truffle
1 carrot

1 onion studded with clove
1 bouquet garni
generous 1 cup / 250 ml whipped cream
1 quart / 1 l light poultry stock
salt, pepper to taste

Legend has it that a Florentine canon once slipped a little pouch of dried beans into the bags of Catherine de Medici and thus introduced the French people to this originally American vegetable. If this is true, the appearance of the bean can be dated back to 1533, the year the fourteen-year old Catherine de Medici arrived in France to marry the Dauphin, the future Henry II. The type, shape, and color of those beans is, however, mostly unknown.

Nowadays, white beans are sold on markets from September. Some come in colorful pink pods, others in yellow ones – the more tender and tasty type, apparently. For this classic French dish, Gérard Vié recommends the smallest of the white beans, the navy bean that is also used in the *cassoulet*, a famous

French stew. Remember that the older the beans are the longer you have to soak them. This has a marked effect on the digestibility of this high-protein dish.

In Chef Gérard Vié's opinion, the beans should be cooked with a piece of bacon so they assume a subtle bacon flavor. They have to be soft and digestible, which requires time and a large amount of water, since beans triple in volume. Scoop off the foam when the bouillon has cooked for fifteen minutes; then cover it and continue cooking over a low heat.

Despite the long preparation period, this warm appetizer is much enjoyed throughout winter.

1. Soak the beans in cold water the night before. The next day, drain them, add the studded onion, the carrot, and the bouquet garni and bring to a boil. Add the light poultry stock and cook over a low heat until the beans are tender.

2. After cooking for about two hours, remove the onion, carrot, and herbs. Continue cooking the beans for a short while, then puree.

with Duck Stomach

3. Add the cream and the reserved stock and bind the beans to a thick soup. Pass through a sieve, cut the duck stomachs into thin slices and heat in the pan.

4. Slice the truffles finely. Pour the hot bean cream into soup plates and arrange the truffle slices on the cream. Finally, add the fried duck stomachs, and serve hot.

Ragout of Caramelized

Preparation time: 4 hours
Soaking time: 12 hours
Cooking time: 2 hours
Difficulty: ★★

Serves four

1 calf's tongue
1 piece of calf's head (about 2.2 lbs / 1 kg)
1 veal sweetbread
2 veal knuckles, boned
2 carrots
2 onions
1 celery stalk
1 quart / 1 l veal stock

1 quart / 1 l red Banyuls
1 quart / 1 l red wine
1 cup / 250 ml port
scant $\frac{1}{4}$ cup / 50 ml oil
1 bouquet garni
salt, pepper to taste

For the garnish:
20 asparagus tips
$3\frac{1}{2}$ oz / 100 g fava beans
1 bunch of young carrots
1 bunch of young turnips
1 bunch of cocktail onions
1 bunch of chervil

In the 17th and 18th centuries, offal was very popular. Calf's head, for example, was prepared in many different ways, some considered fit for a king. With the traditions of those days in mind, our chef, Gérard Vié, presents a most original warm appetizer based on various calf's innards. You can even save it for several days if your guests, against all odds, leave any leftovers.

When you buy offal, both red and white, make sure it is very fresh and in immaculate condition and prepare it straight away. Soak it first for quite a long time to remove the unavoidable bloodstains and marks. Owing to this procedure, this recipe requires a number of steps that should be spread out over two to three days. With regard to the veal sweetbread, the most del-

icate part of the offal, take a few precautionary measures into account. Remove any yellowish fibers, any traces of blood or other tissue, and use only the very white, odorless meat.

Choose tender young vegetables to accompany this ragout. Prepare them individually, according to their requirements, and as late as possible to preserve their full flavor. This refers particularly to the fava beans, which have to be skinned beforehand, particularly if they are older beans with their indigestible white skins. Prepare a few more than planned; you will find that you will be continually tempted to sample them. Banyuls, with its high sugar content, is ideal for caramelizing. The wine will lend the dish a superb flavor.

1. Soak all the offal in cold water overnight to rid it of any traces of blood. Then blanch it and leave it to cool. Drain and clean it, and cut the meat into cubes.

2. To cook the meat in Banyuls, heat all the offal pieces in oil first and add the finely cut carrots, celery, and onions and the bouquet garni.

Offal with Banyuls

3. Brown and spoon out the fat, then add port and Banyuls. Boil down and add the remaining red wine. Reduce again, add the veal stock and cook over a low heat for an hour and a half.

4. Cook the vegetables individually in salted water, then braise them together in a pan with the offal stock. Remove the offal pieces, strain the liquid, and reduce to a creamy sauce. Add the offal pieces again. Serve on deep plates and sprinkle with chives. Garnish with vegetables, and serve very hot.

Preparation time: 1 hour
Cooking time: 2 hours
Difficulty: ★★

Serves four

14 oz / 400 g lasagna noodles (see below)
7 oz / 200 g pig's head
7 oz / 200 g potatoes
2 carrots
1 celery stalk
1 onion

1 lemon
3¹/₂ oz / 100 g Parmesan cheese
¹/₄ cup / 60 g butter
1 cup / 250 ml olive oil
1 tbsp / 15 ml balsamic vinegar
2 fresh oregano sprigs
1 bay leaf
salt, black pepper to taste

In this recipe, our chef, Gianfranco Vissani, prepares the lasagna filling from a pig's head, an ingredient that is highly valued in Italy. He thus adds another novelty to a concept that has a host of varieties. This dish is an illustration of Vissani's own definition of the art of cooking: "Creativity and an enormous amount of technology as well as knowledge of herbs and vegetables, generously seasoned with love."

Choose a fat pig's head. For inexperienced cooks, boning it will take some time, but in the end it is only a matter of patience. The lasagna should be well seasoned to disguise the gelatinous consistency of the pig's head to a certain extent. You could also use thin slices of big eggplants; your guests will appreciate their flavor and color.

Fresh oregano, also called wild marjoram, is widespread in Italy and Crete as well as in other dry areas. This very aromatic herb gives the potatoes a superb flavor. Apparently, even the Romans made use of its medicinal, nerve-strengthening qualities. Today oregano is used in the pharmaceutical field for its tonic effect. The plant also produces an essential oil that is highly valued in perfumery.

See the Basic Recipes at the back of this book for a simple preparation for lasagna noodles – in this case, white noodles. Or, alternately, you may buy ready-made noodles, but only those made from durum wheat flour, and not the tasteless, homogenized variety that masks as real pasta and is ubiquitous on market shelves.

1. Cook the pig's head with carrots, onion, celery, lemon, a bay leaf and a pinch of salt for an hour and a half.

2. Bone the pig's head and cut into slices. If you have prepared lasagna dough, roll it out and cut into 3 in / 8 cm wide long noodles. Cook the lasagna sheets in salted water and drain.

Oregano and Pork

3. Peel and wash the potatoes and cut them into round slices. Brown lightly in olive oil. Right at the end, season with salt and pepper and add fresh, chopped oregano.

4. In a buttered ovenproof dish, layer the potatoes, pork, and lasagna sheets on top of each other, repeating three times and ending with a layer of lasagna. Grate Parmesan; sprinkle the cheese and 2 tbsp / 30 ml tablespoons of melted butter over the lasagna and bake in the oven at 355 °F / 180 °C for ten minutes. Take out and leave to rest for five minutes. Sprinkle with balsamic vinegar and garnish with fresh herbs.

Preparation time: 20 minutes
Cooking time: 2 hours,
                       30 minutes
Difficulty: ★★★

Serves four

14 oz / 400 g egg noodle dough (see below), or
   noodles as desired
generous 1 lb / 500 g rabbit meat
5 oz / 150 g sheep's milk cheese
1 cup / 250 ml vegetable brunoise from celery,
   carrot, onions (see below)

2 cups / 500 ml chicken stock
5 spinach leaves
2 cloves of garlic
1 tomato
1 sprig of rosemary
3 sage leaves
2 bay leaves
1 small chili pepper
1 bunch of chervil
generous $^3/_8$ cup / 100 ml red wine
$^1/_2$ cup / 125 ml extra-virgin olive oil
salt, black pepper to taste

Rabbit meat has been used in numerous dishes since time immemorial. This recipe, from Chef Gianfranco Vissani, is based on culinary traditions that have been passed on right through the whole history of the Italian peninsula. The very prominent flavor of the rabbit meat (preferably a young male specimen) will certainly delight your guests. To make sure that the rabbit is fresh when you buy it, check that its fur is shiny and its paws are still covered with hairs. Do not leave it to hang, as rabbit meat goes off quickly. Or, if you are not keen on game, you might want to use poultry instead of rabbit.

The central component of this recipe is the noodle dough prepared with eggs. Use at least forteen egg yolks for this recipe.

If our chef has his way you will have to use no fewer than thirty egg yolks for two pounds (one kilo) of flour. If this far exceeds the amount you require, you can keep what is left over and use it for lasagna, tagliatelle, ravioli, tortellini, spaghetti or any other traditional noodle recipes at a later stage. As an alternative, you can, of course, also use dry noodles. The freshness of the spinach is of utmost importance, since the structure of the leaves used to line the mold determines the appearance and the success of the whole dish.

1. Heat olive oil in a pan and add the brunoise, the chopped garlic, sage, bay leaves, rosemary, and chili pepper and braise for ten minutes. For the rabbit ragout, dice the rabbit meat and brown lightly in oil.

2. Add a dash of red wine and cook over a low heat for two hours. To prepare the sauce, mix some chopped tomato with the olive oil and thin with a ladle of poultry bouillon. Puree the mixture in the blender and then pass through a sieve. Add to the rabbit ragout.

Rabbit Sauce

3. Before the rabbit ragout has totally boiled down, add the rabbit stock prepared from the rabbit bones and take off the stove. Line small pâté molds with raw spinach leaves. Cook the noodles, drain them, place them in a pan, add rabbit ragout and mix with a fork.

4. Fill the molds with noodles, cover with grated sheep's milk cheese and bake in the oven for five minutes. Turn the pappardelle out of their molds, arrange them on plates and spoon sauce around them. Decorate with tomato cubes and chervil leaves.

Polenta

Preparation time: 30 minutes
Cooking time: 30 minutes
Difficulty: ★★

Serves four

7oz / 200 g sheep's milk ricotta
7oz / 200 g fresh anchovies
4 tsp / 20 g white cocktail onions
1³/₄ oz / 50 g garlic
half a chili pepper
2 tbsp / 30 ml olive oil
1 bay leaf
salt, black pepper to taste

For the polenta:
⁵/₈ lb / 300 g cornmeal
3¹/₄ cups / 800 ml mineral water
scant ¹/₈ lb / 50 g sheep's milk cheese
¹/₂ tsp olive oil
salt, pepper to taste

Traditionally, polenta is a porridge made of fine-grain corn semolina, which, according to historical records, was already a staple food in pre-Columbian civilization. The corn fritters were so popular that cornmeal was called "golden rain" on account of its fascinating beautiful color. Chef Gianfranco Vissani here presents a dish that was originally designed for pork ragout, but is now prepared with onions and anchovies in keeping with Sicilian tradition.

You should use small fresh anchovies with firm and shiny bodies that are easy to clean. As soon as the head is removed, you should be able to take out the backbone without any difficulty. Outside the main fishing grounds in Spain, Italy or the French Midi, fresh anchovies are extremely hard to find.

It is an Italian custom to invite friends for the preparation of a polenta: they are then enlisted in helping to stir the flour slowly into the boiling water. The polenta must be liquid and creamy and not have any lumps. It must also be served as soon as it is cooked, which requires last-minute preparation. The same applies to the mixture of anchovies and onions. The anchovies can be substituted with tomatoes and garlic, but that is a matter of taste and personal choice.

Ricotta, available in any good cheese shop, is a very versatile sheep's milk cheese with a surprisingly light consistency. In this recipe, as Vissani insists, it should not be replaced by any other cheese.

1. Add a drop of olive oil, the grated sheep's milk cheese, and salt and pepper to the mineral water. Bring to a boil. Add the cornmeal and cook over a low heat for 20 minutes, stirring it with a wooden spatula. Sauté the cocktail onions with chopped garlic, bay leaf, and the half of a chili pepper in a pan with oil and brown lightly.

2. Clean and wash the anchovies, cut them into small cubes and combine them with the onions. Cook for a maximum of two minutes and take off the stove.

with Ricotta

3. Spread a $^1/_2$ in / 1 cm thick layer of cooked polenta in an ovenproof dish. Place the onion and anchovy mixture on top, and sprinkle with the oil of that mixture.

4. Scatter the diced ricotta and the rest of the grated sheep's milk cheese over the polenta. Slide under the grill for a few minutes. Take it out, sprinkle with fresh grated garlic, and serve hot.

Preparation time:	15 minutes
Cooking time:	20 minutes
Difficulty:	✭

Serves four

¾ lb / 350 g fresh tuna, such as bluefin, cut from the center portion of the fish
3½ oz / 100 g sun dried tomatoes
generous ⅜ cup / 100 g lentils
1 clove of garlic
10 saffron threads

2 bay leaves
1 sprig of fresh thyme
1 tbsp / 15 ml extra-virgin olive oil
salt, white pepper to taste

We owe this recipe to the red tuna from Calabria, which is two to three times larger than white tuna and is caught in trawl or ring nets (*tonara* in Italian). When creating this recipe, our chef, Gianfranco Vissani, was influenced by Japanese cooking. The Japanese rate second worldwide in tuna fishing and in the consumption of tuna, and have many ways to prepare the fish, from serving it raw to cooking it through.

The red portion of the tuna, usually from a bluefin, spoils easily and must be bought very fresh. The center portion of the fillet is removed, cooked, and then cut into smaller fillets. A little touch of saffron harmonizes exquisitely with an accompaniment of lentils and tomatoes, rounding off this appetizer in style.

The lentils should only cook for about fifteen minutes to stay *al dente*. Our chef recommends Castellucio de Norce, a type of lentil with an earthy taste that provides strong competition for the maritime flavor of the tuna. If these are unavailable, look for red, gray, or green small lentils. The sundried tomatoes used here are easy to prepare, and also serve to round off the aroma. It normally takes a month to dry tomatoes; less in summer when it is very hot. Nowadays sundried tomatoes are available in markets; to prepare them for cooking, soak them briefly in warm water, or a mixture of warm water and olive oil, and they will moisten nicely. Sundried tomatoes can be stored in a dry place for about a year.

You can also use canned tomatoes, but their flavor is less concentrated. The tuna may be substituted with crayfish or shrimps, if desired, but again, the impact will not be the same.

1. Soak the sun dried tomatoes in water for half an hour. Drain and cut into fine strips.

2. Cook the lentils and herbs in water for 15 minutes. Drain and fry in a pan with the fresh thyme.

Sundried Tomatoes

3. Place the tuna fillets, cut from the center portion of the fish, into a different pan with hot oil. Add bay leaves, garlic, salt and pepper and fry over a low heat.

4. Spoon the thinly cut tomatoes with the saffron threads onto the plates. Arrange tuna fillets on top. Sprinkle with lentils and freshly chopped garlic. Serve hot with olive oil, garnished with chopped chives.

Red Beets in Beer Batter

Preparation time: 20 minutes
Cooking time: 40 minutes
Difficulty: ★

Serves four

1¼ lbs / 600 g small red beets
scant ¼ cup / 50 ml tarragon vinegar
pinch of caraway seeds
1 bunch of parsley
salt to taste

For the batter:
⅝ lb / 300 g flour
scant 5 tbsp / 70 g butter

3 eggs, separated
1¼ cups / 300 ml pale lager beer
2 pinches of salt

For the horseradish sauce:
1 fresh horseradish root
1 shallot
generous 2 cups / 500 ml white wine
scant ¼ cup / 50 ml Noilly Prat (vermouth)
1¼ cups / 300 ml vegetable stock
⅝ cup / 150 g butter
¼ cup / 60 ml cream
salt, pepper to taste

The bulk of German red beets are produced in Bavaria. In this recipe, which could have been invented by dedicated followers of vegetarian cooking, our chef, Heinz Winkler, makes use of all the possibilities inherent in this remarkable vegetable. Rich in sugar, calcium, and iron, it was once the issue in a fight between the Greeks and the Romans, who could not agree on where it originally came from. Whatever the case may have been, the Europeans welcomed the red beets with great enthusiasm. The French eat them raw or cooked in salads, the English fill them, the Norwegians serve them with herrings, the Russians make them into soup, and the Americans boil them and slice them into thin rounds.

There are four types of beets: round, flat, half-long and long ones. Heinz Winkler recommends the small, fairly young beets, which hide their fleshy roots under large green leaves.

Tarragon vinegar lends them a delicious aroma and the art only lies in covering them in sufficient batter to conceal a surprise for your guests.

The batter will turn pleasantly crisp when deep-fried if you add some butter to it and leave it to stand for a while. Grate the fresh horseradish just before you stir it into the sauce, otherwise it will lose the sharp flavor that gives this dish that extra something.

Some gourmets will probably frown at this "sweet adventure" which – though delicious – might be a little too imaginative for their taste. You may use alternatives like asparagus or salsify for this recipe, but in that case the horseradish sauce must be left out.

1. For the deep-fry batter, blend egg yolks and beer in a bowl. Melt the butter in a pan and add to the batter. Add salt, whip the egg whites and carefully fold into the mixture. Leave the batter to stand at room temperature for 30 minutes.

2. For the horseradish sauce, chop the shallot, add to a saucepan with wine and Noilly Prat and bring to a boil. Add the vegetable stock, reduce to a third of its original volume, and stir in butter and seasoning. Clean, peel, and grate the horseradish. Reheat the sauce, stir, and fold in 1 tbsp / 15 g of horseradish as well as some whipped cream.

with Horseradish Sauce

3. Clean the red beets and bring to a boil in a pot with water, tarragon vinegar, salt, and caraway seeds. Cook over a medium heat for 35–40 minutes. Drain, rinse under cold water and peel. Heat oil in a deep-fat fryer to 320 °F / 160 °C, roll the red beets in flour, dip them into batter and deep-fry them for one to two minutes.

4. Lift the "doughnuts" out with a skimmer and dry them on paper towels. Deep-fry the parsley for decoration. Pour the horseradish sauce onto the plates and arrange the deep-fried red beets and parsley on top.

Potato Mousseline

Preparation time: 15 minutes
Cooking time: 30 minutes
Difficulty: ☆

Serves four

⁵/₈ lb / 300 g potatoes
2 oz / 60 g fresh Périgord truffles
³/₄ cup / 180 g butter
generous ³/₈ cup / 100 ml cream
salt to taste

The term *mousseline* requires some explanation. It is the French word for *muslin*, and generally refers to certain types of thin cotton material, as well as to a specific kind of opaque glass. In cooking, it refers to a variety of savory and sweet sauces made with whipped cream or whipped egg white. In the case of this dish, presented by our chef, Heinz Winkler, *mousseline* stands for a more refined and lighter preparation of the classic puree.

The Germans did not wait for Parmentier to discover the qualities of the potato though, Sir Walter Raleigh had already planted the supposedly notorious vegetable on his farm in Ireland. The Grand Duchy of Hesse made a statistical record of this plant as early as 1648. But while this dish may appear simple, since made from such a humble plant, this recipe actually has highbrow qualifications. For one, you have to choose a suitable kind of potato. Heinz Winkler recommends Nicola potatoes, a type with a firm consistency that does not become watery when cooked. If unavailable, look for firm, early potatoes. Add some grated nutmeg and enough melted butter to give the puree a creamy and soft texture.

Since the flavor of the truffles is of utmost importance in this recipe, nothing but the famous *Tuber melanosporum*, the black truffle from the Périgord, should be used. These so-called Périgord truffles are found predominantly in Provence (in the area around Aups or Carpentras) where truffles are not only a culinary specialty but also a legendary delicacy with many admirers. Choose nice specimens of one and a half to two ounces (fifty to sixty grams) each when truffles are in season, from December through January. The degree to which their flavor is absorbed by the mousseline depends on how finely the truffles are sliced – for this purpose, a grater works well.

1. Bring water to a boil in a saucepan. Peel, quarter, and cook the potatoes and drain.

2. To make the puree, pass the potatoes through a fine sieve or process in a blender.

with Périgord Truffles

3. Heat the butter and mix together with the cream into the potato puree. Blend and season to taste.

4. Make small dumplings of the potato mousseline and arrange on plates. Slice the truffles thinly with a grater and place evenly on top of the mousseline.

Pike Dumplings

Preparation time:	*1 hour, 30 minutes*
Chilling time:	*1 hour*
Cooking time:	*30 minutes*
Difficulty:	✶✶

Serves four

12 large crayfish
3 each leeks, carrots, stalks of celery
1–2 tbsp / 20 g coarse salt
1 quart / 1 l fish stock

For the pike filling:
5¼ oz / 150 g pike fillet
1 egg white
generous ³/₈ cup / 100 ml cream
salt, pepper to taste
juice of 1 lemon

generous ³/₈ cup / 100 ml whipping cream

For the sauce:
crayfish carcasses
2 tbsp / 30 ml vegetable oil

2 shallots (to yield ¼ cup / 60 g diced)
1 oz / 30 g each diced carrot, celery, fennel, tomato.
2 coriander seeds, 2 peppercorns
1 bunch of fresh dill
1¼ cups / 300 ml Riesling (wine)
generous ³/₈ cup / 100 ml Noilly Prat (vermouth)
2½ tbsp / 40 ml port
4 tsp / 20 ml cognac
generous 1 cup / 250 ml fish stock
generous 1 cup / 250 ml cream
juice of 1 lemon
6 tbsp / 80 g butter

For the garnish:
1 carrot, 1 leek, 1 stalk of celery
scant ⅛ lb / 50 g snowpeas

The German *knödel* and the French q*uenelles*, both meaning dumplings, basically differ only in shape and are generally made from similar ingredients, such as minced meat, fish, or vegetables. Whether French or German, the mixture is then bound with eggs and poached, often in broth.

In this recipe the pike takes the lead role, accompanied by vegetables cut into diamond-shaped pieces – you should wind up with a quarter of a pound (one hundred and twenty grams) when all is cut. Considered a superb eating fish, pike is easily recognizable by its hammer-shaped mouth and light, silvery belly. This predatory fish makes its home in freshwater, and is extremely clever, adapting to the color of its surroundings and camouflaging itself to better surprise its chosen prey. In lakes with lush vegetation the pike has a greenish color, whereas it is

yellower in brackish water. If you want to serve a pike whole choose a medium-sized one of a maximum of six pounds (three kilos) to make sure it will retain its tenderness and flavor when cooked. For our recipe, larger pikes are recommended, since their fillets are more suitable for the preparation of dumplings (and pike is the fish customarily used in *quenelles*). Removing the bones with which the pike has very generously been endowed by nature requires a lot of patience.

The sauce is easy to prepare if all the numerous ingredients are available and of good quality. This frothy cream with its Mediterranean herbs (fennel, coriander) and subtle flavors (Riesling, Noilly Prat, port, and brandy) will doubtlessly delight your guests. So long as they are fresh, the origin and type of the crayfish is of no major importance.

1. For the pike filling Dice the pike fillets and season with salt and pepper. Refrigerate for an hour, then blend in a food processor with egg white and cream to make a smooth filling. Season to taste, add a few drops of lemon juice, strain and refrigerate. Cook the crayfish and the vegetables in salted water for four minutes, reserving the crayfish shells. Cut the vegetables into diamonds, blanch and rinse under cold water.

2. For the crayfish sauce sauté the crayfish shells in oil, add vegetables, spices, and, dill. Add white wine, vermouth, port and cognac and reduce. Pour the fish stock over and reduce to a third. Add the cream and cook over a low heat for ten minutes. Season to taste, strain and add the juice of a lemon.

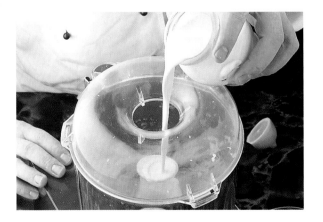

with Crayfish

3. Heat the crayfish sauce and add the crayfish and vegetables. Stir in the butter.

4. Fold the whipped cream into the cooled pike filling. Heat the slightly salted fish stock. Form 12 pike dumplings with a tablespoon and poach them for 12–14 minutes. Place the dumplings onto the plates, garnish with crayfish and vegetables and sprigs of dill and pour the sauce over the whole arrangement.

Preparation time: 15 minutes
Soaking time: 12 hours
Cooking time: 2 hours,
30 minutes
Difficulty: ☆

Serves four

⁵/₈ lb / 300 g borlotti beans, dried
⁵/₈ lb / 300 g potatoes
⁵/₈ lb / 300 g onions
2 cloves of garlic

3¹/₂ oz / 100 g Parma ham (the end piece)
2 tbsp / 30 g butter
¹/₄ lb / 50 g Parmesan
¹/₂ cup / 125 ml olive oil
1 bundle of sage
1 zucchini
1 bunch of parsley
salt, pepper to taste

Aside from the summer months, this dish is never taken off the menu of the Vecchia Lanterna, Armando Zanetti's restaurant in Turin. Its preparation has been strongly influenced by traditions that can be traced back to the 14th century in the Piemont region. Minestrone is a simple, economical, and nourishing dish that can claim popularity among all social strata. Some of the restaurant's most famous regular customers (politicians, actors, journalists) order it the minute they come through the front doors.

Minestrone (Italian for "big soup") is basically a soup made of a mixture of different coarsely chopped vegetables such as carrots, potatoes, and celery, the combination varying depending on the chef and the region. It is often prepared with noodles or rice. Thus, as Zanetti encourages, choose the ingredients as whim directs you: add large amounts of beans or fried boletus, like our chef's grandmother used to do, or cook it with pieces of bacon or ham like a Sunday soup from the old days, or do both. In this recipe, our chef processes the ham into small dumplings to add them to the minestrone. Parma ham, being both tasty and lean, is well suited for this purpose.

It is no coincidence that our chef recommends borlotti beans, as they have regional significance for him, being grown in the Italian province of Belluno. They are light red and slightly speckled and their taste is evocative of chestnuts. But if they are unavailable, substitute pinto beans, small kidney beans, or even adzuki beans instead. If you substitute Parma ham with pork or veal knuckle, the soup can be served as an appetizer, and the knuckle with the beans as a main dish.

1. Soak the beans overnight in lukewarm water. The next day, bring to a boil with the potatoes and the Parma ham. Top up with water and add salt.

2. Sauté the garlic and the tied-up sage in a pan with olive oil and butter.

Beans Piemont Style

3. Peel and slice the onions, add to the pan with garlic and sage bundle and braise.

4. Stir everything into the beans and cook over a low heat for about two and a half hours. Serve in soup plates with milled pepper, chopped parsley, and a tablespoon of olive oil, and decorate with zucchini strips. Add a little grated Parmesan on top, or serve on the side for your guest, to use as they desire.

Preparation time: 20 minutes
Cooking time: 30 minutes
Difficulty: ☆

Serves four

For the savarin:
scant ¹/₈ lb / 50 g durum wheat semolina
generous 2 cups / 500 ml whole milk
1 egg
generous 2 tbsp / 30 g Parmesan (grated)
4 tsp / 20 g butter
a pinch of salt

For the artichokes:
2 artichokes
scant ¹/₄ cup / 50 g butter
1 bunch of parsley
salt, pepper to taste

For the fonduta:
1¹/₄ cups / 300 ml milk
7 oz / 200 g Emmental cheese
5 tsp / 25 g butter
5 tsp / 25 g flour
2 egg yolks
salt, pepper to taste

The Italian *fonduta* is the counterpart of the cheese fondue. In Piemont it is called *fondua* and made of Fontina, a rich semi-soft cooking cheese made from full-cream cow's milk that is similar to Raclette. The *fonduta* is always bound with an egg yolk and seasoned with pepper, unlike similar cheeses in Switzerland or the French mountainous regions.

If you are unable to get hold of Fontina, our chef recommends using Raclette cheese with butter added to make it into a nice and smoothly bound paste. However, if you find the cheese too fatty, just add a little water to give the *fonduta* the right consistency. Emmental, available almost anywhere in Europe (it is even produced in Brittany) and in many North American markets, generally also complies with all the requirements of

this recipe. The gentle touch of Parmesan, however, or preferably even Parmesan Grano Padano, is irreplaceable for rounding off this small semolina cake.

The savarin in this recipe is exclusively prepared of durum wheat semolina – couscous semolina is unsuitable. If possible, use a savarin mold that is suitable for an attractive presentation of a rice accompaniment. The sliced artichokes may be replaced by forest mushrooms, boletus or topinambur.

This appetizer can be served on its own or with meat in sauce and allows for numerous variations, such as the addition of sliced white truffles, a popular Piemont specialty.

1. To prepare the savarin, bring the milk to a boil, add butter and salt, sprinkle in the semolina and stir with a whisk for a minute. Cook for 15 minutes. Take off the stove and stir in egg yolk and grated Parmesan.

2. Butter four molds, fill to the rim with the semolina mixture and refrigerate.

Artichokes and Fonduta

3. Prepare the artichoke hearts and cut them into thin slices. Heat the butter and add the artichoke hearts, chopped parsley, salt and pepper. Braise over a low heat for about 15 minutes.

4. For the fonduta, heat the butter with the flour. Add the milk, bring to a boil and stir in the Emmental cheese. When the cream is even and smooth add the egg yolks, salt, as well as pepper if desired. Cover the base of the plates with fonduta, place the semolina savarin in the middle, and heap the fried artichokes on top.

Cream of Pinto Bean

Preparation time:	30 minutes
Soaking time:	12 hours
Cooking time:	1 hour, 30 minutes
Difficulty:	☆

Serves four

generous 1 cup / 250 g pinto beans
14 oz / 400 g blood sausage
3¹/₂ oz / 100 g bacon
2 tsp / 10 g chorizo (sausage from pork)
half a head of white cabbage
1 clove of garlic
scant ¹/₄ cup / 50 ml olive oil

For the vegetable bouillon:
1 leek stalk
1 onion
1 carrot
2 small red peppers, dried
1 clove of garlic

This recipe, from Chef Alberto Zuluaga, features characteristic elements of the Basque region such as leeks and peppers, as well as pinto beans, even though they are – falsely – accused of being hard to digest.

The traditional combination of bacon, chorizo, and red beans is very popular in Spain. Though the beans should still be soaked, a pressure cooker reduces the cooking period to one and a half instead of three and a half hours. Exchange the water when it has come to a boil – three times altogether. After blending the cream in a food processor, pass it through a very fine sieve to give it an even consistency without lumps.

Alberto Zuluaga recommends using a vegetable bouillon made of onions, red peppers, and leeks to thin the cream. Since it keeps well, you can prepare it in advance and focus all your attention on cooking the beans. The Spaniards use a particularly nice and mildly flavored red onion that keeps exceptionally well.

You can prepare chickpeas or lentils the same way, using these instead of pinto beans without showing too much disrespect for tradition. And note that this simple recipe is suitable for any season.

1. Pre-soak the beans the night before. On the day of preparation, wash the cabbage, slice it finely, and wash it again. Sauté in a pan with oil and garlic and keep warm.

2. Place the soaked beans, bacon, chorizo, and blood sausage into a pressure cooker. Cover with water and cook for about one hour. If necessary, add water occasionally. Cook a vegetable bouillon from the ingredients indicated to thin the bean puree.

Soup with Morcilla

3. When cooked, take out the chorizo, bacon, and blood sausage. Mix the rest in a blender or food processor and then pass through a fine sieve.

4. Pour the bean puree back into the pressure cooker and thin with the vegetable bouillon to obtain a creamy consistency. Place some cabbage into each plate, pour the very hot bean cream around the cabbage, and add the blood sausage slices.

Marmitako

Preparation time: 45 minutes
Cooking time: 50 minutes
Difficulty: ☆

Serves four

3 lbs / 1¹/₂ kg bonito tuna (saving the head and tail
   for the fish stock)
3 lbs / 1¹/₂ kg potatoes
6 tomatoes
3 red onions
6 green chili peppers
5 dried red peppers

generous ³/₈ cup / 100 ml oil
salt, pepper to taste

The term *marmitako* refers both to the container used for the preparation of this Basque specialty and to the dish itself – a tasty combination of bonito, onions, potatoes, and red peppers. Its origin goes back to the first fishermen from Bermeo, a well-known harbor on the Bay of Biscay that is famous for its sea pike and bonito fishing. These tough fishermen who went out to sea for days on end had no choice but prepare their catch with the only vegetables they could preserve.

The bonito tuna is a red-fleshed fish, a relative of the white tuna; they both belong to the family of osseous fish. The best kind does not grow large and is caught in the vast Cantabrique. Wherever it is a rarity or unavailable, it can be substituted with any other type of tuna to obtain a similar result. Other fish with a relatively high fat content like salmon are also suitable for this dish.

Our chef, Alberto Zuluaga, cautions that this dish is not exactly simple. The red peppers of the Basque region are sometimes difficult to preserve, as they contain more water than the usual Andalusian peppers. It is also not easy to remove the skin from the flesh required for the preparation of this dish. Make sure the onion does not caramelize when it is grilled. Also, the potatoes should remain firm when cooked to prevent the marmitako from turning into mush.

1. Immerse the five dried red peppers into boiling water and blanch three times, rinse well, and remove the skin. In the meantime make a fish stock from the head and the tail of the bonito.

2. Sauté the chopped red onions in a pot over a high heat until golden brown. Sauté the tomatoes and the flesh of the red peppers separately in oil. Cook over a low heat for 30 minutes and puree in a blender.

with Bonito

3. Add the chopped chili peppers and the diced potatoes to the fried onions. Stir well. Pass the fish stock through a sieve and add to the pot to just cover the potatoes. Season with salt.

4. As soon as the potatoes are cooked, add three small ladles of pepper and tomato puree as well as the diced bonito. Combine well and cook for 3–4 minutes. Season to taste, and serve on pre-warmed soup plates.

Basic Recipes

Puff Pastry

Recipes: Duck Liver Pie with Truffles – Jean Fleury

Master Chiquart's Filled Puff Pastry Pockets – Guy Martin

Oxtail Soup with Puff Pastry Hat – Roger Jaloux

Snails in a Puff Pastry Hat – Jean Crotet

Vaudois Pie with Leeks – Étienne Krebs

Ingredients for 4 people:
generous 2 cups / 500 g flour – 1 tbs / 15 g salt – generous 1 cup / 250 ml water
To layer: generous 2 cups / 500 g butter

Preparation:
Heap the flour onto the working surface in a circular pile, placing salt and water in the center. Mix rapidly, processing into a ball of dough. Set aside for twenty minutes, then roll the dough into a rectangle. Place 2 cups of soft butter on top, fold the dough sides over the butter, roll into a rectangle again. Repeat this process six times at 20 minute intervals.

Shellfish Vinaigrette

Recipe: Warm Salad of Marinated Shellfish – Jean & Jean-Yves Schillinger

Ingredients:
salt pepper – scant $^7/_8$ cup / 200 ml balsamic vinegar – $^1/_2$ cup shellfish stock – $1^2/_3$ cups / 400 ml olive oil – 2 tomatoes – 1 shallot – 1 bunch of chives – 1 bunch of dill

Preparation:
Dissolve salt and pepper in a bowl with vinegar, and add the shellfish stock. Stir well with a whisk and add oil. Skin and seed the tomatoes and chop finely. Chop the shallot, chives and dill finely as well. Combine the tomatoes, shallot, and herbs with the vinaigrette just before serving.

Pasta Dough

Recipe: Tortelli with Pumpkin Filling – Nadia Santini

Ingredients:
generous 1 cup / 250 g durum wheat flour – 2 whole eggs – 2 egg yolks – scant 1 tsp / 4 g salt

Preparation:
Heap the flour onto the working surface, make a well in the center and add the eggs, egg yolks, and salt. Combine well with both hands. Shape the dough into a ball and refrigerate for an hour before processing it.

Hollandaise Sauce

Recipe: Black Salsify with Fresh Walnuts – Philippe Groult

Ingredients:
scant $^7/_8$ cup / 200 g butter – 4 egg yolks – 4 tbs water – salt – pepper – 1 pinch of cayenne pepper – 4 dashes of almond milk

Preparation:
Melt the butter in a saucepan. In a different saucepan, whip egg yolks and water over a low heat until frothy. Remove from the stove and gradually stir in the melted butter. Season with salt, pepper, and cayenne pepper; add four dashes of almond milk.

Mornay Sauce and Béchamel Sauce

Recipe: Moussaka with Mediterranean Sea Perch – Nikolaos Sarantos

Ingredients:
For the Béchamel sauce: scant $^1/_4$ cup / 50 g butter – scant $^1/_4$ cup / 50 g flour – $2^1/_2$ cups / 600 ml whole milk – salt
For the Mornay sauce: 2 eggs – 2 tbs / 30 g, grated Parmesan – scant $^1/_4$ cup / 50 g butter – salt – pepper

Preparation:
To make a roux for the Béchamel sauce, melt butter in a saucepan, add flour and mix with a whisk. Sauté over a very low heat for about five minutes, then leave to cool. Bring the milk to a boil and gradually add the cold roux to the boiling milk. Cook over a low heat for ten minutes and repeatedly stir with a whisk.
For the Mornay sauce, separate the eggs, remove the Béchamel sauce from the stove and whip the egg yolks quickly into the boiling sauce. Add Parmesan. Pass through a fine sieve, add $3^1/_2$ tbsp / 50 g butter and fold in the whipped egg whites. Season to taste and keep warm, but keep the sauce from boiling again.

White Champagne Sauce:

Recipe: Leipziger Medley with Vegetables – Lothar Eiermann

Ingredients:
scant $^7/_8$ cup / 200 ml veal sweetbread stock – 4 tsp / 20 ml Noilly Prat (vermouth) – 2 tbs / 30 ml champagne – 1 shallot – 4 tsp / 20 g butter – half a bay leaf – salt, pepper – two white peppercorns, crushed – 1 lemon – generous $^3/_8$ cup / 100 ml crème fraîche – generous $^3/_8$ cup / 100 ml cream

Preparation:
Reduce the fish stock with the chopped shallot, bay leaf, and salt to half its volume, add the cream and reduce again. Pass through a fine sieve and add vermouth. Bring to a boil again, add crème fraîche, butter, and finally, the champagne. Season to taste.

White and Black Lasagna Doughs

Recipes: Spanish Txanguro Lasagna – Pedro Subijana

Lasagna: with oregano and pork – Gianfranco Vissani.

Ingredients:
For the white lasagna: scant $^7/_8$ cup / 200 g flour – 1 egg – 2 egg yolks – 2 tsp / 10 ml olive oil – a pinch of salt
For the black lasagna: scant $^7/_8$ cup / 200 g flour – 1 egg – 2 egg yolks – 2 tsp / 10 ml olive oil – a pinch of salt – 3 octopus or squid ink sacs, or 3 oz / 90 ml bottled octopus or squid ink

Preparation:
For the white lasagna dough, heap the flour onto the working surface, make a well in the center and add two egg yolks, an egg, olive oil and salt. Knead well with your hands to make an even dough; when it no longer sticks to your fingers, it is done. Refrigerate for an hour before turning into noodles. Proceed similarly with the black lasagna dough, dying it with ink.

Introducing the Chefs

Fernando Adría

born May 14, 1962

Restaurant: **El Bulli**
Address: 30, Apartado de Correos Cala
Montjoi 17480 Rosas, Spain
Tel. (9)72 15 04 57; Fax (9)72 15 07 17

As a young, talented 21-year-old back in 1983, Fernando Adría received two Michelin stars for his culinary achievements in *El Bulli*, his restaurant on the Costa Brava, whose kitchens had previously been run by his friend Jean-Louis Neichel. Awarded 19 points and four red chef's hats by Gault-Millau, Adría has also fared well with the Spanish restaurant guides: four stars in Campsa and 9.5/10 in Gourmetour. A winner of the Spanish national gastronomy award, Fernando Adría also received the European culinary grand prix in 1994. When his work leaves him time, this chef is a great supporter of the Barcelona soccer team.

Hilario Arbelaitz

born May 27, 1951

Restaurant: **Zuberoa**
Address: Barrio Iturrioz, 8
20180 Oyarzun, Spain
Tel. (9)43 49 12 28; Fax (9)43 49 26 79

Born in the heart of the Spanish Basque country, whose gourmet traditions form the emphasis of his cooking, Hilario Arbelaitz began his career in 1970 at Zuberoa, where he became chef in 1982. Since then, he has received numerous French and Spanish awards: two Michelin stars and three red chef's hats and 17 points in Gault-Millau, as well as four Campsa stars. In 1993 he was named Best Chef in Euzkadi (the Basque country), after being named Best Chef in Spain in 1991. He brings equal measures of enthusiasm to the Basque game of pelota and family life, and is very interested in the history and future of his profession.

Firmin Arrambide

born September 16, 1946

Restaurant: **Les Pyrénées**
Address: 19, place du Général de Gaulle
64220 Saint-Jean-Pied-de-Port, France
Tel. (0)5 59 37 01 01; Fax (0)5 59 37 18 97

Firmin Arrambide has been at the helm of this restaurant not far from his place of birth since 1986, garnering two Michelin stars, three red chef's hats and 18 points in Gault-Millau for *Les Pyrénées*. His regionally inspired cuisine won him second place in the 1978 Taittinger awards and carried him to the finals of the Meilleur Ouvrier de France competition in 1982. True to his Basque origins, Arrambide hunts woodpigeon and woodsnipe in the fall, and also loves mountain climbing; occasionally, though, he enjoys simply soaking up the sun by the side of the swimming pool.

Jean Bardet

born September 27, 1941

Restaurant: **Jean Bardet**
Address: 57, rue Groison
37000 Tours, France
Tel. (0)3 47 41 41 11; Fax (0)3 47 51 68 72

Before opening a restaurant in Tours under his own name in 1987, Jean Bardet traversed the whole of Europe, working mainly as a sauce chef at the *Savoy* in London. A member of Relais et Châteaux, Relais Gourmands, and the Auguste Escoffier Foundation, he was awarded four red chef's hats in Gault-Millau (19.5) and two Michelin stars. In 1982 he had the honor of preparing dinner for the heads of state at the Versailles Summit. Jean Bardet is an enthusiastic cigar smoker (American Express awarded him the title of Greatest Smoker in the World in 1984) and in the fall indulges his passion for hunting together with friends.

Giuseppina Beglia

born May 16, 1938

Restaurant: **Balzi Rossi**
Address: 2, Via Balzi Rossi
18039 Ventimiglia, Italy
Tel. (0)18 43 81 32; Fax (0)18 43 85 32

Since 1983 her restaurant has towered over this famous vantage point and the caves of the Balzi Rossi ("red cliffs"), but Giuseppina Beglia herself is just as well known in Italy for the television cookery programs broadcast under her direction between 1985 and 1990. A member of Le Soste, the prestigious Italian restaurant chain, she holds two Michelin stars, three red chef's hats in Gault-Millau (18) and 82/100 in the Italian Gambero Rosso guide. In 1992 she won the first Golden Key of Gastronomy to be awarded by Gault-Millau to chefs outside of France. Giuseppina Beglia is very interested in the flower arrangements in her restaurant, and loves skiing in the nearby Alps.

Michel Blanchet

June 16, 1949

Restaurant: **Le Tastevin**
Address: 9, avenue Eglé
78600 Maisons-Laffitte, France
Tel. (0)139 62 11 67; Fax (0)1 39 62 73 09

After a top-notch training from 1967 to 1971 at *Maxim's*, *Lutétia* and *Ledoyen*, Michel Blanchet took over the reins at *Tastevin* in 1972; today, the restaurant boasts two Michelin stars. Blanchet's talents have more than once carried him through to the final rounds of prestigious awards: the Prosper Montagné prize (1970 and 1972); the Taittinger prize (1974); and the Meilleur Ouvrier de France competition in 1979. Michel Blanchet is a Maître Cuisinier de France and a member of the Culinary Academy of France. A great lover of nature, he enjoys rambles through the woods – during which he sometimes also collects mushrooms – as well as cycling and hiking.

Christian Bouvarel

born April 26, 1954

Restaurant: **Paul Bocuse**
Address: 69660 Collonges-au-Mont-d'Or,
France Tel. (0)4 72 42 90 90;
Fax (0)4 72 27 85 87

The youngest chef at *Paul Bocuse* had famous teachers, training under Raymond Thuillier at *Ousteau de Baumanière* in Baux-de-Provence in 1971 and Paul Haeberlin at the *Auberge de l'Ill* in Illhaeusern in 1972 before coming to work at this celebrated restaurant in Collonges in 1975. Three Michelin stars, four red chef's hats in Gault-Millau (19), four stars in the Bottin Gourmand guide: Christian Bouvarel has also naturally played his part in the success story of this restaurant, and was named Meilleur Ouvrier de France in 1993. A native of Lyons, he is an enthusiastic nature-lover and spends his scarce leisure hours preferably mountain climbing.

Carlo Brovelli

born May 23, 1938

Restaurant: **Il Sole di Ranco**
Address: 5, Piazza Venezia
21020 Ranco, Italy
Tel. (0)3 31 97 65 07; Fax (0)3 31 97 66 20

It was only fitting that the Italian restaurant guide Veronelli should pay tribute to this restaurant with the sun in its name by awarding it this distinction. Looking back on a 120-year-old family tradition, *Il Sole di Ranco* is run in a masterly fashion by Carlo Brovelli, who took over the reins in 1968 after training at the college of hotel management in La Stresa. A member of the Le Soste, Relais et Châteaux and Relais Gourmands chains, Brovelli has received many accolades: two Michelin stars, three chef's hats in Gault-Millau (18), 84/100 in the Italian Gambero Rosso. Carlo Brovelli loves cycling and soccer, as well as his favorite sport, hunting.

Jean-Pierre Bruneau

born September 18, 1943

Restaurant: **Bruneau**
Address: 73–75, avenue Broustin
1080 Brussels, Belgium
Tel. (0)24 27 69 78; Fax (0)24 25 97 26

For a good 20 years now, Jean-Pierre Bruneau has run the restaurant bearing his name that stands in the shadow of the important Koekelberg Basilica in the center of Brussels. The sophisticated creations of this Belgian Maître Cuisinier have won him many distinctions: three Michelin stars, four red chef's hats in Gault-Millau, three stars in Bottin Gourmand and 94/100 in the Belgian restaurant guide Henri Lemaire. He is also a member of Traditions et Qualité. Outside of the kitchen, he enjoys hunting and car racing (first hand); in addition, he collects old cars.

Michel Bruneau

born February 11, 1949

Restaurant: **La Bourride**
Address: 15–17, rue du Vaugueux
14000 Caen, France
Tel. (0)2 31 93 50 76; Fax (0)2 31 93 29 63

"Normandy is proud of herself" – this is the motto of Michel Bruneau, who never tires of enumerating the sumptuous produce of the Calvados region on his exhaustive, tempting menu. Starting off his career in the midst of the plantations in Ecrécy, on the banks of the Guigne (1972–82), he then moved to *La Bourride* in Caen. Here he continues to delight gourmets with his inventive cooking, steeped in regional traditions, which has also impressed the critics: two Michelin stars, three red chef's hats in Gault-Millau (18). In his spare time, Michel Bruneau enjoys cooking for friends.

Alain Burnel

born January 26, 1949

Restaurant: **Oustau de Baumanière**
Address: Val d'Enfer
13520 Les Baux-de-Provence, France
Tel. (0)4 90 54 33 07; Fax (0)4 90 54 40 46

Alain Burnel served his apprenticeship in Beaulieu at *La réserve de Beaulieu* (1969–73), in Nantes at *Frantel* under Roger Jaloux, in Marseilles at *Sofitel* and in Saint-Romain de Lerps at the *Château du Besset*, where he served as chef from 1978 to 1982 before taking over the reins from the famous Raymond Thuillier in Baux, whose restaurant is now owned by the Charial family. Alain Burnel has earned two Michelin stars, three white chef's hats in Gault-Millau (18) and is a member of Traditions et Qualité, Relais et Châteaux, and Relais Gourmands. In his free time this chef is a keen cyclist, and was once even a participant in the Tour de France.

Jan Buytaert

born October 16, 1946

Restaurant: **De Bellefleur**
Address: 253 Chaussée d'Anvers
2950 Kapellen, Belgium
Tel. (0)3 664 6719; Fax (0)3 665 0201

Despite being a dyed-in-the-wool Belgian who has spent a large part of his career in his native country (first at the *Villa Lorraine* in Brussels from 1973–74), Jan Buytaert worked for two years in the kitchens of *Prés et Sources d'Eugénie* in Eugénie-les-Bains under Michel Guérard (1974–75). In 1975, after this French interlude, he opened his current restaurant, which has earned him two Michelin stars and is one of the best in the region. This Belgian Maître Cuisinier loves gentle activities such as hiking and riding, and also enjoys working in the garden.

Jacques Cagna

born August 24, 1942

Restaurant: **Jacques Cagna**
Address: 14, rue des Grands Augustins
75006 Paris, France
Tel. (0)1 43 26 49 39; Fax (0)1 43 54 54 48

This distinguished chef has worked in the most famous restaurants of the French capital (1960 at *Lucas Carton*, 1961 at *Maxim's*, 1964 at *La Ficelle*), and was even Chef to the French National Assembly (1961–62) before opening his own restaurant under his own name in 1975, for which he has received high honors: two Michelin stars, two red chef's hats in Gault-Millau (18) and three stars in Bottin Gourmand. Jacques Cagna is a Knight of the Mérite nationale des Arts et des Lettres. He knows his way around Asia very well, speaks fluent Japanese and is keen on classical music, opera and jazz.

Stewart Cameron

born September 16, 1945

Restaurant: **Turnberry Hotel & Golf Courses**
Turnberry KA26 9LT, Scotland
Tel. (0)1655 331 000; Fax (0)1655 331 706

Since 1981, the kitchens of the *Turnberry Hotel* – one of only two five-star Scottish restaurants – have had a real Scot at the helm: Stewart Cameron, who previously worked at *Malmaison*, the restaurant of the Central Hotel in Glasgow. This chef is also a member of the Taste of Scotland and of the British Branch of the Culinary Academy of France. In 1986 and 1994 he was privileged to play host in his restaurant to the participants of the British Golf Open. When he gets the chance, Stewart Cameron goes hunting or fishing. A rugby fan (of course!), he is one of the Scottish Fifteen's most faithful supporters.

Mario Cavallucci

born May 20, 1959

Restaurant: **La Frasca**
Address: 38, Via Matteoti
47011 Castrocaro Terme, Italy
Tel. (0)543 76 74 71; Fax (0)543 76 66 25

Two Michelin stars, four chef's hats in Gault-Millau (19), one sun in Veronelli, 89/100 in Gambero Rosso: what more could Mario Cavallucci want? Working in perfect harmony with the restaurant's proprietor and cellarman, Gianfranco Bolognesi, this young, energetic chef has already received many accolades. A member of the Le Soste restaurant chain, he has vigorously supported Italy's great culinary tradition since 1978. This extraordinarily busy chef nevertheless manages to find a little spare time for fishing, reading, seeing the occasional movie, and playing cards, soccer, and billiards.

Francis Chauveau

born: September 15, 1947

Restaurant: **La Belle Otéro**
Address: Hôtel Carlton (7th floor)
58, La Croisette
Cannes 06400, France
Tel. (0)4 93 69 39 39; Fax (0)4 93 39 09 06

Although born in Berry in the northwest of France, Francis Chauveau's encounter with Provençal cooking has led to outstanding results, which visitors to the legendary *Palace-Hotel* in Cannes – holder of two Michelin stars – have been enjoying since 1989. Francis Chauveau gained his first experience as a chef in the *Hôtel d'Espagne* in Valencay, continuing his career at the *Auberge de Noves* in 1965. Later, he worked in prestigious restaurants such as the *Auberge du Père Bise*, the *Réserve de Beaulieu*, the *Terrasse* in the Hotel Juana in Juan-les-Pins, and in the famous restaurant *L'Amandier* in Mougins from 1980 to 1989.

Jacques Chibois

born: July 22, 1952

Restaurant: **La Bastide St-Antoine**
Address: 45, avenue Henri Dunant
06130 Grasse, France
Tel. (0)4 92 42 04 42; Fax (0)4 92 42 03 42

During the course of a career involving many moves, Jacques Chibois has met many famous names in French gastronomy: Jean Delaveyne in Bougival, Louis Outhier in La Napoule, Roger Vergé in Mougins, and the famous pastry chef Gaston Lenôtre. Since 1980 he has repeatedly worked under Michel Guérard, and was awarded two Michelin stars during his time at *Gray d'Albion* in Cannes (1981–95). He opened *La Bastide Saint-Antoine* in Grasse in 1995. In his spare time, Jacques Chibois is an enthusiastic cyclist and nature-lover, as well as a keen hunter and angler.

Serge Courville

born: December 9, 1935

Restaurant: **La Cote 108**
Address: Rue Colonel Vergezac
02190 Berry-au-Bac, France
Tel. (0)3 23 79 95 04; Fax (03) 23 79 83 50

Serge Courville names his three teachers – Roger Petit, Robert Morizot, and Jean-Louis Lelaurain – with warmth. Although not much interested in accolades, he has nevertheless reached the final of numerous culinary competitions (Prosper Montagné prize, 1971; Trophée national de l'Académie Culinaire, 1972; Taitinger prize, 1973). Since 1972, he and his wife have run *La Cote 108* together, which in 1982 received one Michelin star. When not working, Serge Courville enjoys cooking for friends; he is also a passionate reader and cyclist and spends a lot of time in the wilds, fishing or hunting for mushrooms.

Bernard & Jean Cousseau

born September 15, 1917 born May 6, 1949

Restaurant: **Relais de la Poste**
Address: 40140 Magescq, France
Tel. (0)5 58 47 70 25; Fax: (0)5 58 47 76 17

Bernard Cousseau embodies the regional gastronomy of Landes. Honorary president of the Maîtres Cuisiniers de France, he serves a fine regional cuisine to his guests at the Relais de la Poste, which openend in 1954 and has been holding two Michelin stars since 1969. On the height of his extraordinary career, the Chef is now an officer of the Mérite Agricole and a Knight of both the Légion d'Honneur and the Palmes académiques. His son Jean has been working with him at the Relais de la Poste since 1970, after an examplary Franco-Hispanic career at the Café de Paris in Biaritz, the Plaza-Athénée in Paris and the Ritz in Madrid.

Richard Coutanceau

born: February 25, 1949

Restaurant: **Richard Coutanceau**
Address: Place de la Concurrence
17000 La Rochelle, France
Tel. (0)5 46 41 48 19; Fax (0)5 46 41 99 45

Richard Coutanceau, whose restaurant boasts a marvelous location in "green Venice" between Marais Poitevin and the Côte Sauvage, started out his career in Paris at *L'Orée du bois* in 1968. He then moved to La Rochelle and the *Hôtel de France et d'Angleterre*, where he worked from 1968 to 1988. This native of Charentais has received many distinctions: two stars in Michelin, three stars in Bottin Gourmand and three red chef's hats and 17 points in Gault-Millau. His restaurant belongs to the Relais Gourmands chain, and he is a member of the Young Restauranteurs of Europe. Richard Coutanceau is an avid tennis player and a keen fisherman.

Jean Crotet

born: January 26, 1943

Restaurant: **Hostellerie de Levernois**
Address: Route de Combertault
21200 Levernois, France
Tel. (0)3 80 24 73 68; Fax (0)3 80 22 78 00

Amidst a splendid park of Louisiana cedar, willow, and ash, through which a small river flows, Jean Crotet offers discerning diners a sophisticated cuisine that has been awarded two Michelin stars and three stars in Bottin Gourmand. He is a Maître Cuisinier de France, as well as a member of Relais et Châteaux and Relais Gourmands chains. In 1988, after working for 15 years at the *Côte d'Or* in Nuits-Saint Georges, he settled down in Levernois, near Beaune. In his spare time Jean Crotet enjoys fishing, flying a helicopter, playing tennis, hunting, and gardening.

Michel Del Burgo

born: June 21, 1962

Restaurant: **La Barbacane**
Address: Place de l'Église
11000 Carcassonne-La Cité, France
Tel. (0)4 68 25 03 34; Fax (0)4 68 71 50 15

This young man from the northern province of Picardy has worked in the kitchens of Alain Ducasse in Courchevel, Raymond Thuillier in Baux-de-Provence, and Michel Guérard in Eugénie-les-Bains, all in the south of France. After a short stay in the Rhône valley and Avignon (1987–90), Michel Del Burgo was in 1991 appointed chef of *La Barbacane* in the center of Carcassonne by Jean-Michel Signoles. In 1995 he was awarded his second Michelin star, the Lily of the restaurant trade and the Gault-Millau golden key, as well as three red chef's hats and 18 points in the latter guide. Michel Del Burgo is fond of music, motor sport, and hiking.

Joseph Delphin

born: September 4, 1932

Restaurant: **La Châtaigneraie**
Address: 156, route de Carquefou
44240 Sucé-sur-Erdre, France
Tel. (0)2 40 77 90 95; Fax (0)2 40 77 90 08

A Maître Cuisinier de France and member of the Culinary Academy of France, Joseph Delphin delights gourmets from the Nantes area with his culinary skills. A knight of the Mérite agricole, this chef has also received the Vase de Sèvres award from the French President. His restaurant, *La Châtaigneraie* (one Michelin star), sits right on the banks of the Erdre, and can be reached by road, river or helicopter... You are sure to be won over by the warmth of the welcome from the Delphin family, as Jean-Louis, a member of the Young Restauranteurs of Europe, works here together with his father.

Philippe Dorange

born: May 27, 1963

Restaurant: **Fouquet's**
Address: 99, avenue des Champs Élysées
75008 Paris, France
Tel (0)1 47 23 70 60; Fax (0)1 47 20 08 69

Does one actually need to introduce the legendary *Fouquet's* in these pages? Surely not, nor the prestigious restaurants in which Philippe Dorange has worked in the past: Roger Vergé's *Le Moulin de Mougins* (1977–81), Jacques Maximin's *Negresco* in Nice (1981–88), and lastly *Ledoyen* in Paris, where he was chef from 1988 to 1992. All in all, a fine career path for a young chef whose Mediterranean origins are reflected in his culinary preferences, a fact that is particularly esteemed by his Champs-Elysées clientele. When not in the kitchen, Philippe Dorange likes to box, drive sports cars or play soccer.

Lothar Eiermann

born: March 2, 1945

Restaurant: **Wald- & Schloßhotel
Friedrichsruhe**
Address: 74639 Friedrichsruhe, Germany
Tel (0)7941 60870; Fax (0)7941 61468

For over 20 years Lothar Eiermann has worked at *Friedrichsruhe*, the summer residence of the Prince von Hohenlohe-Öhringen that belongs to the Relais et Châteaux chain. Before this, he traveled throughout the whole of Europe, working as a chef in Switzerland between 1964 and 1972 in the *Grappe d'Or* in Lausanne and in the *Hotel Victoria* in Glion. He then worked in the *Gleneagles Hotel* in Scotland, traveled south to England, and returned to Scotland, where he managed a hotel from 1972 to 1973. This Bordeaux-wine enthusiast has a degree in Economics from the University of Heidelberg, and enjoys skiing.

Jean Fleury

born: April 22, 1948

Restaurant: **Paul Bocuse**
Address: 69660 Collonges-au-Mont-d'Or, France
Tel (0)4 72 42 90 90; Fax (0)4 72 27 85 87

After a highly promising début in his home town of Bourg-en-Bresse – the chief town of Bresse, a region renowned for its outstanding produce – Jean Fleury achieved fame as a chef in the *Hotel Royal* in Évian (1968–69) and in the Brussels *Hilton* (1971–78). Winner of the Prosper Montagné prize in 1976, he was named Best Chef in Belgium in the same year, and won the Meilleur Ouvrier de France competition in 1979. In 1985 he left the kitchens of the *Arc-en-ciel* in Lyons, following Paul Bocuse to his famous restaurant in Collonges. Jean Fleury loves traveling and hiking and collects antique cookbooks, from which he enjoys drawing inspiration.

Constant Fonk

born: September 1, 1947

Restaurant: **De Oude Rosmolen**
Address: Duinsteeg 1
1621 Hoorn, the Netherlands
Tel (0)229 014752; Fax (0)229 014938

Thanks to Constant Fonk, the town of Hoorn in North Holland has had a two Michelin star restaurant since 1990. After his first highly promising steps in the Amsterdam *Hilton* (1965–66), and the *Amstel Hotel* (1966–67), our chef returned to his home town, where in 1967 he began work in *De Oude Rosmolen*, finally taking over the reins of the kitchen in 1976. A lover of fine cuisine and good wines, he especially enjoys partaking of both with like-minded people. As far as sport is concerned, golf is his favorite form of exercise, and makes a change from the kitchen.

Louis Grondard

born: September 20, 1948

Restaurant: **Drouant**
Address: 16-18, rue Gaillon
75002 Paris, France
Tel (0)1 42 65 15 16; Fax (0)1 49 24 02 15

It is no easy task to have catered for the members of the jury of the prestigious Goncourt literary prize every year since 1990; rather, it requires someone with the skills of this chef, who was named Meilleur Ouvrier de France in 1979. Louis Grondard served his apprenticeship at *Taillevent* and at *Maxim's*, first in Orly, then in Roissy. He then achieved his first successes in the Eiffel Tower restaurant and in the famous *Jules Vernes*. To quote Michel Tournier, "The stars [two in Michelin] fall as his due from heaven." Louis Grondard has also been favored with three white chef's hats and 17 points in Gault-Millau. He loves literature, Baroque music and opera, and enjoys going diving when on vacation.

Philippe Groult

born: November 17, 1953

Restaurant: **Amphyclès**
Address: 78, avenue des Ternes
75017 Paris, France
Tel (0)1 40 68 01 01; Fax (0)1 40 68 91 88

A devoted pupil and colleague of Joël Robuchon at *Jamin* from 1974 to 1985, this native Norman now runs his own restaurant, to the satisfaction of diners and critics alike. Named Meilleur Ouvrier de France in 1982, today Philippe Groult has two Michelin stars and three red chef's hats (18) in Gault-Millau. In 1988 he was a contender in the Culinary Olympics in Tokyo, and one year later took over the reins in the kitchen at *Amphyclès*. He has been a member of Devoirs Unis since 1978. Philippe Groult is a keen traveler, a connoisseur of the Far East, and an enthusiastic martial arts practitioner.

Marc Haeberlin

born: November 28, 1954

Restaurant: **Auberge de L'Ill**
Address: 2, rue de Collonges-au-Mont-d'Or
68970 Illhaeusern, France
Tel. (0)3 89 71 89 00; Fax (0)3 89 71 82 83

This worthy heir to the Haeberlin dynasty will on no account disappoint the gourmets who, once lured by the success of his father Paul, return to this temple of Alsatian cuisine. Three Michelin stars, four red chef's hats (19.5!) in Gault-Millau and four stars in Bottin Gourmand are the impressive distinctions garnered by this former student at the college of hotel management in Illkirch. Completing his training with Paul Bocuse and the Troisgros brothers, he proved his skills in Paris at the *Lasserre* back in 1976. When time allows, Mark Haeberlin occupies himself with painting and cars. In winter he goes downhill-skiing on the slopes of the Vosges.

Michel Haquin

born: September 27, 1940

Restaurant: **Le Trèfle à 4**
Address: 87, avenue de Lac
1332 Genval, Belgium
Tel. (0)2 654 0798; Fax (0)2 653 3131

Not far from Brussels, on the shores of Lake Genval, Michel Haquin successfully pursues a culinary career which began in 1961 in the Belgian capital. There, from 1977 to 1985, he ran a restaurant under his own name. As a Belgian Maître Cuisinier and member of the Culinary Academy of France, this chef was admitted to the Order of the 33 Masterchefs of Belgium and was awarded the Oscar of Gastronomy. The guidebooks have showered him with honors: two Michelin stars, three red chef's hats in Bottin Gourmand and 91/100 in the Belgian guide Henri Lemaire. In his leisure time, Michel Haquin enjoys reading and traveling.

Paul Heathcote

born: October 3, 1960

Restaurant: **Paul Heathcote's**
Address: 104–106 Higher Road,
Longridge PR3 3 SY, England
Tel. (0)1772 784969; Fax (0)1772 – 785713

This young British chef is very open to culinary influences from the other side of the English Channel. After working with Michel Bourdin at the *Connaught*, he spent two years with Raymond Blanc at the *Manoir au Quatr'Saisons* in Oxfordshire, and worked at the *Broughton Park Hotel* in Preston before finally opening his own restaurant (two Michelin stars) in 1990. In 1994, the Egon Ronay guidebook awarded him the enviable title of Best Chef of the Year. An enthusiastic sportsman, Paul Heathcote loves soccer, squash, and skiing.

Eyvind Hellstrøm

born: December 2, 1948

Restaurant: **Bagatelle**
Address: Bygdøy Allé 3
0257 Oslo, Norway
Tel. 22 44 63 97; Fax 22 43 64 20

No other chef in Scandinavia has received as many accolades as Eyvind Hellstrøm. This chef is strongly influenced by French gastronomy, with which he became familiar in the course of his training under famous chefs such as Guy Savoy, Alain Senderens, Bernard Loiseau, and Fredy Girardet. A member of Eurotoques and Traditions et Qualité, Eyvind Hellstrøm was awarded two Michelin stars for his restaurant in 1982. A passionate wine connoisseur and a lover of Burgundies in particular, this chef often visits the wine cellars of Beaune and the surrounding area. He enjoys traveling and skiing, and is a self-confessed fan of the Swedish skier Ingmar Stenmark.

Alfonso Iaccarino

born: January 9, 1947

Restaurant: **Don Alfonso 1890**
Address: Piazza Sant'Agata,
80064 Sant'Agata sui due Golfi, Italy
Tel. (0)81 878 0026; Fax (0)81 533 0226

In 1973, Alfonso Iaccarino named his restaurant, with its marvelous view of the Gulf of Naples and Salerno, after his grandfather. A member of the Le Soste, Relais Gourmands and Traditions et Qualité chains, this chef has garnered numerous honors: two Michelin stars, four chef's hats in Espresso/Gault-Millau, one sun in Veronelli and 92/100 in Gambero Rosso. In 1989 he was awarded the title of Best Winecellar in Italy for his collection of noble Italian and French wines. In his private life, Alfonso Iaccarino is a true sportsman and particularly enjoys racing and cycling. He also loves nature, painting, and traveling.

André Jaeger

born: February 12, 1947

Restaurant: **Rheinhotel Fischerzunft**
Address: Rheinquai 8,
8200 Schaffhausen, Switzerland
Tel. (0)52 625 3281; Fax (0)52 624 3285

André Jaeger can proudly claim to have successfully inspired Swiss and even European gastronomy with an oriental flavor. His restaurant, which he opened in 1975, boasts two Michelin stars and four red chef's hats in Gault-Millau (19). Named 1995 Chef of the Year by Gault-Millau, he was awarded the Golden Key of Gastronomy in 1988 and appointed Chairman of the Grandes Tables in Switzerland. He is also a member of Relais et Châteaux and Relais Gourmands. A connoisseur of wines from around the world, André Jaeger is also very interested in contemporary art and collects cars.

Roger Jaloux

born: May 20, 1942

Restaurant: **Paul Bocuse**
Address: 69660 Collonges-au-Mont-d'Or,
France
Tel. (0)4 72 42 90 90; Fax (0)4 72 27 85 87

As the most loyal among the loyal pupils of Paul Bocuse, Roger Jaloux followed his mentor into the latter's own restaurant in 1965, which incidentally received its third Michelin star in the same year. Everything there is to say about this celebrated restaurant in Collonges and the accolades it has received has already been said: it was here that Roger Jaloux prepared for the competition for the prestigious title of Meilleur Ouvrier de France, which he won in 1976. In his spare time, Roger Jaloux enjoys artistic activities such as painting and singing, and numerous sports, including tennis, cycling, and skiing.

Patrick Jeffroy

born: January 25, 1952

Restaurant: **Patrick Jeffroy**
Address: 11, rue du Bon Voyage
22780 Plounérin, France
Tel. (0)2 96 38 61 80; Fax (0)2 96 38 66 29

A Breton with a penchant for solitude, Patrick Jeffroy settled down in a village in the Côtes-D'Armor département, where he serves innovative, delicious food in his restaurant, established in 1988 and now boasting one Michelin star and three red chef's hats in Gault-Millau (17). The earlier part of his career was spent in Abidjan in the Ivory Coast (1972) and the *Hôtel de l'Europe* in Morlaix back in France (1977–87). Patrick Jeffroy has had his Michelin star since 1984; he is also a Maître Cuisinier de France, and a recipient of the Mandarine Impériale first prize. Outside of working hours, he enjoys going to the theatre and the movies.

Émile Jung

born: April 2, 1941

Restaurant: **Le Crocodile**
Address: 10, rue de l'Outre
67000 Strasbourg, France
Tel. (0)3 88 32 13 02; Fax (0)3 88 75 72 01

Behind the sign of the crocodile – an allusion to Napoleon's Egyptian campaign – can be found Émile Jung's restaurant, highly rated by food lovers and a veritable temple of Alsatian cuisine, boasting no fewer than three Michelin stars, three white chef's hats in Gault-Millau (18) and three stars in Bottin Gourmand. The awards hardly come as a surprise, when one considers that this chef's career took him from La Mère Guy in Lyons to Fouquet's (1965) and Ledoyen (1966) in Paris. Émile Jung is a Maître Cuisinier de France and member of Relais Gourmands and Traditions et Qualité. A passionate enologist, he is particularly well-versed in Alsatian wines.

Dieter Kaufmann

born: June 28, 1937

Restaurant: **Zur Traube**
Address: Bahnstraße 47,
41515 Grevenbroich, Germany
Tel. (0)2181 68767; Fax (0)2181 61122

Dieter Kaufmann harbors a great love of France, and that country knows how to repay him in kind: with two Michelin stars and four red chef's hats in Gault-Millau (19.5) he figures among the most highly esteemed non-French chefs, and was named by Gault-Millau 1994 Chef of the Year. He is a member of the prestigious Traditions et Qualité, Relais et Châteaux and Relais Gourmands chains. With over 30 000 bottles and some remarkable vintages, his restaurant, which he has run since 1962, boasts what is without a doubt the most important wine cellar in Germany. A bibliophile and polyglot, Dieter Kaufmann is also an enthusiastic traveler.

Örjan Klein

born: May 15, 1945

Restaurant: **K.B.**
Address: Smalandsgatan, 7
11146 Stockholm, Sweden
Tel. 86 79 60 32; Fax 86 11 82 83

At the pinnacle of a career based largely in the Swedish capital (Berns from 1966 to 1967 and Maxim's of Stockholm from 1971 to 1979), Örjan Klein joined forces with Ake Hakansson in 1980 to open *K.B.*, which boasts one Michelin star. Named Chef of the Year in 1993, Örjan Klein is also a Nordfishing Trondheim and Swedish Academy of Gastronomy gold-medallist (1976 and 1983, respectively). A nature lover, our chef enjoys gardening and hiking. He also writes (cook)books and keeps fit by playing tennis and skiing.

Robert Kranenborg

born: October 12, 1950

Restaurant: **La Rive/Hotel Amstel Inter-Continental**
Address: Prof. Tulpplein, 1
1018 GX Amsterdam, the Netherlands
Tel. (0)20 622 6060; Fax (0)20 520 3277

One doesn't become chef of *La Rive* (one Michelin star) – the restaurant of the *Inter-Continental*, the most prestigious hotel in Amsterdam – overnight. In fact, Robert Kranenborg had a string of successes as glowing references when he began work there in 1987: *Oustau de Baumanière* in Baux-de-Provence (1972–74), *Le Grand Véfour* in Paris (1975–77) and *La Cravache d'Or* in Brussels (1979-86). In 1994, Robert Kranenborg was named Chef of the Year. When he is able to escape from the kitchen, he enjoys playing the drums or sports – golf being his favorite.

Étienne Krebs

born: August 15, 1956

Restaurant: **L'Ermitage**
Address: 75, rue du Lac
1815 Clarens-Montreux, Switzerland
Tel (0)21 964 4411; Fax (0)21 964 7002

As chef-proprietor of a magnificent house on the shores of Lake Geneva, Étienne Krebs is a happy man: a member of the Young Restauranteurs of Europe and Grandes Tables Suisses, he boasts one Michelin star and three red chef's hats in Gault-Millau (18), as well as the title of Chef of the Year 1995 for French-speaking Switzerland. After training with the greatest Swiss chefs – Fredy Girardet in Crissier and Hans Stucki in Basel – he ran the *Auberge de la Couronne* in Cossonay from 1984 to 1990, before finally opening *L'Ermitage* in Montreux. Étienne Krebs enjoys walking and cycling around the lake, as well as cooking for his family.

Jacques Lameloise

born: April 6, 1947

Restaurant: **Lameloise**
Address: 36, place d'Armes
71150 Chagny, France
Tel. (0)3 85 87 08 85; Fax (0)3 85 87 03 57

The third generation of his family to bear the name, Jacques Lameloise has since 1971 also carried on the tradition of running the family restaurant. Cutting his professional teeth at *Ogier's* in Pontchartrain, from 1965 to 1969 he worked at the Parisian temples of gastronomy *Lucas Carton*, *Fouquet's*, *Ledoyen* and *Lasserre*, not forgetting the *Savoy* in London. Lameloise can boast three stars in both Michelin and Bottin Gourmand, as well as three red chef's hats in Gault-Millau (18), and is a member of the Relais et Châteaux, Relais Gourmands and Traditions et Qualité chains. Our chef is especially keen on antiques and old cars, and enjoys golfing and skiing.

Dominique Le Stanc

born December 7, 1958

Restaurant: **Chanteclerc - Hôtel Negresco**
Address: 37, Promenade des Anglais
06000 Nice, France
Tel. (0)4 93 16 64 00; Fax (0)4 93 88 35 68

Some of the biggest names in the world of gastronomy have watched over the early stages of Dominique Le Stanc's career. After serving an apprenticeship with Paul Haeberlin, he worked with Gaston Lenôtre, Alain Senderens, and Alain Chapel, and became chef de partie under the latter before putting out his own shingle, first at the *Bristol* in Niederbronn-les-Bains (1982–84) then in Monaco and Èze. A member of the Italian chain Le Soste, he has been head chef of *Negresco* since 1989, earning this celebrated establishment two Michelin stars and three red chef's hats in Gault-Millau (18). A keen athlete, our chef takes part in triathlons and water-skis.

Michel Libotte

born May 1, 1949

Restaurant: **Au Gastronome**
Address: 2, rue de Bouillon
6850 Paliseul, Belgium
Tel. (0)61 53 30 64; Fax (0)61 53 38 91

Since 1978, Michel Libotte has presided over the kitchens of *Au Gastronome*, rated 94/100 in the Belgian restaurant guide Henri Lemaire. French critics have also been unstinting in their praise, awarding our chef's establishment two Michelin stars and three stars in Bottin Gourmand. Michel Libotte has won the title of Best Cook in Belgium, and is a member of Eurotoques and the Culinary Academy of France. His restaurant, which lies close to the Franco-Belgian border, serves a highly individual, imaginative cuisine. Michel Libotte collects firearms as a hobby, and keeps fit by swimming and playing tennis regularly.

Léa Linster

born April 27, 1955

Restaurant: **Léa Linster**
Address: 17, route de Luxembourg
5752 Frisange, Luxembourg
Tel. 66 84 11; Fax 67 64 47

Léa Linster is the first, and to date the only, woman to receive the highest gastronomic accolade, the Bocuse d'Or, awarded to her in Lyons in 1989 by the Master himself in well-earned recognition of her daily efforts to make the generous cuisine of Luxembourg better known to the dining public. Converting her parents' inn into an haute cuisine restaurant in 1982, this chef received her master craftsman's diploma in 1987. In addition to her obvious enthusiasm for fine cuisine, Léa Lister enjoys walks in the wild and stimulating conversations with diners in her restaurant.

Régis Marcon

born June 14, 1956

Restaurant: **Auberge et Clos des Cimes**
Address: 43290 Saint-Bonnet-le-Froid, France
Tel. (0)4 71 59 93 72; Fax (0)4 71 59 93 40

In 1995, at only 39 years, Régis Marcon was awarded the Bocuse d'Or, with his neighbor Michel Troisgros serving as godfather – just one more glowing distinction in a career already crowned with accolades: the Taittinger prize in 1989, the Brillat-Savarin prize in 1992 and several-time finalist in the Meilleur Ouvrier de France competition (1985, 1991, 1993). In 1979 our chef opened a restaurant in his village that has earned him three red chef's hats in Gault-Millau (17), and which was designed to resemble "a cloister bathed in light". Here one recognizes the eye of the painter, a one-time ambition Régis Marcon, who is a great sportsman and medal-winning skier, as well as a passionate lover of nature.

Guy Martin

born February 3, 1957

Restaurant: **Le Grand Véfour**
Address: 17, rue de Beaujolais
75001 Paris, France
Tel. (0)1 42 96 56 27; Fax (0)1 42 86 80 71

It would be impossible to summarize Guy Martin's career in just a few words – two Michelin stars, three white chef's hats in Gault-Millau (18), three stars in the Bottin Gourmand and 18.5/20 in Champérard. This prodigy studied first with Troisgros, then in his native region, chiefly in Divonne. In 1991 he took over the reins of *Le Grand Véfour*, that jewel among Parisian restaurants at which the litterati of the French metropolis have rubbed shoulders for over 200 years, made famous by Raymond Oliver. Guy Martin remains true to the memory of his mother and to his native region of Savoy, of whose culinary history he is a fervent devotee. He also loves music, painting and Gothic art.

Maria Ligia Medeiros

born August 9, 1946

Restaurant: **Casa de Comida**
Address: 1, Travessa das Amoreiras
1200 Lisbon, Portugal
Tel. (0)1 388 5376; Fax (0)1 387 5132

Since 1978, Maria Ligia Medeiros has run the kitchens of a cozy restaurant owned by Jorge Vales, a former stage actor of the Casa de Comedia theater – hence the pun of the restaurant's name (*comida* = "food"). There, in the heart of the historic Old Town of the capital, she dishes up traditional Portuguese dishes with skill and flair, for which she was awarded a Michelin star several years ago. In addition to haute cuisine, our chef loves classical music and spends a large part of her leisure hours reading.

Dieter Müller

born July 28, 1948

Restaurant: **Dieter Müller**
Address: Lerbacher Weg,
51469 Bergisch Gladbach, Germany
Tel. (0)2202 2040; Fax (0)2202 204940

Dieter Müller had already beaten a career path across several countries and continents by the time he settled down in his native Germany in 1992: from 1973 onward he served as head chef of various establishments in Switzerland, Australia (Sydney), Japan, and Hawaii, collecting numerous awards along the way, including the title of chef of the Year in the Krug guidebook in 1982 and in Gault-Millau in 1988. Today, he boasts two Michelin stars and four red chef's hats (19.5), as well as a National Gastronomy prize. A member of Relais et Châteaux and Relais Gourmands, his hobbies are photography and collecting old recipes, as well as playing ice hockey and soccer.

Jean-Louis Neichel

born February 17, 1948

Restaurant: **Neichel**
Address: Beltran i RÛzpide, 16 bis
08034 Barcelona, Spain
Tel. (9)3 203 8408; Fax (9)3 205 6369

Thanks to his training under such culinary celebrities as Gaston Lenôtre, Alain Chapel, and Georges Blanc, Jean-Louis Neichel is a European chef *par excellence*. For 10 years he brought his invaluable experience to bear while running *El Bulli* in Rosas, where Fernando Adría is now head chef, before opening his own restaurant in Barcelona in 1981, esteemed in particular for its collection of old Armagnacs and Cognacs. Awarded two Michelin stars and 9/10 in Gourmetour, Jean-Louis Neichel is also a member of Relais Gourmands. His leisure hours are devoted to oil painting (landscapes), his family, and sports (tennis, cycling, skiing).

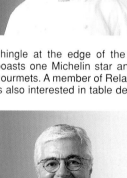

Pierre Orsi

born July 12, 1939

Restaurant: **Pierre Orsi**
Address: 3, place Kléber
69006 Lyons, France
Tel. (0)4 78 89 57 68; Fax (0)4 72 44 93 34

Pierre Orsi's career reads like a dream: named Meilleur Ouvrier de France in 1972, he has worked with the culinary greats of his generation: with Bocuse from 1955 to 1958, then at *Lucas Carton*; with Alex Humbert at Maxim's, and at *Lapérouse* in Paris. There followed a stint in the USA from 1967 to 1971, after which he returned to Lyons and put out his shingle at the edge of the *Tête d'Or* quarter. His superb restaurant, which boasts one Michelin star and three stars in Bottin Gourmand, is a mecca for gourmets. A member of Relais Gourmands and Traditions et Qualité, Pierre Orsi is also interested in table decoration and collects art objects and antiques.

Georges Paineau

born April 16, 1939

Restaurant: **Le Bretagne**
Address: 13, rue Saint-Michel
56230 Questembert, France
Tel. (0)2 97 26 11 12; Fax (0)2 97 26 12 37

Georges Paineau had the unusual good forture to start off his career under Fernand Point at *La Pyramide* in 1960. Since then, he drew ever closer to Brittany, stopping off in *La Baule* (1962) and Nantes (1963), before settling at Le Bretagne in Questembert, close to the Gulf of Morbihan, where he now collects stars (two in Michelin and four in Bottin Gourmand) and Gault-Millau chef's hats (four red, 19 points). Our chef works with his son-in-law, Claude Corlouer. His restaurant, an old coaching inn, is a member of Relais Gourmands and Relais et Châteaux. A gifted painter, Georges Paineau also loves literature and rugby.

Paul Pauvert

born July 25, 1950

Restaurant: **Les Jardins de la Forge**
Address: 1, place des Piliers
49270 Champtoceaux, France
Tel. (0)2 40 83 56 23; Fax (0)2 40 83 59 80

Professionally speaking, Paul Pauvert took his first steps at the *Café de la Paix* in Paris; from 1972 to 1974 he served a stint in the kitchens of the Transatlantic Shipping Company's famous ocean liner *Grasse*, after which he worked at the *Hotel Frantel* in Nantes at the invitation of Roger Jaloux. In 1980 he opened his own restaurant in his home town, on the same spot where his ancestors had once run a forge. The holder of one Michelin star, Paul Pauvert is also a member of the Culinary Academy of France and the Young Restauranteurs of Europe. The border area between Anjou and Nantes where our chef lives offers ample opportunity for the hunting, fishing, and riding that he enjoys.

Horst Petermann

born May 18, 1944

Restaurant: **Petermann's Kunststuben**
Address: Seestraße 160,
8700 Küsnacht, Switzerland
Tel. (0)1 910 0715; Fax (0)1 910 0495

After serving his apprenticeship in Hamburg, Horst Petermann continued his career in Switzerland, in Saint Moritz, Lucerne and Geneva. He cooked in the kitchens of Émile Jung at *Le Crocodile* in Strasbourg, and at the Culinary Olympics in Tokyo in 1985, where he figured among the prizewinners. Further accolades received were the Golden Key of Gastronomy in 1987, Chef of the Year in 1991, four red chef's hats in Gault-Millau (19) and two Michelin stars. The success of his restaurant is also ensured by his master pastrycook, Rico Zandonella. As well as being a keen sportsman, Horst Petermann enjoys cultivating the friendships he has made through his work.

Roland Pierroz

born August 26, 1942

Restaurant: **Hôtel Rosalp-Restaurant Pierroz**
Address: Route de Médran,
1936 Verbier, Switzerland
Tel. (0)27 771 6323; Fax (0)27 771 1059

Since 1962, Roland Pierroz has worked in this popular winter-sports resort in an equally popular restaurant. The holder of one Michelin star, four red chef's hats and 19 points in Gault-Millau, and three stars in Bottin Gourmand, he was awarded the Golden Key of Gastronomy in 1980 and named Chef of the Year in 1992. Roland Pierroz trained in Lausanne (Switzerland) and London, and is a member of Relais et Châteaux and Relais Gourmands, as well as vice-chairman of the Grandes Tables Suisses. A native of the Valais, he enjoys hunting and golf.

Jacques and Laurent Pourcel

born September 13, 1964

Restaurant: **Le Jardin des Sens**
Address: 11, avenue Saint Lazare
34000 Montpellier, France
Tel. (0)4 67 79 63 38; Fax (0)4 67 72 13 05

Though specializing in different areas, these inseparable twins underwent the same training, serving apprenticeships with Alain Chapel, Marc Meneau, Pierre Gagnaire, Michel Bras, Michel Trama, and Marc Veyrat. Together with their business partner, Olivier Château, they opened the *Jardin des Sens* in a house made of glass and stone in 1988, since when they have collected stars in various guides: two from Michelin and three red chef's hats in Gault-Millau (17). Both chefs are Maîtres Cuisiniers de France and members of Relais Gourmands.

Stéphane Raimbault

born May 17, 1956

Restaurant: **L'Oasis**
Address: rue Honoré Carle,
06210 La Napoule, France
Tel. (0)4 93 49 95 52; Fax (0)4 93 49 64 13

After working for several years in Paris under the watchful eye of Émile Tabourdiau at *La Grande Cascade*, followed by a stint with Gérard Pangaud, Stéphane Raimbault spent nine years in Japan, where he ran the *Rendez-vous* restaurant in the *Hotel Plaza d'Osaka* in Osaka. After returning to France in 1991, he took over *L'Oasis* in La Napoule, with his brother as pastry chef. The recipient of two Michelin stars and three red chef's hats in Gault-Millau (18), he was also a finalist for the title of Meuilleur Ouvrier de France. In addition, he is a Maître Cuisinier de France and a member of Traditions et Qualité.

Paul Rankin

born October 1, 1959

Restaurant: **Roscoff**
Address: 7, Lesley House, Shaftesbury Square, Belfast BT2 7DB, Northern Ireland
Tel. (0)1232 331 532; Fax (0)1232 312 093

Paul Rankin has had an international career, working first in London with Albert Roux in Le Gavroche, then in California and Canada. It was not, however, in Canada, but on a cruise in Greece that he got to know his Canadian wife Jeanne, whose skills as pastry chef have delighted diners at *Roscoff* since 1989. Named Best Restaurant in the United Kingdom by the Courvoisier guidebook in 1994–95, it is only a wonder that Roscoff has just one Michelin star. Paul Rankin also presents the BBC television program "Gourmet Ireland". Our chef loves traveling and wine, plays soccer and rugby and practices yoga.

Joël Roy

born November 28, 1951

Restaurant: **Le Prieuré**
Address: 3, rue du Prieuré,
54630 Flavigny-sur-Moselle, France
Tel. (0)3 79 26 70 45; Fax (0)3 86 26 75 51

In 1979, while still in the employ of Jacques Maximin at the *Hôtel Negresco* in Nice, Joël Roy won the Meilleur Ouvrier de France competition. Shortly afterwards, he became head chef at the *Frantel* in Nancy. In 1983 he opened *Le Prieuré*, which looks like a modern cloister with its arcades and garden. His one-Michelin-star establishment is in the Lorraine, a region he loves for its traditions and natural beauty. An expert on fish, he is especially fond of river angling, and also enjoys cycling in his spare time.

Santi Santamaria

born July 26, 1957

Restaurant: **El Racó de Can Fabes**
Address: Carrer Sant Joan, 6
08470 San Celoni, Spain
Tel. (9)3 867 2851; Fax (9)3 867 3861

Since 1981, Santi Santamaria has taken great pleasure in serving specialties from his native Catalonia to his discerning clientele. His restaurant, which is just a stone's throw away from Barcelona, at the foot of Montseny national park, has been awarded three Michelin stars and 8/10 in Gourmetour. In addition, Santi Santamaria is a member of Relais Gourmands and Traditions et Qualité. Our chef also organizes gastronomic seminars, on herbs in the spring and on mushrooms in the fall. These gourmet workshops are always a great success. In his free time, Santi Santamaria enjoys reading.

Ezio Santin

born May 17, 1937

Restaurant: **Antica Osteria del Ponte**
Address: 9, Piazza G. Negri
20080 Cassinetta di Lugagnano, Italy
Tel. (0)2 942 0034; Fax (0)2 942 0610

Ezio Santin's culinary talents have been common knowledge since 1974, when he became chef at the *Antica Osteria del Ponte*. Three Michelin stars, four red chef's hats in Gault-Millau (19.5), one sun in Veronelli and 92/100 in Gambero Rosso: these honors justify the high regard in which he is held by his fellow Italian chefs, who have elected him chairman of Le Soste, an association of the best restaurants in Italy. Ezio Santin enjoys reading in his spare time. An enthusiastic fan of Inter Milan soccer club, he is also interested in modern dance.

Nadia Santini

born July 19, 1954

Restaurant: **Dal Pescatore**
Address: 46013 Runate Canneto sull'Oglio, Italy
Tel. (0)376 72 30 01; Fax (0)376 70304

Since 1974 Nadia Santini has presided over the kitchens of *Dal Pescatore*, which was opened in 1920 by her husband's grandfather. Its outstanding reputation is impressively documented in both Italian and French restaurant guides: two Michelin stars, four red chef's hats in L'Espresso/Gault-Millau (19), one sun in Veronelli and 94/100 in Gambero Rosso. A member of Le Soste, Relais Gourmands and Traditions et Qualité, she was awarded the prize for the Best Wine Cellar of the Year by L'Espresso/Gault-Millau in 1993. Nadia Santini is interested in history, especially the history of the culinary arts. She also loves hiking in the mountains.

Maria Santos Gomes

born August 10, 1962

Restaurant: **Conventual**
Address: Praça das Flores, 45
1200 Lisbon, Portugal
Tel. (0)1 60 91 96; Fax (0)1 387 5132

The Conventual is located in the historic Old Town of Lisbon, right by the Parliament. There, in 1982, Dina Marquez engaged the young chef Maria Santos Gomes – to the great delight of Lisbon politicians, who dine there regularly. Much of the restaurant's decor comes from the former convent of Igreja (hence the restaurant's name). Maria Santos Gomes' inventive cuisine has already earned her one Michelin star; in 1993, she won first prize in the Portuguese Gastronomy Competition, which always takes place in Lisbon. In addition to cooking, she loves literature, going on walks, and traveling.

Nikolaos Sarantos

born December 5, 1945

Restaurant: **Hôtel Athenaeum Inter-Continental**
Address: 89–93, Syngrou Avenue
117 45 Athens, Greece
Tel. (0)1 902 3666; Fax (0)1 924 3000

From 1971 to 1988, Nikolaos Sarantos traveled around the Mediterranean and the Middle East, honing his culinary skills in the various *Hilton Hotels* in Teheran, Athens, Corfu, Kuwait City, and Cairo before finally settling down at the *Athenaeum Inter-Continental* in 1988. Nikolaos Sarantos is a member of the jury at international cooking competitions in San Francisco, Copenhagen and Bordeaux. Chairman of the Chef's Association of Greece, he is also a great sports fan, and a keen tennis, soccer, and basketball player.

Fritz Schilling

born June 8, 1951

Restaurant: **Schweizer Stuben**
Address: Geiselbrunnweg 11,
97877 Wertheim, Germany
Tel. (0)9342 30 70; Fax (0)9342 30 71 55

A chef since 1972, Fritz Schilling opened his restaurant in the Main valley near the romantic little town of Wertheim in 1990. His refined and versatile cuisine, which cultivates the best German gastronomic traditions, has already earned him two Michelin stars and four red chef's hats in Gault-Millau (19.5). A member of Relais et Châteaux and Relais Gourmands, his restaurant is one of the best in Germany. In his spare time, Fritz Schilling loves listening to pop music. A passionate driver, he enjoys playing golf and likes most beach sports.

Jean and Jean-Yves Schillinger

born January 31, 1934   born March 23, 1963
died December 27, 1995

Jean Schillinger was Chairman of Maître Cuisiniers de France and a symbol of Alsatian gastronomy; his restaurant in Colmar (1957–95) boasted two Michelin stars, three red stars in Gault-Millau (17), and three stars in Bottin Gourmand. A Knight of the Ordre de Mérite, he raised the profile of French cuisine throughout the world, from Japan to Brazil and Australia.

His son Jean-Yves belongs to the fourth generation of the restaurant family and has worked all his life in famous restaurants: the *Crillon* and *Jamin* in Paris, and *La Côte Basque* in New York. From 1988 to 1995 he worked in the family-owned restaurant in Colmar.

Rudolf Sodamin and Jonathan Wicks

born April 6, 1958; June 14, 1958

Restaurant Passenger Ship *Queen Elizabeth II* Home port: Southampton, Great Britain

These two chefs work for the shipping company Cunard Line, which owns several liners apart from the *Queen Elizabeth II*. The Austrian Rudolf Sodamin is chef de cuisine and chief pastry chef. He has attracted the notice of many restaurants in Austria, France, Switzerland, and the United States. In New York he worked in the famous *Waldorf Astoria*.

Jonathan Wicks has worked in several London restaurants, among them the *Mayfair Intercontinental*, *Grosvenor House* in Park Lane, and the *Méridien* in Piccadilly. In 1987 he was appointed chef de cuisine of the *Queen Elizabeth II*.

Roger Souvereyns

born December 2, 1938

Restaurant: **Scholteshof**
Address: Kermstraat, 130
3512 Stevoort-Hasselt, Belgium
Tel. (0)11 25 02 02; Fax (0)11 25 43 28

Since 1983, Roger Souvereyns has presided over the *Scholteshof*. This 18th-century farmstead has a large vegetable garden that used to be tended by his friend and gardener Clément, and which is the source of the wonderful fresh fruit and vegetables used in his cooking. Roger Souvereyns has two Michelin stars, four red chef's hats in Gault-Millau (19.5), three stars in Bottin Gourmand, and 95/100 in the Belgian restaurant guide Henri Lemaire. A member of Relais et Châteaux, Relais Gourmands and Traditions et Qualité, he is a collector of antiques and old pictures. He also loves opera, and enjoys swimming and cycling.

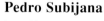

Pedro Subijana

born November 5, 1948

Restaurant **Akelaré**
Address: 56, Paseo del Padre Orcolaga
20008 San Sebastian, Spain
Tel. (9)43 21 20 52; Fax (9)43 21 92 68

Since 1981, Pedro Subijana has had his own restaurant overlooking the Bay of Biscay. Awarded two stars in Michelin and 9/10 in Gourmetour, he was named Best Cook in Spain in 1982. Subijana underwent a traditional training at the coliege of hotel management in Madrid and at Euromar college in Zarauz, and became a cooking teacher in 1970. In 1986 he became Commissioner General of the European Association of Chefs, whose headquarters is in Brussels. He presents food programs on Basque television and on Tele-Madrid. Pedro Subijana loves music and the movies.

Émile Tabourdiau

born November 25, 1943

Restaurant: **Le Bristol**
Address: 112, rue du Faubourg Saint-Honoré
75008 Paris, France
Tel. (0)1 53 43 43 00; Fax (0)1 53 43 43 01

Since 1964, Émile Tabourdiau has worked only in the most famous of restaurants: First at *Ledoyen*, then at *La Grande Cascade*, and finally, since 1980, at *Le Bristol*, located in the immediate vicinity of the Élysée Palace and boasting magnificent large gardens. A former pupil of Auguste Escoffier, Émile Tabourdiau is a member of the Culinary Academy of France, and was the winner of the Prosper Montagné prize in 1970 as well as Meilleur Ouvrier de France in 1976. He restaurant has one Michelin star. In his spare time he loves painting, and enjoys playing tennis and spending time in his garden.

Romano Tamani

born April 30, 1943

Restaurant: **Ambasciata**
Address: 33, Via Martiri di Belfiore
46026 Quistello, Italy
Tel. (0)376 61 90 03; Fax (0)376 61 82 55

Romano Tamani is the only one of our top chefs to hold the coveted title of Commendatore della Repubblica Italiana, a distinction conferred on him by his native Italy in 1992. This Lombardian, who learnt his craft in London and Switzerland, is without doubt one of the most skillful representatives of Italian gastronomy to be found. Together, he and his brother Francesco have run the *Ambasciata* since 1978. Accolades include two Michelin stars, three chef's hats in Espresso/Gault-Millau, one Veronelli sun and 90/100 in Gambero Rosso, as well as membership of the prestigious Italian chain Le Soste. It is hardly surprising, therefore, that cooking is Tamani's consuming passion.

Laurent Tarridec

born May 26, 1956

Restaurant: **Le Restaurant du Bistrot des Lices**
Address: Place des Lices,
83990 Saint-Tropez, France
Tel. (0)4 94 97 29 00; Fax (0)4 94 97 76 39

That this Breton, a pupil of Michel Rochedy, could set himself up on the Côte d'Azur of all places, and after only one year (1995) walk off with one Michelin star and three red chef's hats in Gault-Millau (18), is testimony to his extraordinary adaptability. Before this, he honed his skills in Brittany at the *Lion d'Or*, in Paris, and in the Rhone valley at the *Beau Rivage*. Laurent Tarridec is interested in politics, as well as anything related with the sea. He also skis, rides a motorcycle, and, since living in Saint-Tropez, has discovered the game of boules.

Dominique Toulousy

born August 19, 1952

Restaurant: **Les Jardins de l'Opéra**
Address: 1, place du Capitole
31000 Toulouse, France
Tel. (0)5 61 23 07 76; Fax (0)5 61 23 63 00

Dominique Toulousy has only been resident in Toulouse since 1984. From the Place du Capitole, he reaped accolades by the dozen: Golden Key of Gastronomy (1986), three red chef's hats in Gault-Millau (18) and two Michelin stars, as well as the title of Meilleur Ouvrier of France (1993). Before this, he had his first successes in Gers, a region known for its generous cuisine. Dominique Toulousy is a member of the Young Restauranteurs of Europe, the Prosper Montagné association, Eurotoques, and Traditions et Qualité. He enjoys poring over old cookbooks and loves gardening, tennis and swimming.

Gilles Tournadre

born June 29, 1955

Restaurant: **Gill**
Address: 8 & 9, quai de la Bourse
76000 Rouen, France
Tel. (0)2 35 71 16 14; Fax (0)2 35 71 96 91

Even a Norman can occasionally be persuaded to leave his native region in order to learn his craft: Gilles Tournadre started out his career at *Lucas Carton*, followed by the *Auberge des Templiers* of the Bézards and *Taillevent*, before finally winding up – on his own two feet – in Bayeux, and lastly in 1984, back in his home town. His career successes have justified all these changes: the young gastronome can boast two Michelin stars and three red chef's hats (17 points) for his restaurant right near Rouen cathedral. A member of the Young Restauranteurs of Europe, this enthusiastic sportsman loves judo, golf, and motor sports, and is also a passionate conservationist.

José Tourneur

born January 4, 1940

Restaurant: **Des 3 Couleurs**
Address: 453, avenue de Tervuren
1150 Brussels, Belgium
Tel. (0)2 770 3321; Fax (0)2 770 8045

The three colors that José Tourneur chose in 1979 as the logo and name of his restaurant are those of the Belgian national flag. The restaurant, which is wholly dedicated to Belgian cuisine, has one Michelin star and was awarded 88/100 in the Belgian restaurant guide Henri Lemaire. A self-taught cook, Tourneur gained experience in Brussels and Nice, won the Prosper Montagné prize in 1969, and was chef de cuisine at the Brussels *Carlton* from 1969 to 1979. He is also a member of the Order of the 33 Masterchefs of Belgium, the Culinary Academy of France, and the Vatel Club. His other interests all revolve around the sea: he loves ships, and enjoys fishing and waterskiing.

Luisa Valazza

born December 20, 1950

Restaurant: **Al Sorriso**
Address: Via Roma, 18
28018 Soriso, Italy
Tel. (0)322 98 32 28; Fax (0)322 98 33 28

Taking their cue from the name of the restaurant that she and her husband Angelo have run since 1981 in their home town in the Piedmont region, the food critics have all "smiled" on Luisa Valazza, awarding *Al Sorriso* two Michelin stars, four chef's hats in Espresso/Gault-Millau (19.2), one sun in Veronelli and 90/100 in Gambero Rosso. Our chef, who is also a member of the Le Soste chain, remains modest in the midst of this avalanche of praise, carefully cooking the recipes she has amassed since 1971 in the Europa in Borgomanero. Luisa Valazza is passionately interested in art. A keen museum-goer, she is also an enthusiastic practitioner of winter sports.

Freddy Van Decasserie

born October 10, 1943

Restaurant: **La Villa Lorraine**
Address: 75, avenue du Vivier d'Oie
1180 Brussels, Belgium
Tel. (0)2 374 3163; Fax (0)2 372 0195

Freddy Van Decasserie started off at *La Villa Lorraine* in 1963 as a kitchen boy and worked his way up the hierarchy until finally becoming head chef and the recipient of numerous awards: two Michelin stars, three red chef's hats in Gault-Millau (18), three stars in Bottin Gourmand and 92/100 in Henri Lemaire. He is a Maître Cuisinier de Belgique and a member of the Culinary Academy of France and Traditions et Qualité. In his spare time, he stays fit by being a training partner to the racing cyclist Eddy Merckx. He also swims and attends the occasional soccer match.

Geert Van Hecke

born July 20, 1956

Restaurant: **De Karmeliet**
Address: Langestraat, 19
8000 Bruges, Belgium
Tel. (0)50 33 82 59; Fax (0)50 33 10 11

Geert Van Hecke was introduced to his craft by Freddy Van Decasserie at the *Villa Lorraine* in 1977, then served a stint with Alain Chapel at the famous *Cravache d'Or* in Brussels, finally opening his own restaurant in a renowned historic house in the heart of Bruges, the "Venice of the North". To date, his cooking has earned him two Michelin stars, three stars in the Bottin Gourmand, three red chef's hats in Gault-Millau (18) and 92/100 in Henri Lemaire. A winner of the Best Chef in Belgium award, he is also a member of Traditions et Qualité. He particulary enjoys Bruges, a well preserved medieval town and popular tourist destination, as he is interested in art and enjoys visiting museums.

Gérard Vié

born April 11, 1943

Restaurant: **Les Trois Marches (Trianon Palace)**
Address: 1 boulevard de la Reine
78000 Versailles, France
Tel. (0)1 39 50 13 21; Fax (0)1 30 21 01 25

The incomparable chef of the *Trois Marches* (since 1970) started his career at the tender age of 13 at Lapérouse. There followed stints at *Lucas Carton* and the *Plaza-Athénée* in Paris and *Crillon Tower's* in London, as well as three years with the Compagnie des Wagons-Lits (1967–70). Today, Gérard Vié can boast two Michelin stars and three red chef's hats (18). Recipient of the Silver Table award from Gault-Millau in 1984, he was presented with the Golden Key of Gastronomy in 1993. An enthusiastic fan of the arts, he collects paintings and is a Chevalier des Arts et Lettres. He also loves hiking and swimming.

Gianfranco Vissani

born November 22, 1951

Restaurant: **Vissani**
Address: 05020 Civitella del Lago, Italy
Tel. (0)744 95 03 96; Fax (0)744 95 03 96

With a rating of 19.6 and four chef's hats, Gianfranco Vissani got a near-perfect report card from Espresso/Gault-Millau – the best in all of Italy. Two Michelin stars, one Veronelli sun and 87/100 in Gambero Rosso complete the guidebook honors showered on the restaurant run by Vissani since 1980 as a family concern together with his wife, mother, and sister. One of the selling points of his establishment is his own olive oil, an indispensable seasoning in his Mediterranean cooking. In his spare time, this gourmet collects clocks and relaxes by listening to classical music or reading. In addition, he is an unconditional fan of the AC Milan soccer club.

Heinz Winkler

born July 17, 1949

Restaurant: **Residenz Heinz Winkler**
Address: Kirchplatz 1,
83229 Aschau im Chiemgau, Germany
Tel. (0)8052 17990; Fax (0)8052 179 966

At only 31 years of age, Heinz Winkler already boasted three Michelin stars: how on earth did he do it? Perhaps by training at the *Victoria* in Interlaken, under Paul Bocuse, and at *Tantris* in Munich, before opening the *Residenz Heinz Winkler* in 1991. To crown it all, this gastronome has three white chef's hats (18) and was Chef of the Year in 1979 as well as Restauranteur of the Year in 1994 in Gault-Millau. Heinz Winkler is a member of Relais et Châteaux, Relais Gourmands, Traditions et Qualité, and the Italian chain Le Soste. He enjoys poring over old cookbooks, playing golf and skiing.

Harald Wohlfahrt

born November 7, 1955

Restaurant: **Schwarzwaldstube**
Address: Tonbachstrasse 237,
72270 Baiersbronn, Germany
Tel. (0)7442 49 26 65; Fax (0)7442 49 26 92

Harald Wohlfahrt started work at the *Schwarzwaldstube*, the restaurant of the *Hotel Trauben-Tonbach* in the heart of the Black Forest, in 1976, and has been chef there since 1980. He learned his trade at *Stahlbad* in Baden-Baden and *Tantris* in Munich. Voted Chef of the Year in 1991 by Gault-Millau, he currently boasts three Michelin stars and four red chef's hats (19.5). He is also a member of Relais Gourmands and Traditions et Qualité. While his main interests, unsurprisingly, are eating and cooking traditions, Harald Wohlfahrt is also an outstanding athlete, with swimming, soccer and cycling being his favorite sports.

Armando Zanetti

born December 11, 1926

Restaurant: **Vecchia Lanterna**
Address: Corso Re Umberto, 21
10128 Turin, Italy
Tel. (0)11 53 70 47; Fax (0)11 53 03 91

A native Venetian, Armando Zanetti ran the *Rosa d'Oro* in Turin from 1955 to1969 before opening the evocatively named *Vecchia Lanterna* ("Old Lantern") restaurant in the same city in 1970. Today, our chef, who devotes himself chiefly to the traditional cuisine of his native country, now proudly boasts two Michelin stars and four chef's hats in Espresso/Gault-Millau (19.2/20). In his spare time, Armando Zanetti tirelessly researches European cuisine of bygone eras. He derives especial pleasure from trying new dishes, both his own and those of his fellow chefs.

Alberto Zuluaga

born March 31, 1960

Restaurant: **Lopez de Haro y Club Nautico**
Address: Obispo Orueta, 2
48009 Bilbao, Spain
Tel. (9)4 423 5500; Fax (9)4 423 4500

As a Basque from the Spanish province of Vizcaya on the Bay of Biscay, Alberto Zuluaga is especially proud to be able to exercise his profession in the true capital of his native province. He has been chef of the five-star luxury restaurant *Club Nautico* in the banking district of Bilbao since 1991. Before this, from 1987 to 1991, he cultivated his love of Basque cuisine and culinary traditions at the *Bermeo* in the same city, earning the title of "Best Cook in Euzkadi" (the Basque Country) in 1988. It goes without saying that our chef enjoys playing Basque boules in his spare time, but he also likes car racing. He is also an enthusiastic mushroom-hunter when time allows.

Glossary

ADD LIQUID: adding liquid such as wine or broth to the contents in the frying pan to loosen them from the base of the pan.

ADJUST SEASONING TO TASTE: seasoning a dish toward the end of preparation, or seasoning its components as you complete their preparation, with salt, pepper, spices, or herbs according to taste rather than measurement.

AÏOLI: a Provençal garlic mayonnaise (in French, ail meants garlic) served traditionally with steamed fish, hard-boiled eggs, or vegetables, such as crudités.

AL DENTE: to keep pasta or vegetables from being overcooked, and thus render them too soft to slightly resist a diner's bite, Italians instruct they be cooked "to the tooth."

AMERICAN SAUCE: a sauce made with well-roasted root vegetables and crushed lobster shells; the sauce is flambéd with brandy, white wine is added, and it is finally whisked with butter. It is traditionally served with fish and shellfish, particularly crustaceans such as lobsters and langoustines.

ASPIC: a flavored jelly, often made from clarified meat juices (but also from vegetables or fish) that sets to form a clear or semi-clear elastic mixture, prepared with pectin or gelatin. Used as a base for molded dishes as well as a garnish – served, for example, as a cubed accompaniment next to a terrine that is based on the same aspic.

BAIN-MARIE: an extremely delicate method of cooking ingredients, such as custards or sauces, that will turn if subjected to a sudden change in temperature. A pot, bowl, or pan of food is placed in a larger pot that is filled with warm water (sometimes boiling, sometimes at a lower temperature); the combination is then cooked in an oven or on the stove. Saucepans with double-walls are also manufactured, containing a cavity between their walls that is filled with water.

BAKE AU GRATIN: to sprinkle cooked dishes with bread crumbs, cheese, or pats of butter and bake at high heat from above, allowing a crust to form.

BASTE: to moisten roast meat (such as roast beef, roast duck, suckling pig, roast turkey, etc.) with the meat's own juices to prevent the meat from drying out while in the oven; basting is also done encourage skin to become crispy or a crust to build up.

BÉCHAMEL SAUCE: one of the French "mother sauces," made with flour, butter, and milk (the proportions determine its consistency, which may vary), blended into a creamy sauce and served hot. Named after its inventor, the Marquis de Béchamel, court master to King Louis XIV.

BIND IN A ROUX: to bind (or thicken) sauces or bind vegetables together in a heated mixture of equal amounts of flour and butter.

BLANCH: a technique with two purposes: the first is to cook ingredients, particularly vegetables, in boiling water for just a moment to either soften a harsh flavor or scent, or kill germs or enzymes. The second is to pour boiling water over fruit, vegetables, or nuts to facilitate peeling or shelling; alternately, they may be dipped in the boiling water for a moment (as in blanching tomatoes).

BLINI: the traditional small Russian pancakes made with buckwheat flour, usually served with soured cream, caviar or smoked salmon.

BOUQUET GARNI: a bunch of herbs that are tied together and used for seasoning soups, casseroles, etc. The traditional bundle consists principally of thyme, bay leaf and parsley, but rosemary, marjoram, lovage, fennel, leek, or celery might also be used, depending on the recipe and the region.

BRAISE: a technique (in the oven or on the stove) of cooking vegetables or meat, although it may also be used on certain kinds of fruit. The ingredients are first browned in butter, oil, or lard, then a small amount of liquid (such as water, broth, stock, or wine) is added, the pan is tightly covered, and the ingredients are slowly cooked. The ingredients thus cook in fat, liquid and vapor, with tender, flavorful results.

BREAD: to roll meat, poultry, vegetables, or fish in a mixture of flour, eggs and bread crumbs, for subsequent frying or deep-frying.

BRIEFLY FRY: to fry meat or other ingredients in a little hot fat, just until brown.

BROTH: a spiced cooking broth that is the result of having cooked meat, fish, or vegetables in water; the cooking ingredients impart their flavor into the water and turn it into stock that can then be used for cooking other ingredients.

BROWN: to cook briefly over a high or medium-high heat, usually in a buttered or oiled frying pan on top of the stove. Often used to cook a tender piece of meat or a slice of bacon, or thin slices of vegetables such as potatoes; the method browns the exterior but enables the interior to remain moist.

BRUNOISE: a mélange or mixture of vegetables that have been either shredded, grated, or diced finely, and are then slowly cooked in butter, to be used primarily to flavor sauces or soups.

CARPACCIO: a classic Italian dish with a legendary history (see *carpaccio* recipes throughout this volume), in which extremely thin slices of filleted, raw meat (usually beef) are dressed with oil and lemon juice, with a mayonnaise or mustard dressing, or with an olive oil vinaigrette, and served as an appetizer; the term has come to include types of fish and shellfish as well.

CARVE: to slice meat, poultry or fish, or to cut these for presentation, traditionally in front of the dining guests. A large and very sharp knife and a large carving board are required for carving.

CHANTILLY: part of the French culinary vocabulary, meaning dishes (*à la chantilly*), from sweet puddings to savory appetizers, that are served with or mixed with whipped cream. The dessert Chantilly cream is a sweetened whipped cream, often flavored with a liqueur or vanilla extract.

CHARLOTTE: though there are many stories about its provenance (some say the dish was originated in France, some say it was originated in Russia for Czar Alexander), the definition remains the same. A charlotte is multi-layered; a form begins with spongecake, finger biscuits (ladyfingers), waffle, or buttered bread base, topped with layers of either a pudding of pureed fruit, or whipped cream or custard.

CHARTREUSE: a pie made with chopped meat, vegetables and bacon, cooked in a bain-marie, and served cold. There is also a liqueur of the same name, that comes in green or yellow varieties and was originally developed by the monks of La Grande Chartreuse in France.

CLARIFY: to make a cloudy liquid, such as a soup or sauce, clear, by stirring in slightly whisked egg white, carefully heating, cooling, and, finally, straining through a seive or cheescloth; the egg whites attract the sediment.

CLARIFIED BUTTER: butter that is slowly melted, causing it to divide, into milky solids at the bottom of the pan and clear liquid on the surface; the top is skimmed of any foam, and the clear liquid is poured off to be used in cooking.

COCKLES: molluscs of the family *cardium*, who have striped and ribbed brown-and-white (to varying degrees) shells in the shape, roughly, of a valentine; at home in the flat coastal waters of the Atlantic and the Mediterranean; wash thoroughly to clean them of substantial amounts of sand, and served raw with lemon juice, fried, or steamed.

CONSOMMÉ: in French: consommer means to consume; a meat or vegetable broth, cooked and reduced for a long time and finally clarified until it is clear. Served cold or hot, and often used as the base for a stock or soup.

CORAL: the roe of crustaceans, from lobsters to scallops, so named because when cooked it turns a salmon-pink resembling the color of some ocean coral; regarded by gourmets as a particular delicacy.

CROUTONS: roasted or toasted diced bread, used to garnish soups, baked dishes or salads; often browned in garlic, herbs, or spices.

CRUDITÉS: (French for raw vegetables) raw vegetables, usually cut into strips, served as an appetizer with dips, a cold dressing, or sauce.

CUSTARD: sauce for puddings made with confectioners' sugar, the yolk of an egg, milk, and a pinch of salt, rounded off with cream. Often cooked in a bain-marie.

DEEP-FRY: to cook (usually until crisp and brown) ingredients, usually vegetables, fish, or meat, by immersing them in extremely hot oil or other fat. The exterior crust formed seals in the food's flavors and moisture.

DIJONNAISE: French term for dishes prepared with light Dijon mustard, a special, creamy kind of mustard made with mustard grains soaked in sour, fermented juice of unripe grapes, and hailing originally from Dijon, France. A mayonnaise with mustard flavor, served with cold meat, is also called a Dijonnaise.

FLAMBÉ: though often a technique of presentation intended to impart a sense of drama to a dish-the word is French for "flaming," it may also be a step during the cooking process. Either way, it involves pouring liquor on top of foods still cooking and lighting the alcohol to better render the food's aroma.

FOLD IN: to mix ingredients carefully without vigorous stirring, as in folding roe into a cream sauce, or a warm ingredient into a cool one.

GALANTINE: a classic French layered dish, often consisting of a spicy pie that is cooked rolled in cloth or thin strips of meat, or in an appropriate form.

TO GARNISH: an art that completes the plate; to arrange accompaniments decoratively around the main part of a dish, often referring back to the dish's ingredients or flavorings.

GAZPACHO: a cold vegetable soup of Spanish origin traditionally made with ripe tomatoes, red peppers, cucumber, olive oil, garlic, and bread crust.

GLAZE: to glaze dishes with their own juices, aspic, or sugar.

TO GRILL: a method of cooking that retains a certain freshness in the food, either on wood or charcoal over a grill.

HOISIN SAUCE: a spicy reddish-brown sauce from China made from fermented soy beans, flour, salt, sugar, and raw rice. Its natural coloring lends visual depth to many Chinese dishes.

JELLY: (also see aspic) clear or semi-clear elastic mixture, prepared with pectin or gelatin; also meat juices set to form a jelly.

JULIENNE: to cut vegetables (often raw) into thin strips often about matchstick size; some chefs prefer to julienne by hand, some use a slicer. Julienned vegetables are the primary component in crudités.

LANGOUSTINE: a French term for a crustacean that is wholly different from either a prawn, a crayfish, or a shrimp. Langoustines have pink or pale-red bodies and elongated, but pronounced front claws; their flavor is both sweet and subtle, and lends them well to dishes such as terrines. Unfortunately, langoustines can not survive for too long out of water, and so are often sold cooked in regions far from the coast.

LARD: to lace or wrap lean meat with strips of bacon, truffle slices, or cloves of garlic to prevent it from drying out, and to impart additional flavors.

MARINATE: a technique known in virtually every cuisine in which fish, meat, poultry, vegetables, or even fruit are coated with a mixture of, usually, oil, vinegar, and lemon juice flavored with herbs and spices. As the food absorbs the flavors of the marinade, it also tenderizes, thus reducing cooking time, and in some cases even replacing the cooking process.

MOUSSE: a French word for foam. A mousse is an airy yet substantial sweet or savory dish that owes its soft, delicate and fluffy structure to egg whites that have been whisked until stiff, or whipped cream. To further bind a mousse, gelatin may be added as well.

PARFAIT: in French the word means perfect or complete; a cold dish made with a delicate stuffing, bound with gelatin or egg white, filled into forms and inverted after chilling. A sweet parfait is a chilled pudding, usually composed of ice cream, jelly, egg cream, a lacing of syrup or liqueur, and cream, served in a special high glass.

PERSILLADE: from the French word for parsley; a mixture of finely chopped parsley and garlic or of thin strips of cold beef and vinegar, oil and plenty of parsley.

PHYLLO DOUGH: a dough made with sticky flour (wheat), water, and oil (fat) that is rolled out paper-thin, cut into slices, brushed with oil, and stacked, often between layers of wax paper. Used frequently in the Near East, Turkey, Greece, Austria, and Hungary. It is similar to puff pastry, which may be used instead.

POACH: to cook ingredients by immersing them in a small amount of liquid over low heat, often used for fish or dumplings.

PRAWN: an often-confusing term, sometimes used to describe any large shrimp, or to refer to langoustines (see langoustines), or to refer to freshwater shrimps. However, prawns in the strictest sense of the word are both salt and fresh water dwellers, migrating from one to the other to spawn. They are larger than shrimp and have longer legs and narrower bodies. King prawns may also be marketed as jumbo shrimps, particularly in the United States.

PUREE: to work soft ingredients into a smooth and even mixture, usually using either a blender or a food processor.

REDUCE: to cook a sauce or gravy for so long that its liquid content evaporates, resulting in a distilled, thick, and more intensely aromatic sauce.

RÉMOULADE: a sauce; essentially an herb mayonnaise and mustard blend seasoned with chopped tarragon, chervil, parsley, gherkin pickles, and capers. It is available in some shops as a ready-made product, and often accompanies cold meat, fish, and crustaceans.

RINSE WITH COLD WATER: a technique used to arrest the cooking process immediately rather than let a just-cooked ingredient keep cooking in its absorbed heat. Invaluable for keeping vegetables crisp and green, and pasta *al dente*.

ROAST: often a misunderstood term, to roast something simply means to cook it in the oven uncovered, that is to say in dry heat, until brown and crisp. Nuts and kernels become more aromatic through roasting; tender pieces of meat or vegetables benefit from it as well.

SAFFRON: spice harvested from the stamen of the saffron flower (a kind of purple crocus). As the tiny dust threads containing the saffron powder can only be picked by hand it is the world's most expensive spice. Fortunately, only extremely small amounts are required to add its pungent flavoring or unique, yellow color to, for instance, fish and rice dishes, curries and puddings.

SAUTÉ: to briefly fry ingredients over direct heat in a little butter or oil until slightly brown.

SCALLOPS: a mollusc with a characteristic flat shell. It moves about with the shell open, using a large muscle; that muscle is the part that is consumed, along with the orange coral. Scallops are usually prepared and served in their shell, and come in two basic types: the small, delicately flavored bay scallop, and the larger, slightly stronger-flavored sea scallop.

SCOOP: a technique of scooping out dumplings, balls and similar shapes with a specially fashioned scoop or a spoon, sometimes for further blanching.

SCORE: to make incision on both sides of a piece of meat or fish for decorative reasons, also useful for preventing food from splitting and achieving even cooking on all surfaces.

SHRIMP: the most popular crustacean in the United States is actually a grouping of hundreds of subspecies. Essentially, a shrimp is a small crustacean without claws or shears, with slim legs and a large, plump body. The color varies according to species, but most turn orange-red when cooked. Shrimps exist in cold and warm waters and in fresh water as well as in sea water. They form the basis for a variety of dishes in many countries, and range in size from colossal to miniature.

SIMMER: to cook ingredients in liquid over a low heat to prevent the liquid from boiling, or to reduce the heat from ingredients that have reached a boil down to a slower rate of cooking.

SKIM: to remove the fat floating on the surface of a liquid (usually soups or sauces) with a skimming spoon or by straining the liquid; sometimes also used when clarifying sauces or butter.

SOUFFLÉ: a light, airy dish based on eggs from the French term for inflating. Can be sweet or savory, served hot (which may require some delicate handling) or cold. The airy and fluffy structure is achieved by folding whisked egg whites that are very stiff into a warm sauce or puree. Often cooked in a special round and straight-sided soufflé dish.

STEAM: a technique that has gained in popularity in the past decade or two. To steam food is to cook it over vapor rising from boiling stock or liquid, using a steamer equipped with a rack, or in multi-layered metal or bamboo steam pots. Also used to describe the process of cooking ingredients in their own juices, with perhaps a very small amount of liquid or fat added.

STOCK: the juices produced by meat, poultry, vegetables, or fish during cooking, used to form the base of sauces. Can be purchased ready-made, or made far in advance and kept chilled or frozen until ready to use.

STRAIN: to pass ingredients (mostly liquid) through a sieve; a technique often used for clarifying sauces and stocks.

STUFFING: a mixture of chopped meat or fish with herbs and spices for filling pies or poultry. Rice, vegetables, bread crumbs, or eggs mixed with meat or entrails are also used for stuffing.

SWEAT: to cook vegetables, in particular onions, or flour, over a low heat in fat without allowing them to turn brown, but only until they soften and begin to glisten, as if sweating.

TARTARE: traditionally, a dish comprised of raw ground beef prepared with finely chopped onions, gherkins, capers or parsley, pepper and salt; increasingly, chefs are discovering other ingredients to present as tartares, such as fish.

TERRINE: a dish made with finely chopped meat, poultry, game, fish, or vegetables (or a combination of any of these), cooked in a deep dish or form with straight walls (also called a terrine, or a terrine form). Terrines are usually served cold, and are often bound in aspic.

GARNISH: the decoration of a dish, considered a crucial aspect in many cuisines; also used to refer to ingredients added to a soup or sauce, such as cream or chopped onions in soup, or chopped herbs in a sauce.

THICKEN: to thicken or bind simmering sauces by stirring in egg yolk and cream, milk, or butter.

TRUFFLES: this delicacy includes quite a few varieties, the most famous of which is the black truffle. Essentially, a truffle is a large wild edible mushroom with a bulbous stem and a fleshy red-brown cap, but its sublime flavor and the effort involved in harvesting it have helped to make it one of the most luxurious ingredients used in cooking. It is found by truffle dogs or pigs in the fall, under oak and chestnut trees.

VELOUTÉ: another of the "mother sauces" from French cuisine, so named for its velvety consistenty (in French, *velours* means velvet). This white, thick sauce is made with butter, flour, veal or chicken stock, and seasoned with salt and pepper. Available ready-made.

VINAIGRETTE: a salad dressing based on a combination of vinegar and oil, often laced with herbs, deepened with mustard, and finally seasoned with salt and pepper.

ZABAGLIONE: a Italian treat, this light, airy, foamy sauce is made with egg yolk, sugar, and white wine or Champagne. Served hot or cold with puddings, and also called *sabayon* in France.

Index